Louisa Blair, Patrick Donovan, and Donald Fyson

Iron Bars And Bookshelves
A History of the Morrin Centre

Foreword by Louise Penny

ISBN 978-1-77186-080-2

Cover and book design by Hugues Skene (KX3 Communication inc.)

Legal Deposit, 2nd quarter 2016

Bibliothèque et Archives nationales du Québec
Library and Archives Canada

Published by Baraka Books of Montreal.
6977, rue Lacroix
Montréal, Québec H4E 2V4
Telephone: 514 808-8504
info@barakabooks.com
www.barakabooks.com

Printed and bound in Quebec

We acknowledge the support from the Société de développement des entreprises culturelles (SODEC) and the Government of Quebec tax credit for book publishing administered by SODEC.

SODEC
Québec ✚✚
✚✚

Financé par le gouvernement du Canada
Funded by the Government of Canada | Canadä

Trade Distribution & Returns
Canada and the United States
Independent Publishers Group
1-800-888-4741 (IPG1);
orders@ipgbook.com

CONTENTS

FOREWORD

THE MORRIN CENTRE IS A TREASURE

Louise Penny

The Morrin Centre is a treasure. And, like most treasures, it isn't always easy to find. But once found, it enriches beyond measure.

I first came across this magnificent place in the late 1980s, when I was hosting the CBC morning radio program. I went there to interview someone. I'm afraid to admit, I can't remember the person, or the interview. But I do remember, clearly, my astonishment at walking into the Literary and Historical Society Library.

It was a very clear sense of coming home.

The dark wood bookcases. The double-height room, the tall windows. The spiral stairs. The leather sofa and intimate seating area. It felt like a library in an old manor home. A place to snuggle in, choose a volume, and get comfortable.

When it came time to set one of my books in Quebec City, I knew where I wanted the setting. The Morrin Centre. The old library.

My husband Michael and I spent a month in Quebec City, researching. Walking the narrow streets in the heart of winter. During Carnival.

But always we found ourselves back in the library. Warming up. Sitting on the sofa. Taking in the atmosphere.

And asking questions. Question after question.

What's the history of the place?

Who founded it?

Tell us about the building.

Tell us about the books.

Can we see the basement?

The volunteers and staff could not have been more patient and gracious and helpful. Until finally, it was time to write the book. It became *Bury Your Dead*. And in it, Chief Inspector Armand Gamache is recovering from an as yet unnamed event, that has clearly left him deeply wounded, physically and emotionally.

He has come to Quebec City, to find peace. And where better than this remarkable, unknown place. A library. A place of thoughts and ideas.

Here is part of Gamache's reflections, as he sits on the sofa, a heavy book in his hands.

> *The sun was already setting on the walled city and the old library within the walls.*
>
> *Gamache was reminded of a nesting doll. The most public face was North America and huddled inside that was Canada and huddled inside Canada was Québec. And inside Québec? An even smaller presence, the tiny English community. And within that?*
>
> *This place. The Literary and Historical Society. That held them and all their records, their thoughts, their memories, their symbols. Gamache didn't have to look at the statue above him to know who it was. This place held their leaders, their language, their culture and achievements. Long forgotten or never known by the francophone majority outside these walls but kept alive here.*
>
> *It was a remarkable place almost no francophone even knew existed. When he'd told Emile about it his old friend had thought Gamache was joking, making it up, and yet the building was just two blocks from his own home.*
>
> *Yes, it was like a nesting doll. Each held within the other until finally at the very core was this little gem.*

The Morrin Centre is a gem, where books and thoughts and heritage are treasured.

And this treasure is worth celebrating. And supporting. And protecting.

Louise Penny

February 2014

ACKNOWLEDGMENTS

Thanks to Lise Bissonnette, Christian Drolet and Normand Charbonneau of Bibliothèque et Archives nationales du Québec (BAnQ) for helping to launch this book project, and to Simon Jacobs for taking it to Septentrion and Baraka Books after BAnQ saw its publishing budgets cut. Thank you to Gilles Herman and Robin Philpot for taking on and producing this book, and to Sophie Imbeault for her editorial assistance and photography. Thanks also to Barry McCullough, Marie Rubsteck, and the Morrin Centre staff for their patience in dealing with three demanding co-authors over the last few years, and to the LHSQ Council and Executive for supporting the project throughout. Our special thanks to the R. Howard Webster Foundation for their generous financial support.

Louisa Blair

I wish to thank my co-authors for their cooperation, patience and generosity; Leah Blythe and Jillian Tomm for their research help; the staff at the Morrin Centre and at BAnQ Quebec; my friend and mentor Bob Chodos; the late Robert Aitken for his gentle company during the writing process; Donald Hembroff for his unending support and encouragement; and my brother David for his infectious love of the Lit & His.

Patrick Donovan

I want to thank Lorraine O'Donnell for setting me on the road to researching Morrin College; Susan Bronson and Jean-Claude Marsan, for their help and encouragement with the earliest incarnation of this research; France Cliche, for trusting me as a 27-year-old to help manage the multimillion dollar Morrin Centre restoration project and allowing me to become immersed in the building history; Helen Meredith and David Blair, who helped me mull over the controversy around the building's sale. Thanks to the Morrin College board of governors for granting me access to their archives, especially Reverend Stephen Hayes, who provided encouraging feedback about my early Morrin College research (he also taught this lapsed Catholic the important distinction between a priest and a pastor). Thank you to my two co-authors for their valuable help in revising my manuscript. Many thanks to my perfectionist girlfriend Anne-Frédérique Champoux for feedback throughout the writing process. Finally, thanks to Renée Lamontagne and Donald Donovan for being the best parents ever.

Donald Fyson

My portion of this project, on the prison, would not have been possible without the help and encouragement of a long list of people: colleagues, other historians, archivists, librarians, museologists, student researchers, and others. So, my thanks and gratitude to Patrick Baker, Mario Béland, André Charbonneau, Maxime Chouinard, François Fenchel, Peter Gagné, Marc Grignon, Patricia Kennedy, Paul Kennedy, Maude-Emmanuelle Lambert, Gilles Laporte, Rénald Lessard, Frank Mackey, Didier Méhu, Luc Noppen, Larry Ostola, Thierry Petit, Didier Prioul, Marc Vallières, and Brian Young, and all the staff at BAnQ Quebec and Library and Archives Canada. My two co-authors also deserve praise for their help and their patience. A special thanks to those dedicated volunteers who over the years have patiently entered the information in the Quebec prison registers into a massive database, and notably Claudette Laberge and Raymond Blanchette. I also want to acknowledge the memory of Jean-Marie Fecteau, the pioneer of the scholarly history of the Quebec City prison. Finally, my thanks to Sovita Chander, my wife, and also former president of the LHSQ, for believing in and supporting the project.

INTRODUCTION

Louisa Blair, Patrick Donovan, Donald Fyson

Un jour viendra sans doute où toutes les prisons seront changées en collèges. C'est lorsque l'instruction, cette grande moralisatrice, aura banni l'ignorance et la misère qui sont la cause de tous les crimes. Il faut pour cela que l'instruction soit libre, qu'elle soit dirigée par des hommes qui veulent faire d'autres hommes, et non par une caste ambitieuse qui ne cherche qu'à faire des esclaves afin de leur commander.

[The day will no doubt come when all prisons will be changed into colleges. Then education, that great force for morality, will banish ignorance and poverty, the cause of all crime. But education must be free, and teachers must be men who want to make men of others, rather than an ambitious caste who want to create slaves so they can dominate them.]

-Arthur Buies, *La Lanterne*, October 1, 1868

In 1868, journalist Arthur Buies was stunned at the dramatic transformation of Quebec City's Common Gaol, which he recalled as a miserable building with "wobbly floors, humid cells, and worm-eaten ceilings." The building had indeed long been considered an eyesore that did not belong in the respectable streets of the walled upper town. Built between 1808 and 1813 on the remains of a French-régime defensive redoubt that had itself served as a prison, the new gaol was supposed to reflect the Enlightenment ideas of British prison reformer John Howard. In large part, the plan failed. Within a few years, officials complained that the building made reform impossible: it was overcrowded, poorly laid out, and in constant need of repair. And it smelled. While far better than the prisons that preceded it, the gaol was considered a disgrace to the district until the day it closed in 1867.

In his section on the history of the common gaol, Donald Fyson goes beyond the usual focus on noteworthy criminals and the sixteen men executed in front of the building to provide a broad social and institutional history of the gaol. He reminds us that while some people were incarcerated for serious offences such as murder and burglary, the vast majority of the 60,000 or so prisoners who passed through its doors were ordinary men and women whose "crimes" were offences like vagrancy or prostitution. The gaol also housed a wide variety of other prisoners: disobedient sailors and apprentices; American prisoners of war; insolvent debtors; even a few political prisoners.

The gaol was not just a place of punishment. In the absence of charitable institutions willing to take them in, many poor and homeless people got themselves committed as a means of simply surviving. Prisoners developed their own form of society in gaol, and it was also a place of work for the staff who ran the institution. Finally, in a town with a majority francophone population, the gaol was very largely a British institution, with three quarters of the prisoners and most of the staff being of Irish, English or Scots origin.

In the fifty-five years of the Quebec gaol's existence, vast changes took place in the social structure of the city. The population grew exponentially, thousands of British and Irish migrants settled in Quebec, and religion took a more prominent place in daily life. This latter change meant that the Catholic clergy became increasingly intrusive, seeking to control what books could be read and what subjects could be taught. Some of Quebec's English-speaking Protestant minority felt they must defend liberal intellectual life in the face of this challenge. They wanted their own institutions. This is in part why prominent Quebec City Presbyterians founded Morrin College, affiliated with McGill University. This English-language college, the first in the city, moved into the remodeled old prison in 1868.

But it wasn't just Protestants who objected to the creeping tendrils of the Catholic clergy. Journalist Arthur Buies, the French-speaking Catholic quoted above, speaks of the "abundant and happy light" shining through the Morrin College building. The reference to light works on many levels: Buies' education in Paris had instilled the anticlerical spirit of the French Enlightenment in him, and his Scottish father's influence may have added to this. But did Morrin College live up to its promise of being a beacon of light in Quebec City?

Patrick Donovan's section on the College attempts to answer this question by bringing the small institution to life, and highlighting its successes and failures. Morrin College faced persistent financial problems, and the school became increasingly irrelevant in the face of the declining Protestant population of Quebec City. This prompted its closure as an educational institution in 1902, after which it continued as a charitable foundation. Nevertheless, Morrin College was the first school in the city to grant university degrees to women, and the college board still provides scholarships to students today. Their stewardship of the former college building throughout the twentieth century ensured the building's preservation and eventual transformation into the Morrin Centre.

The final section, by Louisa Blair, looks at the Literary and Historical Society of Quebec, founded in 1824. Like the college and the prison, it owes its existence to the Age of Enlightenment. Its founder, the Earl of Dalhousie, governor-in-chief of British

North America, hoped it would "open new views, and new sentiments more suited to the present state of the civilized world."

As Canada's oldest existing learned society, it gathered historical documents, republished rare manuscripts, encouraged research, published scholarly essays, and lobbied for the preservation of the country's heritage. In its heyday it also had a large museum, held public lectures and science demonstrations, and gave prizes for artistic endeavour. In 1868, it moved into the renovated prison at the same time as Morrin College. A succession of presidents and councils, including some of Quebec's most colourful and powerful scientists and *literati*, argued their way down the centuries about what Society members should be reading, learning and thinking about.

Throughout the twentieth century, the Society became more of a community institution that centred on the services of its lending library. It provided access to English-language books in a largely French-speaking city. By the end of the century, it was struggling to make ends meet.

In recent years, the Literary and Historical Society of Quebec has been given a new lease on life. It broadened its mandate to preserve and promote the history of the three diverse vocations of the long-neglected building where it had been a tenant since 1868, spearheaded its restoration, and created the Morrin Centre. This cultural centre not only houses the library but also acts as Quebec City's main English-language cultural centre.

The Society was the main driving force behind the original historical research included in this publication. The three authors provide new perspectives on a building whose history serves to illustrate the broader evolution of criminal justice, education, scholarship, and the place of Quebec City and its English-speaking minority within our country.

PRISON REFORM AND PRISON SOCIETY: THE QUEBEC GAOL, 1812-1867

Donald Fyson

INTRODUCTION

Today, the Morrin Centre is a lovely old neoclassical building in the heart of Quebec City's historic district, housing a library and a cultural centre. But it started out life as something quite different. Between 1812 and 1867, tens of thousands of women, men, and children passed through its doors and became prisoners in what was then Quebec City's main civil prison, or "common gaol." "Gaol" was the usual spelling of "jail" at the time, and was pronounced the same. The Quebec gaol was also home to the gaolers (jailers), turnkeys, and guards who kept the prisoners, and was visited by a steady stream of prisoners' friends and relatives, lawyers, doctors, jurymen, philanthropists, prison inspectors, and many others. Though the building is considered an architectural gem today, that was not the case at the time. Instead, it was virulently denounced in letters, reports and newspaper articles.

Traces of the Quebec gaol are still visible in the building. The stone window-frames have stopped-up holes where bars used to be. Hefty hinges and thick door-frames on the top floors remind us of the heavy doors that used to hang there, locking up disorderly women and disobedient sailors. And most spectacularly, there are two surviving cell blocks on the ground floor, with low-vaulted ceilings, worn wooden floorboards incised with prisoners' graffiti, and rings attached to the ground where men and women condemned to death were once chained. But most reminders of the gaol were wiped away when the building became Morrin College in the late 1860s. The inner walls of the main cell blocks were taken down and floors removed, to create the lofty spaces of the library and of College Hall. Gone is the small cell over the front entrance, where those condemned to death were readied for their final moments, along with the door that led out to the execution platform in front and the platform itself. The malodorous privies that hung off the back of the gaol have been sliced off, leaving only their outlines.

The women's prison and the guardhouse in the old exercise yard have become condos. Even the infamous inscription over the front door, *"Carcer iste bonos a pravis vindicare possit"* ("May this prison deliver the good from the bad"), on which passing schoolchildren would practice their Latin, has been utterly destroyed.

And yet, while the architects and builders hired by the trustees of Morrin College at the end of the 1860s erased much of the gaol's architectural heritage, they couldn't erase the experiences of the vast multitude of people who lived, suffered, and, in some cases, died in the gaol. What was the Quebec gaol like? Where did the idea for the gaol come from, and how well did it fulfil the plans of its builders? Who were these prisoners: were they all just criminals? And what was it like to be there as a prisoner, or to work there as gaoler, guard, matron, doctor, or sheriff? These are some of the questions this chapter aims to answer.

But before we begin, let's turn to two stories.

James Cockburn, "The Jail on St. Stanislas Street" (c.1830).
This watercolour is the best existing depiction of the building while it was a gaol.

16

STORIES

Professional, academic historians talk about overall trends, averages, the big picture. This is important, because it gets us away from cherry-picking examples that serve our argument: history is so vast, one can find almost anything in it. But the big picture sometimes makes us forget that history is made up above all of stories: the stories of a multitude of people, of a multitude of lives lived. So before turning to the story of the Quebec gaol, let's remember the lives of two real people who were locked up in it.

PHILIPPE AUBERT DE GASPÉ

Philippe Aubert de Gaspé was a member of Quebec's landowning seigneurial elite, and is best remembered as one of Quebec's most famous writers, the author of classics such as *Les Anciens Canadiens* (1863). Before becoming a writer, he was a lawyer, and in 1816 he became sheriff of the district of Quebec. One of his many responsibilities as sheriff was to oversee the district gaol. He hired the gaoler, he established the rules, he paid the gaol's expenses and submitted his accounts to the government, and so on. Aubert de Gaspé didn't last long as sheriff, and was replaced in 1822. In part, this was because he had built up a huge debt to government (connected to his work in civil suits), which he couldn't pay back. At the time, debtors could be put in prison by their creditors until they paid. This is exactly what happened to Aubert de Gaspé almost fifteen years later. In 1838, after a very long and complicated court case stemming from his debt to government, Aubert de Gaspé was arrested and put in gaol – the very gaol he had himself run two decades before! The irony is stunning. Unable or unwilling to pay his debt, Aubert de Gaspé remained in prison for more than three years, finally being released in 1841. In *Les Anciens Canadiens*, he paints a grim picture of being able to see the house his family was in from the window of his cell:

> I knew my children were dying, and I was only separated from them by the width of the street. During those long sleepless nights, I could see people moving about by their bedsides, and the lights being carried from room to room; and every moment I dreaded to see these signs of life disappear, for they announced to me that my children still required being nursed with maternal love. I am ashamed to acknowledge that I was often so overcome by despair, that I was tempted to dash out my brains against the bars of my window.

Some authors have wondered whether this scene was just made up by Aubert de Gaspé decades later, for effect. But we now know that this is almost certainly a true tale, especially because he recounted almost exactly the same story in a private letter written while he was in prison.

Philippe Aubert de Gaspé in about 1860, two decades after he was imprisoned in the Quebec gaol.

LUCY NOYES

Aubert de Gaspé's time in gaol is well known and often told. Nobody remembers Lucy Noyes. An Irish or English immigrant (she described herself as both), she was in and out of the Quebec gaol over forty times between 1831 and 1840, including fourteen times during the period Aubert de Gaspé was locked up. Like many of the gaol's most habitual inmates, Lucy was incarcerated for being a prostitute or a vagrant, though she was formally charged with the catchall offense of being "loose, idle and disorderly." The routine was almost always the same. She was swept up off the city streets by constables or watchmen. One of the city's magistrates then sentenced her to one or two months at hard labour in the gaol. She got out at the end of her sentence, and either a few days or a few weeks later, the same thing happened again. Lucy spent about two thirds of her life between 1831 and 1840 in the gaol. The last time she was imprisoned, in September 1840, she was very sick, and five days later she died. She was about twenty-eight years old. The gaol doctor, Joseph Morrin (founder of Morrin College), said he knew her well and was not surprised by her death, which he diagnosed as being caused by "dropsy" (unspecified edema). Joseph Morrin had not only tended to Lucy as gaol doctor. On two occasions, acting as a magistrate, he had committed her to the gaol himself. In Lucy's case, as with many other destitute women, there were probably many times when she was relatively happy to be committed to gaol, especially during the long winter months. When Quebec City's port was frozen over, there were fewer clients, and with no social services for "fallen" women like her, she would have had nowhere else to turn and most likely sought out imprisonment in order to survive. But at other times, it was clearly the frowning might of Quebec's polite society that drove the police to arrest her and lock her up. Women like Lucy Noyes were not meant to be seen on Quebec City's streets.

* * *

The difference between the experiences of our two prisoners is striking. Aubert de Gaspé, as a debtor and as a member of Quebec's elites, had access to the best the gaol could offer, such as it was. He would have been housed in one of the special rooms in the gaol reserved for higher-class debtors. He would have had food and even alcohol brought to him by family and friends, who could visit him very frequently. He had access to books, writing paper, pen, and ink, and wrote lengthy missives from his cell. Not so Lucy Noyes. She would have been crowded into one of the wards of the women's prison, a small building in the back of the gaol yard. She would only have been allowed the standard gaol allowance of food, consisting of bread, potatoes, and gruel. And while she might have had access to a Bible, she was illiterate. Philippe Aubert de Gaspé and Lucy Noyes probably saw each other many times, if only through gaps in the wooden fence that separated the men's and women's exercise yards. But a gulf separated them. Both experienced the gaol we're about to describe, but how they lived it was very different. Still, while they were prisoners, both saw the world through the bars of their windows. And perhaps most importantly, neither were really criminals in the modern sense. Instead, they were both, each in their own way, victims of a harsh system.

BEFORE THE GAOL

Before the Quebec gaol, there was ... the Quebec gaol! The Morrin Centre is often described as Quebec's first prison. If this were the case, where were all the prisoners kept before the building opened in 1812? In fact, there were several prisons before then, stretching back to the French regime.

French prisons in Canada

Prisons of one sort or another have been a feature of justice systems in Europe since at least the time of ancient Greece. Europeans brought these institutions with them to North America, much to the surprise and disgust of the Native populations. In what is today Quebec, there was a prison in each of the three main judicial districts: Quebec, Montreal and Trois-Rivières. In Quebec City, the prison was part of the complex of buildings around the palace of the intendant, the main civil government official. The prison was in part of a storehouse called the *magasins du roi*; a couple of the low, vaulted cells still exist today, although they are not open to the public. As in Europe, it was mainly used to house accused who were awaiting trial, or those awaiting punishment after being convicted.

In the French criminal justice system that was in place before the British conquered the colony, there were four main ways to punish condemned criminals. First, there was capital or corporal punishment, notably public hangings and whippings. These were meant to provide spectacular examples to deter others from committing crimes. Secondly, criminals might be banished from the colony, or forced into service on the royal galleys. Third, offenders might be fined, especially for minor offenses. Finally, some criminals

21

might also be forced to publicly acknowledge their crime and seek forgiveness from God. It was rare, though not unknown, for imprisonment to be used as punishment. Still, the French colony needed and used its prisons.

Conditions in these institutions were very poor. One American prisoner, Susannah Willard Johnson, briefly found herself in Quebec's criminal prison in the 1750s. She was aghast: "This jail was a place, too shocking for description. In one corner sat a poor being, half dead with the small pox; in another were some lousy blankets and straw; in the centre stood a few dirty dishes, and the whole presented a scene miserable to view."

On some occasions, French authorities had to house much larger numbers of prisoners. These were British soldiers or American colonists (like Johnson) captured during the many conflicts between New France and the British colonies to the south of Canada. When the normal prisons became overstretched, other buildings were pressed into service. One was the Royal Redoubt in Quebec City, which stood on the grounds occupied today by the Morrin Centre. Along with the similar Dauphin Redoubt, the

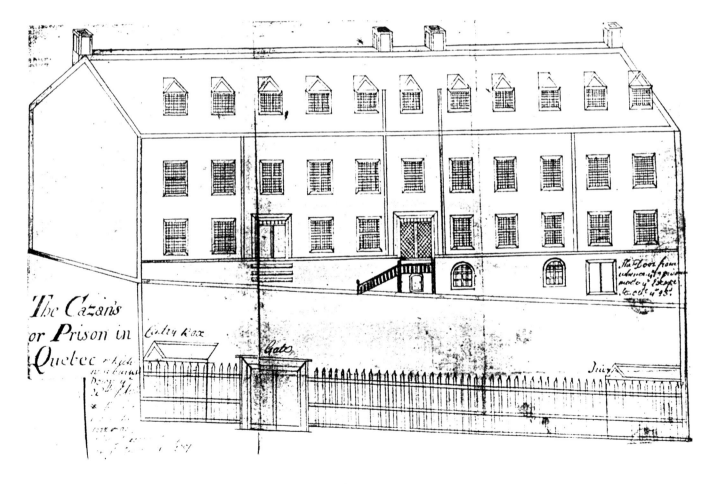

Royal Redoubt was part of the city's early fortifications, designed and built by French military engineers Josué Dubois Berthelot de Beaucours and Gaspard-Joseph Chaussegros De Léry. During the 1740s, its defensive role was superseded by fortifications built further out, and it was used as a barracks. It also housed British and American prisoners of war.

Conditions in the Royal Redoubt were difficult, though probably less miserable than in the criminal prison. Up to two hundred men, women, and children might be crowded into its relatively small space. Disease was rampant, and many died; although many more survived. The memoirs kept by a few prisoners are poignant reminders of the horrors of war.

BRITISH PRISONS IN QUEBEC

When the French colony of Canada fell to British conquerors in 1759-1760, British justice replaced French justice. But overall, British justice wasn't really that different. Like French justice before, it relied mainly on well-publicized capital and corporal punishment, on banishment, and on fines. Prisons were used mainly to house prisoners before, during, and after their trials. Still, the British system relied more on imprisonment than the French.

For one thing, the British treated the death penalty differently from the French. Under English criminal law, known as the "Bloody Code," many crimes were punishable by death, including some we would consider minor today. This included not only offenses like murder and rape, but also burglary, robbery, minor thefts, and even some forms of vandalism. In the first few decades following the Conquest, dozens of people in Quebec were sentenced to death for such crimes. However, very few were actually executed. Instead, most were pardoned.

The philosophy of the justice system was very different from what we know now. Today, we want similar crimes in similar circumstances to have similar punishments. But that view only began to take hold in the the late eighteenth century. Before then, capital punishment had two complementary purposes. One was to terrorize potential criminals by making many crimes punishable by death and by regularly conducting public executions. The other was to show that the King was merciful by getting him to pardon most of those sentenced to death. Some pardons were absolute, but most were conditional. In conditional pardons, the punishment of death might be replaced by banishment from

"The Cazan's or Prison in Quebec," an image of the Royal Redoubt that accompanies a journal kept by an unknown American prisoner of war who was imprisoned there in 1746-1748. The image also indicates the basement door through which two American prisoners of war escaped. Escapes were also common when the building was used as a civilian prison under British rule.

the colony, or by a term of imprisonment of several months or even years. This meant that there were often prisoners undergoing imprisonment as a punishment. As well, applications for pardon might take a long time, and during all of that time, the convicted prisoner was kept in gaol. All of this increased the prison population.

The British system also extended the use of imprisonment as a punishment in other ways. Those accused of being "loose, idle and disorderly," usually prostitutes or vagrants like Lucy Noyes, might be locked up in what was called a "bridewell" or a "house of correction" and put to hard labour. Disobedient servants and apprentices could also be disciplined in this way. As well, under English law, creditors could lock up debtors like Aubert de Gaspé who could not pay their debts and thus use the prisons for their private purposes, as long as they paid for the maintenance of their prisoners.

The Royal Redoubt

In England, and especially in London, these different institutions were often separate: criminal prisons, houses of corrections, debtors' prisons, each in their own building. But in smaller jurisdictions, and in the colonies, all these institutions might be together in the same building. This is exactly what happened in Quebec after the British took control. The *magasins du roi*, which housed the prison, had been partially destroyed during the siege, so the British had to look elsewhere. Quite understandably, they fell back on another former French-regime building: the Royal Redoubt (which they also called the King's Redoubt). This was the city's first common gaol under the British. It was at one and the same time a criminal prison housing accused and condemned criminals; a house of correction; and a debtors' prison. In July 1768, for example, the gaol housed at least seventeen prisoners: eleven criminals (some awaiting trial, some under sentence), including three women; four debtors (all men); and two men sentenced to hard labour in the house of correction. Technically, the house of correction and the common gaol were two separate institutions, but when they were together in the same prison, the building was usually referred to simply as the gaol.

At times, the gaol housed some very famous prisoners: it was probably here, for example, that Marie-Josephte Corriveau was confined in 1763, charged with murdering her husband. She was hanged on the Plains of Abraham, and her body "hung in chains" (exposed in an iron cage) at Lévis, across the river. She has entered legend as one of the most notorious figures of Quebec folklore.

Life in a pre-reform prison

As the American prisoners of war had discovered in the 1740s, the Royal Redoubt was not a very comfortable or secure building. Despite regular repairs, the building was always in poor shape, seemingly about to fall apart at any moment. The walls were separating from the roof and the floors, and British authorities had to shore them up with large masonry buttresses, like those that can still be seen today on the Dauphin Redoubt. The cellar floor was covered in mud and cow dung. Water from a spring regularly backed up and flooded the basement, and froze into thick sheets in the winter. Wind whistled through poorly sealed and glazed windows, and snow built up in the garret.

Prisoners of all different sorts were locked up together in what the debtors decried in 1768 as a "dolefull prison." There were eight usable rooms in the building, plus the garret, but only four or five were used for prisoners, including one set aside for debtors. The gaoler himself lived in the gaol, with his family. So too did the public executioner, or hangman, who carried out the occasional but regular hangings, and the more frequent corporal punishments such as whipping. Other rooms were probably used for storage, including at times for the gallows and the pillory (a wooden yoke used to expose criminals on the public market place). The rooms themselves were about twenty feet square, and heated in the winter by wood stoves; they probably had straw on the floor for sleeping.

Though the rooms were regularly swept, whitewashed, and washed with vinegar, and a doctor attended prisoners on occasion, the gaol was not a healthy place. It had a privy, but some prisoners had to use "necessary tubs," which were then emptied outside. The gaol also housed prisoners with contagious illnesses. In 1769, one prisoner was afflicted with leprosy. In 1783, the gaoler complained of "a number of diseased, disorderly women," in other words, sick prostitutes, who were sent to the gaol to undergo a cure. He decried the "intollerable stench which issues from the room where these women are confined." Water for the gaol was often brought up from the river in barrels, since a well in the yard worked only during the summer. For food, prisoners had one pound of bread per day, although those with money could buy extra food and even alcohol from the gaoler, and some sick prisoners got additional food. On special occasions like Christmas, generous townsfolk might even provide a festive meal for the prisoners!

Some prisoners may have had access to a small yard for exercise, but not prisoners sentenced to death. Until they had been pardoned, they were kept chained up, for fear that desperation would make them do anything to escape. This was good business for the blacksmith who had the prison contract: his accounts show a steady stream of charges for "putting a man in irons," "taking a man out of irons," and so on. But it was undoubtedly painful for the prisoners themselves. Even if they were pardoned, as most were, they had already undergone a very severe form of punishment. Still, gaol officials had every reason to be concerned about escapes, since the building was not at all secure. Prisoners escaped with alarming regularity, and often in groups. As the gaoler complained in 1783, the prisoners were "confined in the same room, where they consult with one another and enter into plots for breaking the Goal, to make their escape."

Overall, the gaol and the way it functioned corresponded closely to other pre-reform prisons throughout the North American colonies, and even in many parts of Britain: repurposed, ill-adapted old buildings; no attempt to classify and separate prisoners according to their crimes; very poor living and sanitary conditions; and overall, an experience that was harsh punishment in itself.

Other prisons

At various times, other buildings in Quebec City were also used as temporary prisons. At the beginning of the American Revolutionary War (1775-1783), the Americans invaded Quebec and laid siege to Quebec City. In a failed attack on the city on December 31, 1775, several hundred American officers and men were captured by the British. The officers were imprisoned in the town's Seminary. Most of the ordinary soldiers were held first in the Recollect convent, and then locked up either in the Royal Redoubt (just like their predecessors in the 1740s) or in the Dauphin Redoubt (which was very similar to the Royal Redoubt) - the sources aren't quite clear on which was used. Others were imprisoned in part of the Artillery Barracks. Later in the war, American POWs were also locked up in prison ships moored in the harbour or the environs and even in temporary structures within the bastions of the town's fortifications. Some political prisoners were also held in these makeshift prisons, including Pierre du Calvet, famous for his opposition to Governor Frederick Haldimand.

Replacing the Old Gaol

As early as the 1770s, British military engineers deemed the Royal Redoubt unfit as a gaol, and discussions were held on replacing it with a new, purpose-built building. By the 1780s, the situation of what became known as the "Old Gaol" was so desperate that the gaoler himself denounced the building as having "long been found too small to hold debtors and felons." British officials decided that the gaol absolutely had to be moved elsewhere. But there was no money for a new building.

New gaol building proposed by Quebec City mason John Bell in 1772. The new prison would have been safer and more spacious than the Royal Redoubt, with thick walls and twelve large cells on two floors, but otherwise would have followed the same pre-reform system. For example, it would have had no separate lock-up cells for individual prisoners. It was never built.

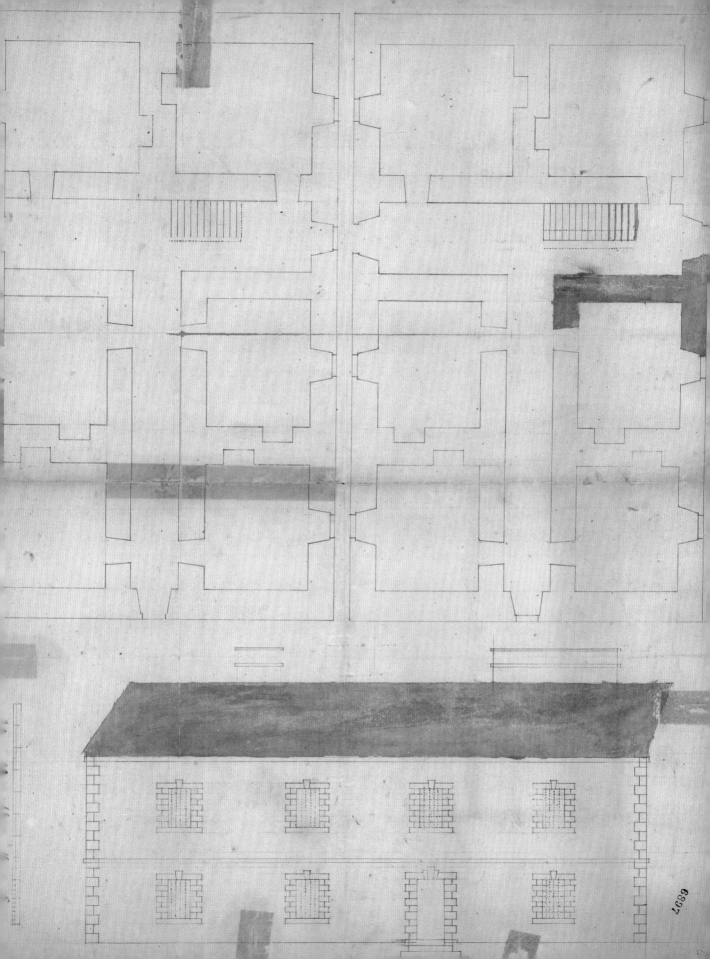

The Artillery Barracks

Colonial administrators chose instead to repurpose another pre-Conquest French military building: the Nouvelles Casernes (New Barracks). Known to the British as the Artillery Barracks, it is still standing today. The easternmost part of the building, abutting what is today the Côte du Palais, had already served as a military prison, and was also where some American POWs were held during the Revolutionary War. Its conversion into a civilian prison wasn't that difficult, and the prisoners were transferred there in April 1787. The Old Gaol became a storehouse for the British army.

Whatever the intentions of the authorities, the new gaol was not much better than the previous one, and in some respects it was worse. There was no exercise yard at all, and no privies; prisoners had to use "stool tubs" which were emptied into the adjoining yard, causing noxious smells. There were no beds and no bedding, so that prisoners had to sleep directly on the floor, in their clothes. It was also not much more secure than the Old Gaol: within the first few months, prisoners had made a breach in one of the walls around the windows in an escape attempt.

A description of the gaol from December 1802, made by the grand jurors of the colony's highest criminal court, gives a good flavour of this pre-reform gaol. On the ground floor, in the front, there were three rooms and a kitchen occupied by the gaoler and his family. In the back, across a long corridor piled with firewood, there were six windowless cells, each about ten feet by six feet. The only heating for these cells was a stove in the corridor, which didn't really keep the cells warm. In one cell was Henry Stationer, an insane man accused of murder who had been there since 1788 and would remain until his death in 1811. The other cells were empty but

The Artillery Barracks (the long building) as sketched by British Army officer Sempronius Stretton in 1805, when part was being used as the gaol. The gaol occupied the last few sections on the right-hand side of the building.

were probably used as needed for those condemned to death, or as punishment cells. The second floor, where most of the prisoners were confined, was only a little better. There were four large rooms, each about 12 feet by 20 feet, along a corridor 10 to 12 feet wide. Each room could in turn be divided in half by double doors, and each had its own stove. Trusted prisoners could walk up and down the corridor in summer months, their only form of exercise.

There were thirty-two prisoners in all, mixed almost indiscriminately. In one room, there were four men convicted of unlawful assembly and two convicted of larceny, all sentenced to the gaol for prison terms; three men sentenced to hard labour in the house of correction (which was still in the same building as the common gaol); three "negroes" awaiting trial as accessories to murder; one man indicted for perjury, also awaiting his trial; and one man committed for lack of bail. In another room, there were four women, all committed to the house of correction: three for being loose, idle, and disorderly and the fourth as a vagrant. In the third room, there were seven men convicted of unlawful assembly and sentenced to terms in the gaol, and two men convicted of larceny and sentenced to the house of correction, along with three men awaiting their trials (one for stealing on the high seas and two for plundering a wreck). Finally, in the fourth room, there were only two men. One was a debtor. The other had been charged with murder on the high seas, and had spent the last fourteen months in prison, desperately trying to go to trial.

Apart from the women's room, all of the rooms were dirty. None of the prisoners sentenced to hard labour actually did any, as there was nothing for them to work on. The prisoners complained of being very cold: they didn't have enough wood for heating, and the windows in all of the rooms were in bad shape, with many panes of glass missing and large gaps around the frames.

One prisoner said that the gaoler demanded money to allow his son to visit. The gaoler, John Hill, confirmed this, saying that he was constantly harassed with such applications and that at his age (he was about 72), he couldn't go up and down the stairs so frequently without a fee, especially since he was paid only £20 per year. At the same time, the jurors felt that Hill acted with humanity and attention towards the prisoners. But they decried the state of the gaol and its utter unfitness for reforming prisoners: "the prisoners sentenced to hard Labour in this nominal House of Correction under these circumstances appear to suffer no other punishment than deprivation of Liberty; their friends or relatives being allowed to carry them all sorts of provisions, and from their remaining so long in a state of idleness, mixed as they now are with other offenders, they are in great danger of leaving the Gaol, at the period of their Confinement, more hardened in Vice than they were when committed." They concluded that, "all these facts and observations clearly demonstrate the present insufficiency of the Gaol and the necessity of Legislative interference to cure an evil of such serious importance." Which is exactly what happened next.

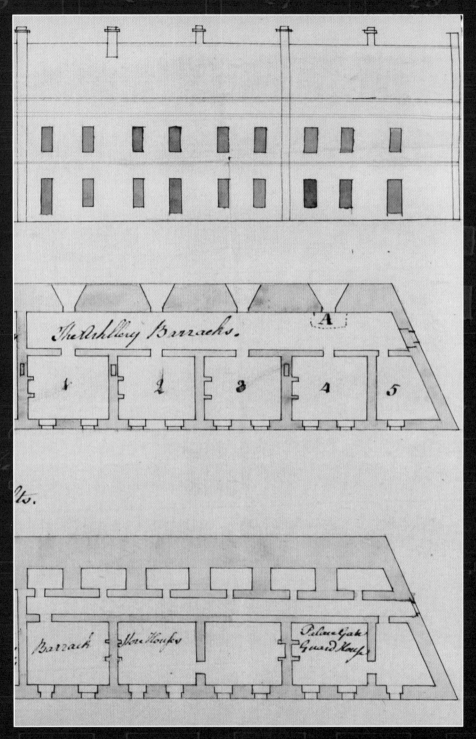

This plan of the eastern end of the Artillery Barracks made in 1771 by Army engineer John Marr shows the part later used as a gaol. The six windowless cells on the ground floor were set into the thick outer wall, which served as part of the fortification of the city. The gaoler and his family (on the ground floor) occupied as much space as the cells (the rooms numbered 1-4) for prisoners on the floor above.

BUILDING THE GAOL

The Morrin Centre looks the way it does today because of decisions that were made during the planning and the construction of the Quebec gaol over two centuries ago. These decisions were based on new and changing theories of punishment that first developed in Europe. At the same time, the building was the end product of financial constraints, political considerations, and even concessions to Quebec's harsh climate. The results may seem pleasing to us today, but at the time, even the building's architect was disappointed with the result.

CHANGING ATTITUDES TOWARDS CRIME AND PUNISHMENT

When the grand jurors complained in 1802 about the state of the Quebec gaol, they were reflecting profound changes that were taking place in the theory of punishment. In Europe, attitudes towards crime and punishment began to shift rapidly during the second half of the eighteenth century. Enlightenment ideas brought condemnation of what were seen as old, barbaric practices.

In 1764, a young Italian nobleman, Cesare Beccaria, called for the abolition of torture and of the death penalty, on philosophical and moral grounds. His book, *On Crime and Punishment*, was an instant hit. It was translated into many languages, including English, and was read throughout Europe. While Beccaria said little about imprisonment, he did argue it should be as mild as possible, since most people in prison had not yet been convicted. Other reformers also argued that prisons should seek to reform criminals rather than to punish them.

In England, a retired merchant and landowner named John Howard took a more practical approach, focusing on the specific reforms needed in prisons. He made an extensive tour of both British and European prisons, and was dismayed by what he saw. In 1777, he published a detailed report on the state of prisons in Britain and on the Continent, which shocked the reading public. He made a series of concrete suggestions as to how imprisonment should be transformed, partly inspired by prison reforms already underway in some parts of Europe. Prisoners, he argued, should be treated with humanity. They should not be put in chains, nor subjected to exactions by their gaolers. Gaols should be well situated and airy, with a decent water supply, and constantly kept clean. Prisoners should be separated according to their crimes and their delinquency, so that old, hardened offenders didn't influence young prisoners inside for minor crimes. Debtors should be separated from other prisoners, and men from women. Prisoners should sleep in separate locked cells at night, in part to prevent them plotting escapes. If they were sentenced to hard labour, they should come together during the day in common areas to perform it. Howard even published a set of plans for a prison that reflected his ideas.

John Howard's "A Plan for a County Gaol," from his 1777 book *The State of the Prisons in England and Wales*. The plan shows the whole prison complex, including the yard, surrounded by a wall. Different types of prisoners were to be housed in separate buildings (marked by the small squares) that stood on arches above the ground. This open plan was not suited to Quebec's harsh climate.

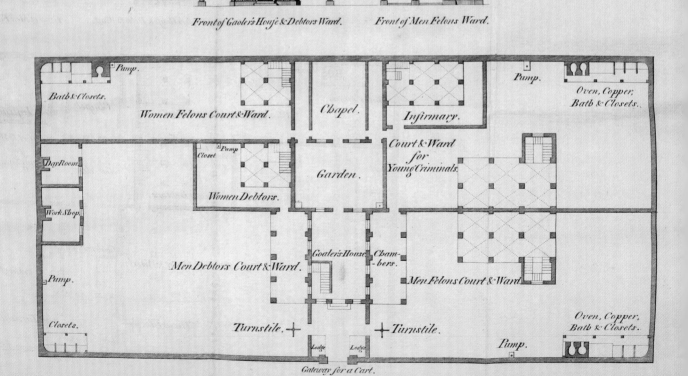

John Howard comes to Quebec

These revolutionary ideas soon found their way across the Atlantic. Beccaria was quoted extensively by the men behind the American Revolution, and his book was for sale in Quebec as early as the 1780s. Howard's ideas also found their way to Quebec, and the Quebec Library had copies of his books. But from ideal to practice was a big step. A new prison cost money, which the colonial government had little of. Even a plan to finance a new prison in Montreal by public lottery failed. Budget-conscious administrators focused instead on fixing up existing prisons, while affirming, against all evidence, that the current buildings were fundamentally sound and well-adapted.

But as ideas like those of Beccaria and Howard slowly percolated through colonial society, attitudes began to change. The 1802 Quebec grand jury report was echoed by a similar report from Montreal, denouncing the gaol there. Robert Shore Milnes, the colony's lieutenant-governor, listened, and in 1803 he presented the issue to the colony's legislature, including elected House of Assembly. The Quebec gaol, he stated, was "unequal to the furnishing such accommodations as both humanity and policy require." The Assembly set up a committee to study the issue and to recommend the best locations for new gaols. For Quebec City, they recommended the ground occupied by the Old Gaol, the Royal Redoubt (although they mistakenly called it the Dauphin Redoubt). They also suggested that a separate house of correction should be set up, perhaps on the grounds of the old intendant's palace (a plan that was never put into effect).

POLITICS AND BUREAUCRACY

Everything seemed to be on track. But political disputes and bureaucratic bickering got in the way. First, the old Quebec-Montreal rivalry raised its hoary head. Montreal assemblymen asserted that while they definitely needed a new gaol, all that Quebec City needed was to repair the current gaol ... the very gaol whose wretched condition had been so denounced by the grand jury! The committee ended up deciding that Montreal needed a new gaol more urgently than Quebec City, although both should eventually be built. The British army then refused to give up the Royal Redoubt, despite requests by Milnes and by his successor, Thomas Dunn. Next there was the problem of paying for the new buildings. In the Assembly, this led to a bitter fight between the mainly French-speaking *Canadien* party (which dominated the Assembly) and the mainly British mercantile interests. Would money for the gaols come from a tax on land (which would directly affect the mainly *Canadien* farmers and landholders), or from increased customs duties (which would hurt the predominately British import/export merchants)?

The fight became wrapped up in a larger political battle between the two factions. In the end, the *Canadien* party won out, and the colonial legislature passed a law in 1805 that financed the new gaols out of duties on imports of tea, spirits, wine, and molasses. Still, construction didn't start immediately. First, the British merchants opposed to the law tried to have it blocked in London. Though they were ultimately unsuccessful, the gaols remained in a sort of political limbo until the King finally approved the financing law in 1807. As well, the army still refused to give up the Royal Redoubt. It took the arrival of a new governor, Sir James Craig, in the fall of 1807, to get the army to budge. Unlike his predecessors, Craig was also commander in chief of the British forces in Canada, and so he simply ordered the military to give up their building.

PLANS AND ARCHITECTS

Five years after the Quebec grand jury had made its report denouncing the horrible conditions in the Artillery Barracks gaol, it was finally time to begin building the new gaol. In December 1807, Craig appointed three commissioners to oversee the construction process: Henry Allcock, the colony's Chief Justice; Louis de Salaberry, a *Canadien* seigneur, and the member of the House of Assembly who had sponsored the 1805 gaols bill; and John Blackwood, a prominent Quebec City merchant and assemblyman. Allcock died not long after, and was replaced by Quebec City lawyer and assemblyman Michel-Amable Berthelot d'Artigny, who had vigorously argued for a new gaol in Quebec City during the debate with the Montreal assemblymen.

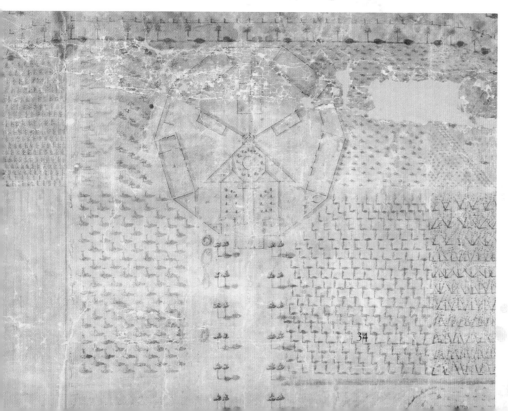

Part of François Baillairgé's 1807 plan for a model house of correction set in the countryside. This shows the radial prison building, an idea imported from continental Europe and later used in penitentiaries in the United States. The commissioners opted instead for John Howard's English ideas.

34

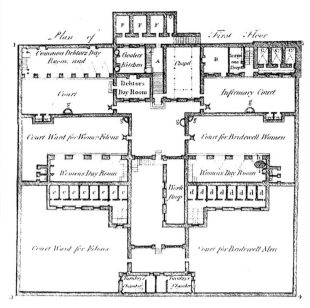

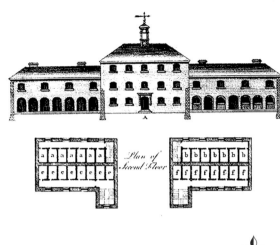

John Call's 1779 plan of Bodmin Gaol, in Cornwall.
This plan was available in Quebec City when
Baillairgé was designing his gaol and was probably
the one given him by Chief Justice Allcock. It was a
more detailed illustration of how John Howard's ideas
might be concretely implemented. While the ideas
most likely inspired Baillairgé and the Quebec gaol
commissioners, the gaol they built was very different.

To design the new gaol, the commissioners turned to a well-established Quebec City architect, François Baillairgé. Baillairgé came from a prominent artistic family. He had trained as an artist in Paris, and initially worked mainly as a painter and a wood-carver. But he also developed his talents as an architect, designing houses for wealthy Quebec City residents and working on public buildings such as the Quebec City courthouse, completed in 1804. Baillairgé had also developed an interest in prison architecture. In 1807, at the behest of Joseph-François Perrault (who later played a part in the imprisonment of Aubert de Gaspé), he drew up the plans for a house of correction in the countryside near Quebec City. It was inspired by the radial design then in use in places like Ghent, in Flanders, which John Howard had reproduced in his book. Though this plan was never built, Baillairgé was still the natural choice to design the new gaol.

It was John Howard's ideas that were meant to inspire the design of the new gaol. In January 1808, Chief Justice Allcock met with Baillairgé, and handed him a plan of a prison based on Howard's ideals. Instead of the plan in Howard's book, this was more likely a plan of Bodmin Gaol in Cornwall, built in the late 1770s. A copy of this plan was in the Quebec Library in 1808, and it also inspired the new gaol then being built in Montreal. Baillairgé also no doubt had access to Howard's book on prisons, with its detailed recommendations and plans. Baillairgé came back to the commissioners with several different plans, along with a scale model of the gaol for use during construction. All of these were discussed, altered, laid before Governor Craig for his comments, discussed and altered again, and finally submitted to Craig for the final choice. Craig seems to have had a keen interest in prison reform. While we don't know what he said about the Quebec gaol, his detailed comments on the Montreal gaol show that he had an excellent understanding of Howard's principles.

Baillairgé versus Howard

In many respects, the gaol designed by Baillairgé did indeed follow Howard's ideas. Sitting high on the hillside above Saint-Jean Street, it was well aired. The solid stone building was divided into twelve different wards, which should have been enough for separating the different types of prisoners. Each ward had a central common room surrounded by cells that could be locked up at night, as Howard suggested. It had a source of running water (the same spring that used to flood the Royal Redoubt), and a pump to move the water up to a reservoir in the attic. It had an exercise yard in the back. It even had an oven; not for baking bread (bread for the prisoners was bought from a baker in the town) but probably, as Howard suggested, for heating up prisoners' clothes and bedding so as to kill vermin like fleas, lice, and bedbugs.

In other ways, though, Baillairgé's building was a compromise. It didn't look anything like the proposed county gaol in Howard's book, or the gaol in Bodmin designed by John Call. Howard wanted his building sitting up on arches, to encourage ventilation and to stop prisoners from escaping through tunnels. This was not suited to Quebec's cold climate. Howard and Call designed their gaols with separate buildings for the different types of prisoners; Baillairgé's gaol was all in a single building. Howard insisted that an ideal prison "should not be surrounded by other buildings, nor built in the middle of a town or city." This part of his advice was completely ignored, and as we will see, caused no end of problems. Howard insisted that the prison hospital be entirely separate from the main building. In the Quebec gaol, a separate building was never built, and the hospital ended up occupying one of the twelve wards. Howard wanted separate exercise yards for the different types of prisoners; the Quebec gaol initially had a single exercise yard, where debtors mixed with felons, and, at the beginning at least, it was used by both men and women. Howard recommended a large workshop for debtors; there was initially no such space in the Quebec gaol. While Howard insisted that the gaoler had to live near the gaol, it was to be in a separate house. In the Quebec gaol, another one of the wards was appropriated as living quarters for the gaoler and his family.

Even the outside appearance of the building represented a compromise, this time between English and French architectural taste. Overall, Baillairgé adopted the Palladian style then in vogue for official buildings in provincial England. The building was rigorously symmetrical with a central block that came forward from the wings; the decoration was neoclassical, such as the central round window under the peaked roof, an *oeil de bouc* (ram's eye), as Baillairgé and his contractors called it. But Baillairgé also called on his Parisian training, drawing inspiration from the French architectural theorist Philibert de l'Orme. In his personal copy of de l'Orme's book, he wrote that he relied on it when designing the façade of the gaol.

CONSTRUCTION BEGINS

Work on the Quebec gaol finally began in earnest in March 1808, when the Royal Redoubt was emptied of its military stores and Louis Gauvreau was hired to demolish it. In May, Pierre Plante began to excavate the bedrock for the foundations of the new gaol, and in June, the commissioners entered into notarized agreements with the main contractors who would work on the project: masons Edward Cannon and his sons Lawrence and John for the stonework; carpenter Jean-Baptiste Bédard for the joists, the floors and the roof; joiners Charles Marié and Pierre Faucher for the rest of the woodwork, such as the frames for the doors and windows, the doors themselves, and the tables and benches for the wards; glazier Pierre Romain for the windows and for painting the gaol; and blacksmiths Pierre Lefrançois and Louis Cérat for the bars and iron grills for the doors and windows, along with the other ironwork.

Though inspired by English and French models, the gaol was very much a local production. The architect and most of the contractors and workmen were francophones. The most lucrative contract went to the Cannons, who were anglophones, but they were Irish Catholic immigrants who had developed close links to Quebec City's francophone Catholic population. John Cannon, for example, married Angèle Grihaut dit Larivière the year he began working on the gaol. The Cannons were among Quebec City's most prominent stonemasons, and had already worked on public buildings such as the Anglican cathedral, as well as Catholic parish churches. Some of the other contractors also had surprising family connections to the gaol. Pierre Romain's father had done glazing work for the old gaol in 1775. Carpenter Jean-Baptiste Bédard was the brother of Pierre-Stanislas Bédard, the head of the *Canadien* party. Pierre-Stanislas was locked up for sedition by Governor Craig between 1810 and 1811, in the Artillery Barracks gaol, while Jean-Baptiste was building the new gaol that Craig had planned!

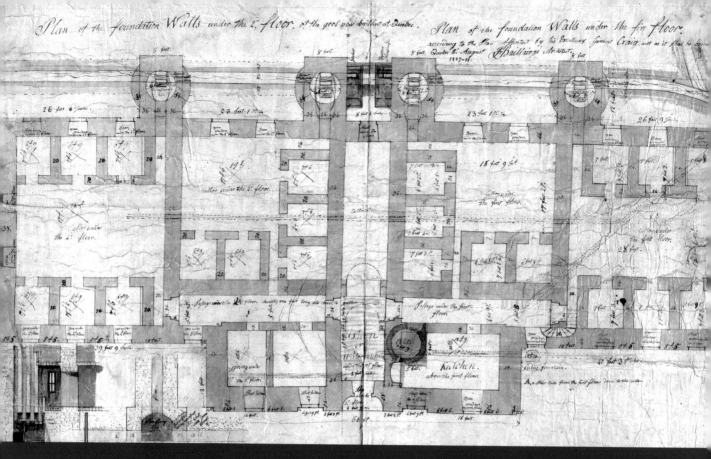

The only remaining working plan of the gaol by Baillairgé, drawn in 1808. It mainly shows the foundations that were to be built by the Cannons, under the cell blocks. The four towers at the back are the privies, with a large drain connecting them. At the bottom left is Baillairgé's sketch of how the privies would work, with an individual chute for each floor.

Most of the materials used in the gaol were also locally produced. The stone was quarried from specialized quarries around Quebec City, at Beauport, L'Ange-Gardien, Pointe-aux-Trembles, and on the Chaudière River. All the ironwork was locally produced, from the bars on the windows to the rings in the floors. The stoves came from the ironworks at Batiscan, up-river. Only a few items remind us that Quebec City was part of a wider empire. The pump and the roofing tin were specially imported from England; the window panes and the paint were probably also imports.

Laying the cornerstone

The cornerstone of the gaol was laid in June 1809, once the foundations had reached ground level. The ceremony was led by Governor Craig, and conducted by the city's freemasons, while a military band played. The newspapers commented favourably on the "brilliant display of Female Beauty" in attendance. Craig himself laid the cornerstone,

Was the Quebec gaol Canada's first?

The Quebec gaol is often described as the first purpose-built prison in Canada and the first to be inspired by John Howard's principles. Neither of these is true. First, there were purpose-built prisons in Canada under the French regime. Second, work started on two gaols in 1808, one in Quebec City, designed by Baillairgé, and the other in Montreal, designed by Louis Charland. Both were inspired by Howard. But the Montreal gaol, located near where City Hall is today, was finished first, in the spring of 1812, and was already housing prisoners as early as 1811. This was because Montreal's situation was more urgent than Quebec City's. The old building used as a gaol in Montreal had burnt down in 1803, and the prisoners were housed temporarily in vaults under the courthouse. In Quebec City, while the existing gaol in the Artillery Barracks was far from ideal, it was nevertheless thought adequate to serve its purpose until construction of the new gaol was finished in the late fall of 1812.

along with a selection of gold, silver, and copper coins, and a pewter plaque with a Latin inscription composed by Louis de Salaberry, one of the commissioners. Then there was a grand speech by Alexander Spark, the Presbyterian minister and chaplain of the freemasons, whose own church was quickly going up just across from the gaol. Spark's speech focused on the gaol's role in suppressing vice and punishing the guilty in order to protect the innocent, although he did mention the need to "reclaim the vicious" in this "mansion of Sin and repentance." This was in the same spirit as the public inscription put up a year later over the main door, "May this prison deliver the good from the bad." De Salaberry's inscription, hidden away in the cornerstone (which has never been found), focused much more on reforming prisoners: the end read "May God grant that from this house of punishment, all may leave free from their punishment and live happily and well!!"

Completing the building

As construction continued, there were further delays. Disagreements arose between Baillairgé and the contractors, especially the Cannons. Baillairgé often changed his mind during construction. For example, at first he planned to have not just one *oeil*

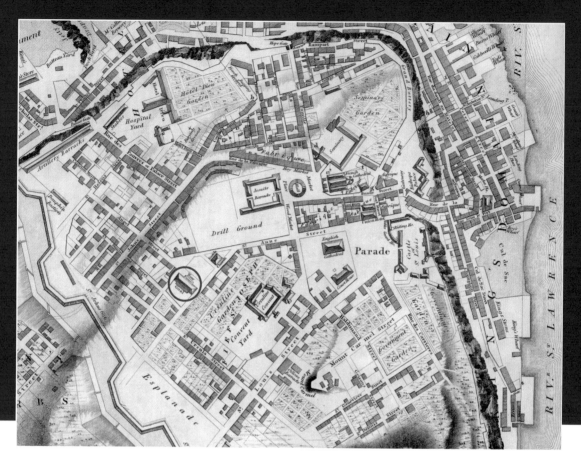

The gaol in the city in 1815, soon after it opened, as drawn by Joseph Bouchette. The Artillery Barracks, previously used as a gaol, are at the top left of the map.

de bouc window, but three, but then couldn't fit two of them in. He also wanted more elaborate decoration on the the building's exterior, including pilasters between each set of windows in the wings, but had to cut back to save costs. The project as a whole led to massive cost over-runs that stopped construction for over a year, and eventually more than doubled the initial budget from £9000 to almost £20,000. The building wasn't completed until the fall of 1812, and the prisoners were most likely transferred to the new gaol in late November. The trouble wasn't over once the building was finished. The Cannons launched a lawsuit against the commissioners, claiming extra expenses caused in large part by Baillairgé's constant changes. This dragged on until 1817 and ended up costing an extra £1900.

Once completed, the building did receive some positive comments. Joseph Bouchette, surveyor general of Lower Canada and author of a detailed description of the colony, who had followed classes given by Baillairgé, called it a "very handsome building" with

Cells in the condemned ward as they can be seen today. The iron door on the leftmost cell is original, as is the wooden door on the right; the wooden door on the left is a reconstruction.

an interior "most judiciously planned, as it respects the health, cleanliness, and safe custody of those who are so unfortunate as to become its inmates." But the gaol almost immediately came under fire from the very people who had been responsible for it. In 1815, John Mure, who had replaced Blackwood as one of the commissioners, complained of "the insufficiency of the Materials used and the bad Workmanship in several instances." Even Baillairgé himself declared in 1815 that, while his building was generally in good shape, there were "defects that were inevitable in a building constructed on the Cheap!" Here was the classic response of the architect with a dissatisfied client: you shouldn't have tried to cut costs!

THE BUILDING AS IT BEGAN LIFE

When it opened in late 1812, the outside of the gaol was roughly similar to what it is today, although the windows were smaller and the front entrance was less imposing. It is much more difficult for visitors today to imagine what it looked like inside. There are no surviving pictures or photos of the interior that we know of, and the renovations carried out when the building was converted to a college in 1868 almost completely transformed the internal arrangements. Many assume that the upper floors were similar to the cramped, vaulted wards that still survive on the ground floor. In fact, the wards on the main floors of the gaol had plastered ceilings and larger brick-walled cells. The forbidding wards that still exist were actually meant for exceptional cases: people condemned to death, for example, or prisoners who had misbehaved and were put in solitary confinement. When the building was converted, these cells were not taken down, presumably because the arches supported the floors above.

After some early adjustments, the basic layout of the gaol changed little through to the end. On the ground floor was the main entrance, flanked by one room for the outside turnkey and another for the gaol guard. Directly ahead was the main staircase, which was the only way to get to the upper floors. To the left, the south wing held kitchens for the prisoners and for the gaoler and his family; to the right, in the north wing, were the condemned ward and the so-called "Black Hole," whose cells were used for solitary confinement. On the first floor, the large wards at either end of the south and the north wing were used respectively as the gaoler's apartments and as the hospital. The two smaller central wards were used for ordinary prisoners. In each of these wards, there was a central common room, with five or six cells arranged around the outside. On this floor, a very small room at the front gave onto

the iron balcony used for hangings, while on either side of it, two other small rooms could be occupied by debtors or used for other special prisoners. The second floor was the same as the first, except that the larger wards were used as a chapel and as a debtors' ward, and one of the small front rooms housed the inside turnkey. The top, or third floor had only the two smaller wards; at either end were garrets under the roof which were used to store old rope and other material used for prisoners put to hard labour, who were usually housed on this floor. Each ward had its own separate privy, reached by a special, narrow passage that led to the outside privy towers. Under the ground floor, there was a large unfinished cellar, but despite a persistent legend it was never occupied by prisoners. Above the third floor was a small attic under the eaves, with the water reservoir and the *oeil de bouc* that looked out onto the street.

Interior of one of the cells in the condemned ward. The bed on the right is a recent reconstruction, which follows the original plans. The iron ring on the floor would have been used to chain condemned prisoners.

Reconstructed floor plans of the gaol

These plans are based on an 1837 plan of the ground floor by Edward Hacker, extrapolated to the other floors based on detailed research.

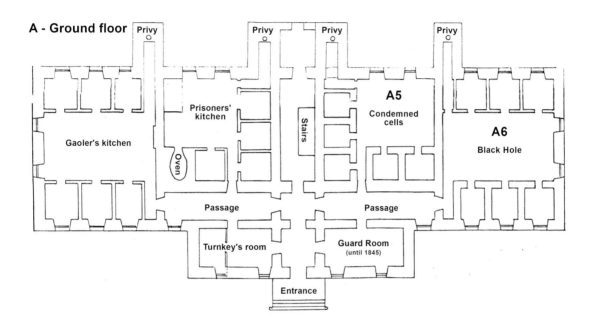

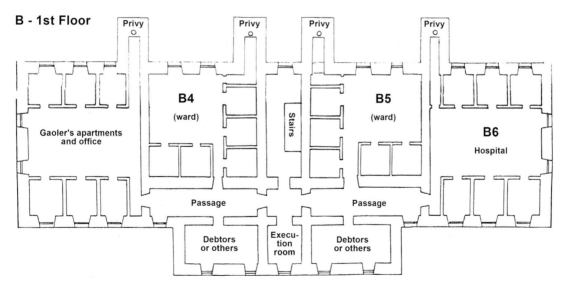

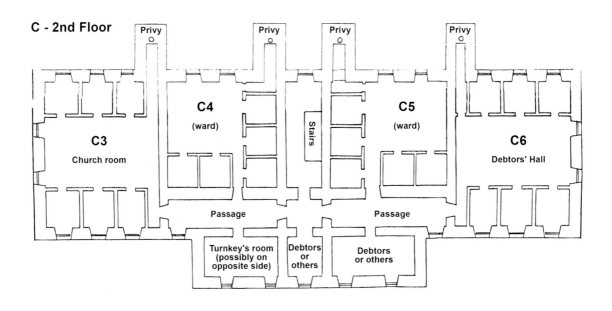

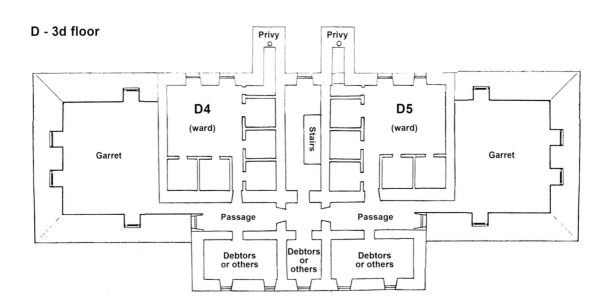

Repairs and additions

After opening, the gaol was frequently in need of repairs. Major renovations were carried out in 1827-1828, in 1843, and in 1847, when the entire roof was replaced. The gaol was also lit by gas in 1849, and hooked up to the city waterworks in 1855. But the building itself underwent no fundamental alterations. Instead, two new buildings were built in the gaol yard to meet special needs.

The first was the women's prison. Up until the 1820s, women and men were both housed in the original building, though in separate wards: the women were up on the third floor. As we will see, there was a rapid increase in the number of prisoners in the 1820s, which made the original gaol too small. As well, there was already a partially completed building in the back of the gaol yard, initially intended to house a treadmill for the prisoners. In 1829 this was converted into a separate prison for women. Though it was sometimes known as the house of correction, in fact, it housed all women prisoners, whatever their status, while men sentenced to the house of correction stayed, as before, in the main gaol building. It had the distinction of being the first separate women's prison established in Quebec, and perhaps even in British North America.

The women's prison was small. It had only four rooms, on two floors. Downstairs, one room housed the matron and her husband. The other served as a kitchen, and possibly at times as a hospital. The prisoners lived in the two rooms upstairs. By the 1850s, the women's prison was so overcrowded that some women had to be placed in the main gaol building. But it remained in use until the gaol closed in 1867. The women also had their own exercise yard, separated from the men's yard by a wooden fence – hardly enough to stop men and women from talking to one another, as the sheriff often complained.

Current photograph of the women's prison, on the corner of Dauphine and Sainte-Angèle streets. Female prisoners would have been housed on the upper floor, but with easy communication with the street. The main gaol building is visible on the left.

The other new building was not for prisoners, but instead for the guards posted outside the gaol. They had first occupied a room at the entrance of the main building. But this was far too small. After repeated complaints, a small guardhouse was built for them in 1845, also in the back of the gaol yard.

There were also other smaller buildings added from time to time in the gaol yard: a shed for firewood; a shed used to dry oakum and possibly also used at times for hard labour; even a small outside kitchen, called a "caboose." This meant that the gaol yard, already small, got very crowded, which reduced the space available for prisoners to exercise.

*　*　*

This was the gaol from when it opened in 1812 until it closed in 1867. But the buildings were just the backdrop for the tens of thousands of lives, with their heavy weight of suffering and sorrow, which flowed through it during the half century of its existence.

The guardhouse in 1950, from the corner of Sainte-Anne and Sainte-Angèle streets. The gaol building is visible behind to the right.

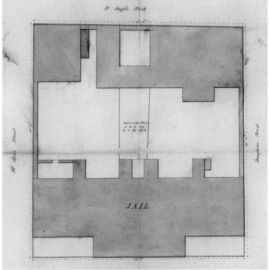

The gaol yard in 1861, a few years before the gaol closed. There was very little space left in the yard for prisoners to exercise in.

THE PEOPLE IN PRISON

The gaol building remains today. The people who passed through it are long dead, and mostly forgotten. But the gaol's excellent records, and historians' methods, can make them live again, if only in our minds. I would even argue that we have a moral obligation to remember them, and to attempt an empathetic reconstruction of these past lives.

Prisoners and their crimes

The most important people in the gaol were the prisoners themselves. Who were the poor souls who found themselves locked up in the Quebec gaol? Were they really all criminals? Above all, they were a very mixed lot. As Sheriff Sewell complained in 1839, the Quebec gaol was "at once a lock-up House, a House of Correction, a receptacle for the Insane, and a refuge for the Destitute – that sailors in vast numbers are its inmates during the Summer Months, and that occasionally, Military Convicts have been kept there for long periods. In addition to which it is the only prison in the District for the Detention of Debtors."

   In the earlier period, most prisoners ended up in gaol for the same wide variety of reasons as in the eighteenth century: mainly those accused of theft or of crimes of violence, along with a sprinkling of morality offenses such as prostitution, a few political prisoners, a regular stream of debtors, and a wide range of other offenders. Most were in gaol awaiting their trials, although some had been sentenced to imprisonment as a punishment. Since the "Bloody Code" remained largely in effect in Quebec until 1841, there was also a regular complement of condemned prisoners awaiting either pardon or execution.

Loose, idle, and disorderly

This picture of the gaol population began to change in the 1820s and 1830s. Quebec City's population exploded in the first decades of the nineteenth century, as it was transformed into a major international port and economic hub. Sailors crowded the streets; poor immigrants from the British Isles poured through the city, mainly on their way elsewhere; soldiers from the large British garrison walked out on leave; and *habitants* from the surrounding countryside sold their wares on the city's markets and used its services and its institutions. Taverns and brothels proliferated to serve the needs of this often-rowdy population. In Quebec City as around the Western world, urban elites grew increasingly frightened by what they saw as the "dangerous classes" who crowded city streets. Behaviours such as public drunkenness, vagrancy, begging, and even simply lounging on the sidewalk, which had mostly been tolerated before, were no longer acceptable. Under pressure from middle-class citizens, people who behaved like this became the target of increasingly professional police forces, and were swept up with other "undesirables" such as rowdy and disobedient sailors and street prostitutes. Following new trends in punishment theory, it was the gaol that became the primary means of disciplining the unruly urban masses. Many of those arrested for what today we would see as petty crimes ended up in the gaol for short terms of imprisonment. In December 1859, two teenagers were committed for sliding in the streets, and another in 1865 for throwing snowballs. By the 1840s and 1850s, the most common reason people were in the Quebec gaol was for the catchall offense of being "loose, idle, and disorderly," which covered just about any form of unacceptable public behaviour along with simply being poor. As with Lucy Noyes, it is very hard to characterize many of these as true criminals; especially since, as we will see, many of those committed for this "crime" actually sought out the prison as a refuge from starvation and cold.

This broadening out of the crimes for which people could be imprisoned had a very significant consequence: severe overcrowding of the gaol. The Quebec gaol had been planned and built just before this surge in imprisonment and was designed for just over one hundred prisoners. This limit was very rapidly surpassed, and reached a peak in the late 1830s and early 1840s. The average number of prisoners committed to the gaol in September 1839, 1840, and 1841 was over two hundred, and a record number was reached on September 23, 1840, when there were over 260 prisoners in the gaol. This meant that at some points, there might be sixty or more prisoners crowded into a ward designed for twelve. There were fewer prisoners in the 1850s, but numbers shot up again in the 1860s. As we will see, this overcrowding had very significant effects on life and society in the gaol.

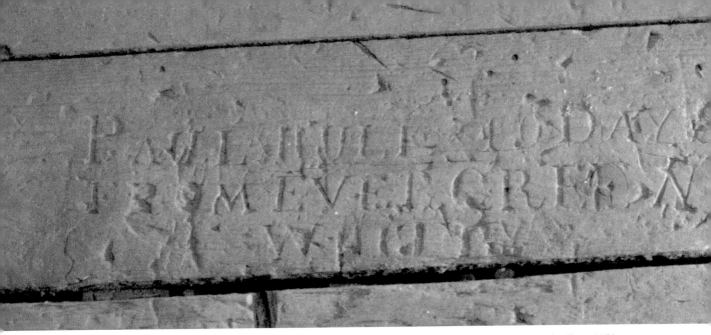

Graffiti scratched by Christopher Paul into the wooden floor of one of the condemned cells in 1850. It reads: "C. Paul Hull 40 days from Evergreen Whitby." This is just one of many graffiti left by prisoners, some of which still survive today.

Disobedient sailors

Each summer, hundreds of sailors were incarcerated for disobeying their masters or deserting their ships. These were men like Christopher Paul, a twenty-two-year-old English sailor who arrived in Quebec City on the ship *Evergreen* in May 1850. Along with several crewmates, Paul refused to work, and the ship's captain, Benjamin Pearson, had them committed to gaol. Paul was sentenced to forty days. He guaranteed his place in history by scratching his name and the details of his story into the wooden planks of one of the cells in the condemned ward. He was probably locked up there because there was simply no space anywhere else. The graffiti is still there today. Paul was let out a month later, just as *Evergreen* was setting sail back to London with a load of timber. It was probably Captain Pearson who got Paul released so that he wouldn't lose his crewman's labour. Two of Paul's crewmates were luckier – they managed to escape from the gaol and were never heard of again. Seamen were also very often incarcerated for other crimes, such as public drunkenness or fighting. In the 1850s, they sometimes made up half of the male prisoners in the gaol in the summer.

Military prisoners, POWs and political prisoners

As Sewell noted, there were also other special sorts of prisoners. The military used the gaol for its own prisoners, such as soldiers convicted of desertion or disobedience, when its own prison was too full. During the War of 1812, the gaol housed several dozen American prisoners of war, though most were incarcerated on prison ships in the harbour. There were also occasional political prisoners, most notably during the rebellions of 1837 to 1838, when thirty-odd Patriotes (rebels) were rounded up and imprisoned in Quebec City.

This was very few compared to the hundreds of Patriotes packed into prisons in Montreal at the same time, but they included some notable figures such as the newspaper editor and politician Étienne Parent and museum owner Pierre Chasseur (whose collections later ended up being taken over by the Literary and Historical Society of Quebec).

Transportees

Up until the early 1840s, the gaol also served as a way-station for prisoners from throughout the colony who were about to be transported to England, on their way to penal servitude in places such as Australia. This was a common punishment for people convicted of serious crimes, and especially those who had been condemned to death but then pardoned by the colony's governor. They also included many military prisoners. For civilians, the practice stopped when prisoners could be incarcerated instead in the penitentiary at Kingston, after the 1841 union of Upper and Lower Canada.

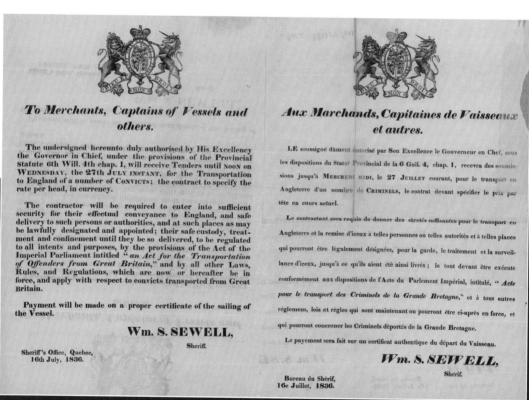

1836 advertisement from Sheriff Sewell seeking a ship on which to transport prisoners then held in the Quebec gaol. Sewell often had great difficulty finding ship captains willing to take on the prisoners, many of whom were seen as being very dangerous. The only way to convince them was to pay out very large sums of money. In all, thirteen convicts were supposed to be shipped out this time, on the aptly named *William Money*. They included James Shuter senior and junior, who had been convicted of murder but pardoned; William Shuter, another son, had been hanged in front of the gaol for the same murder in 1834. Legal wrangling meant that the Shuters were taken off the ship and put back in prison, only to be shipped out the following year.

The old gaol building in 1971, before the recent renovations. The former Methodist church is immediately to the right, just across the street. In the foreground is the roof of Saint Andrew's Presbyterian Church.

The gaol as asylum

The gaol didn't only house people accused or convicted of crimes. As had long been the tradition, it also acted as an overflow institution for housing the insane. People with serious mental illnesses were put in gaol when they couldn't be placed in other institutions such as the Hôpital-Général, which had a few cells for the purpose. When in gaol, they were given no particular care. Usually, they were just placed in the wards with other prisoners, where they might disturb all those around them if they got agitated, and prevent them from sleeping. At best, individual prisoners were asked to take care of their insane fellows, with extra food as a reward. At first, there were no restraints available other than chains, which gaol officials were very reluctant to use. As a result, the insane sometimes committed violent acts. One man tried to cut his own throat with a piece of window glass, another with a blunt breadknife; another stabbed a fellow prisoner during a visit by a grand jury. One woman repeatedly tried to set fire to the straw from her bed. Putting the insane in separate rooms wasn't the answer either. In 1848, the sheriff complained that while he had placed an insane woman in a small room in the main building, "she annoys persons passing along the street by her shouting and throwing water out upon them." This only got worse as the city closed around the gaol: in 1852, the grand jury reported that "the place has become a nuisance to the neighbourhood from the noise and uproar kept up by these insane persons insomuch that the congregation of the Methodist Church opposite ... on last Sunday were so much annoyed by this roaring that it was with the greatest difficulty they could perform divine service." Sheriffs, gaolers, grand juries and prison inspectors regularly complained that the gaol was no place for the mentally ill, but little changed. Even after a regular asylum opened at Beauport in 1845, and insane prisoners were regularly transferred to it, financial concerns and the reluctance of the Beauport asylum to accept the violently insane meant that right up until the gaol was closed, the courts kept on using it as a place to dump the mentally ill.

The gaol as a social service

In the absence of any significant public social services in the colony, the gaol also often served as a receptacle for society's cast-offs. This had already been the case in the eighteenth century, when diseased prostitutes were housed in the gaol while they were being cured, and it continued in the new gaol. In 1815, a grand jury complained that in the wards set aside as a house of correction, there were women who had been sent there simply because they were homeless and destitute. Of course, in almost all cases, the poor would be formally convicted of an offense like vagrancy and sentenced to gaol. This is what authorized the gaoler to keep them in gaol, out of the cold. But in reality, it was a form of judicial charity, a legal fiction that allowed the gaol to be used as a refuge.

The practice shocked well-meaning citizens, for whom the gaol should only serve to punish real criminals. Another grand jury in 1836 proclaimed "the very great necessity of a Penitentiary and proper house of refuge for the poor destitute stranger, seaman and others, as many persons we understand, apply at the close of the summer season to be committed to the gaol as a place of refuge or shelter from the inclemency of the weather during the winter." In 1838, the secretary of the Quebec Jail Association, the reverend Henry Sewell, asserted that half of the 235 people committed for being loose, idle and disorderly were actually seeking food and shelter. This represented about 15 percent of prisoners overall. The practice of using the gaol as a refuge for the poorest of the poor seems even to have become a more important part of the gaol's mission as time went on. By the 1860s, there were more people in the gaol in the winter months than there were in the summer, a reversal of earlier decades when the gaol filled up in summer months with sailors and others passing through the port. The most common way of getting committed was by "voluntary confession" of vagrancy before a local court; in essence, asking the court to be sent to prison. The practice became increasingly common in the 1850s and 1860s. In 1860, for example, almost a quarter of prisoners overall got into the prison in this way, and more than a third during the winter months. Most of these were women: in 1860, more than 40 percent of women prisoners were there at their own behest, and over half during the winter. These "voluntary" prisoners were still convicted by the courts, and were treated no differently than prisoners who were in the gaol involuntarily, but it does mean that a significant proportion of prisoners actually wanted to be in the gaol, rather than out.

A particularly poignant illustration of how the gaol served as a refuge for people who had absolutely no connection with crime is the case of Mary Gray, a poor woman who died in the gaol in March 1847. In December 1846, John O'Connor, a Quebec city carter, heard from neighbours that Gray was perishing from cold and hunger in the garret she occupied on D'Artigny Street, where the Quebec National Assembly building stands today. He found her lying in an armful of straw, covered by an old blanket with no stove and no fuel. She was very sick and hadn't eaten in three days. He tried to take her to the Hôtel-Dieu hospital, but they wouldn't let her in as she was suffering from venereal disease. He then went to the chief of police, Robert Henry Russell, for help. Russell asked O'Connor if he could prove she was a woman of loose character or a vagrant, so that she could be charged, convicted, and committed to gaol. O'Connor replied that he had never known her to conduct herself improperly. Nevertheless, Russell sent two policemen to take her to the gaol. She was so weak that they had to carry her, but she went with them willingly. She was committed without any warrant while waiting for a decision from the magistrates. The next day, the court ordered her discharged, but the gaol physician, Joseph Morrin, refused to release her, as she had huge sores all over her body. She stayed in the gaol for the next three months, in a room by herself in the hospital ward, tended to by two other female prisoners. She was fed a quart of milk a day, and sometimes soup and bread. During her last month she was also given wine to drink. Her sores healed, but she got weaker and weaker; and then she died.

The overall picture

Between 1812 and 1867, we know the reasons for about 58,000 committals to the Quebec gaol. Almost 32,000 committals were for public order offenses such as vagrancy (including those committed on their own request), public drunkenness, or prostitution; about 9000 for various labour related offenses, including disobedience among seamen; about 7000 for various types of theft, burglary, robbery, or forgery; about 5000 for crimes of violence, such as assault, rape, or murder; a little under 2000 for debt; perhaps a thousand for various types of political offenses or acts of resistance against the state; about 600 military prisoners; about 350 committed as insane; and the remainder a hodgepodge of various offenses, including one poor fellow imprisoned in 1858 for "hunting a snipe."

How many prisoners?

It's not easy calculating just how many prisoners passed through the doors of the Quebec gaol. The official registers record just over 59,000 committals of prisoners between September 1813, almost a year after the gaol opened, and May 1867, when it closed. All of these names are available in an online database at Bibliothèque et Archives nationales du Québec. But there were many other prisoners who didn't get recorded in these registers. The American prisoners of war in the gaol in 1812-1815 were recorded separately by military authorities. Many children who accompanied their mothers into the gaol show up in bread accounts and death records, but not in the registers. Prisoners brought in drunk and disorderly at night by city watchmen or police, but released the next day without being charged, passed through almost without a trace. At some points, prisoners nominally committed to the house of correction weren't recorded in the gaol registers either, but instead, in separate registers, to keep up the fiction of these being separate institutions. Overall, there must have been many thousands more people who experienced imprisonment in the gaol building than shown in the registers. At the same time, many of those committed to the gaol were there more than once; sometimes upwards of fifty or a hundred times. It is very difficult to estimate how many different individuals went through the gaol ("James Brown" was committed sixty times, but how many different people was that?), but a very rough estimate would be at least 30,000.

Extraordinary prisoners

Over its half-century of existence, the gaol housed some very extraordinary figures. Some have even come down to us through legend.

François Marois dit Malouin

François Marois dit Malouin, the "Docteur L'Indienne," was a folk healer who was hanged in front of the gaol in 1829 for murdering a peddler at Saint-Jean-Port-Joli. He had previously escaped from the gaol in 1825, after being convicted on what was probably a trumped up charge of attempted sodomy. After his death, a legend grew up that he was a serial killer, and although there is absolutely no evidence that this was true

Possibly a sketch of François Marois dit Malouin, the "Docteur L'Indienne." It is on the back of one of the documents used at his trial, probably drawn by a court clerk.

(his basement, where bones were found, turned out to be an old graveyard), the legend remains anchored in Quebec folklore.

Charles Chambers

Charles Chambers was the youthful head of the "Chambers Gang." This was a band of thieves active in Quebec City and the surrounding area in the mid-1830s. who went so far as to rob a chapel. Committed to gaol for a first time in 1835 for burglary, sacrilege and murder, Chambers managed to avoid being found guilty on all charges and was released. He was swept up once again in 1836 and on the strength of the testimony of one of his former accomplices, was sentenced to death for burglary in 1837. But after he feigned conversion to Catholicism, dozens of Quebec City's respectable Catholic citizens, including several prominent clerics, signed a petition begging for his life. As a result, his death sentence was commuted to transportation for life to Australia, although he died on the way, in England, later in 1837. His deeds, and those of his gang, were immortalized by author François-Réal Angers in a rollicking, semi-fictional account published immediately after Chambers' transportation. Angers' book was a resounding success right through the nineteenth century.

Cover page from François-Réal Angers semi-fictional account of the exploits of Charles Chambers and his gang, published in 1837. It is considered to be a milestone in Quebec literature. Angers changed Chambers' name slightly, to Cambray.

55

Pierre Belleau

Pierre "Bis" Belleau's name is still scratched on the floor of one of the cells. He was imprisoned in the gaol fourteen times between 1856 (aged 17) and 1860, for offenses such as larceny, burglary, vandalism, riot, and attempted murder. On the last occasion, he cut through the bars of a window, squeezed through, and lowered himself down with a rope, only to be arrested by the guards. After his last stint in gaol, he fled to the United States and became a "bounty jumper," a soldier who signed up to fight in various regiments during the American Civil War, but then deserted once he got the signing bonus. Belleau soon came back to Quebec and started his life of crime again. In 1864, he was caught and sentenced to four years in the Kingston penitentiary; once again, he nearly escaped from the Quebec gaol before being sent off. Coming back to Quebec again in 1869, he was in and out of the new prison on the Plains of Abraham, escaping several times but always being recaptured. All of this made him something of a romantic folk hero, cheered on by crowds as the little guy who fought the system.

Pierre Belleau's name scratched into the floor of one of the cells, probably during one of his stays.

Baron Fratellin

Perhaps the most unusual prisoner has long been lost to popular memory. He was a European confidence trickster, who went by the name of John Bratish Eliovich, Baron Fratellin. Fratellin first appeared in Quebec City in August 1838. He delivered a rousing lecture at Rasco's Hotel, based on travels he had apparently undertaken in Mexico and the United States since 1827. He also claimed to be known throughout Europe and to hold diplomatic rank. A few weeks later, people began to get suspicious, when he made further claims he couldn't back up. In October, Fratellin rented a horse and cart and tried to flee south to the United States. He was arrested, charged with horse theft, and locked up in the gaol, but managed to get released a couple of weeks later. Right about this time, rebellion was breaking out in Lower Canada. In November 1838, for reasons that aren't entirely clear, Fratellin was arrested along with other Quebec City Patriotes and imprisoned once again, this time charged with treason. Probably in order to endear himself to the authorities, he now claimed to have been in cahoots with the rebels for months. He said he had knowledge of a plot to set off a rebellion in the Quebec City area, and also of a larger Russian plan to give military aid to the Patriotes. This was perfect bait for paranoid colonial officials, who saw rebels in every corner. Fratellin was transferred to the prison in Montreal, where he was supposed to give further testimony against rebels imprisoned there. But this time, he refused. At the same time, he befriended some of the imprisoned rebels, including some who were later hanged. He was then transferred back to Quebec City, released in April 1839, and immediately expelled to Maine, protesting bitterly all the while.

The story is murky at best, but it turns out this was neither the first nor the last time Fratellin had made exaggerated claims. Before coming to Quebec, he had bilked people in Boston, Washington, and Philadelphia. He had claimed to have been a general in the Polish, Spanish, and Mexican armies, as well as the Consul-General of Greece, Mexico, Switzerland, and Turkey, and a native of Hungary. In Philadelphia, he had been accused of forgery and horse-theft, and had run off before being arrested. After being expelled from Lower Canada, he went to Portland, Maine, where he once again began his lecture series and his impostures. After this too eventually went sour, he set off back to Europe, where he disappeared into the murk of history; although not before claiming to have been named a general of the state of Maine.

Cover page of a pamphlet published in Portland, Maine in 1840, just after Fratellin was expelled from Lower Canada, by the author and critic John Neal, who was beguiled by Fratellin and believed his tales. A quarter century later, in 1867, Neal published an article in which he admitted that he had been duped by the con-man.

APPEAL

From the American Press to the American People.

IN BEHALF OF

JOHN BRATISH ELIOVICH,

LATE A MAJOR GENERAL IN THE SERVICE OF HER MOST
CATHOLIC MAJESTY, THE QUEEN OF SPAIN:
K. C. C. K. L. H. &c. &c.
AND NOW AN AMERICAN CITIZEN.

BY JOHN NEAL.

ORDINARY PRISONERS

These highly colourful individuals make for good stories. But the stories of most of the people locked up in the Quebec gaol have not been recorded for posterity. However, the lives and the suffering of these very ordinary prisoners were just as important to them. As they should also be for us.

Men and women

The prisoners were a very diverse lot of people. While the majority were men, women made up a significant minority: overall, almost thirty percent of all prisoners committed were women, and in some years as high as forty percent or more. Most of these women were incarcerated for vagrancy offenses, quite a few of which were related to prostitution. At the heart of these so-called "disorderly women" were a small group who cycled in and out of gaol on a very regular basis, on many occasions being incarcerated at their own request. At least eight of these women were imprisoned a hundred times or more; one, Sarah Doyle, an Irish immigrant (as were seven of the eight), was in and out of the gaol over 170 times from the 1830s to the 1860s; sometimes after being arrested by police, other times at her own behest. Overall, at least a third of incarcerations of female prisoners were of women locked up 30 times or more.

British and French

Even though Quebec City always had a majority French-speaking population, the gaol was also a very English-speaking institution. Almost three quarters of the prisoners were of British or Irish descent, over half being Irish. These were not the rich anglophones of legend! Most of the rest were francophones born in the colony, although there were small numbers of other Europeans such as Scandinavians, Germans, or Italians. Significantly, almost all of the prisoners were white. Blacks and Natives made up little more than one percent of the gaol population.

Young and old

Prisoners also varied widely in age. The average age of prisoners was about thirty, and the vast majority were between sixteen and forty years old, but there were prisoners who were both very young and very old. Up until the late 1850s, there were no special institutions for juvenile offenders, and children as young as seven could be convicted and punished for crimes. A few very young "prisoners," some as young as four, were committed for being loose, idle, and disorderly, but these were accompanying parents or relatives. Michael Kelly was in and out of gaol for vagrancy thirty odd times between 1859 and 1867, beginning when he was five or six up until the age of thirteen. Until 1866, he was always committed with Mary Anne Sullivan, probably his mother. After that, he seems to have graduated to being committed on his very own. Many other young children accompanied their mothers (or sometimes their fathers) into gaol without ever being charged with anything. We only know of their presence because in the gaoler's account books, he noted when they were given half rations of bread, along with milk for infants.

There were still younger denizens of the building. Nothing stopped pregnant women from being committed to gaol, and a number gave birth while they were there: at least twenty-five between 1856 and 1867. This caused particular problems in the crowded women's wards, as a grand jury noted in 1845: "Several women, committed from motives of humanity as destitute, so as to entitle them to a place of refuge, have lately given birth to children within the walls and as there is no separate apartment for them, they necessarily disturb during the night the sleep of the able-bodied inmates who are by day engaged in hard labor."

Still, there were many young prisoners who were imprisoned as punishment for crimes, just like adults. Sometimes the imprisonment was obviously just meant to scare them back on to the straight and narrow. This was the case for Jean-Baptiste and Charles Charland, in 1827. Aged fifteen and eleven respectively, they were each sentenced to a day in the house of correction for drunkenness and frequenting a brothel. In other cases, though, the full severity of the law came to bear on very young folk. In 1845, John and Francis Mathers, Irish immigrants also aged fifteen and eleven, were accused of committing a series of thefts and put in gaol while awaiting their trial. Three weeks later they were convicted, sentenced to seven years in the penitentiary at Kingston, and shipped off. They remained there for five years, until they were finally pardoned in 1850.

The iron balcony and beam used to execute prisoners at the Quebec gaol between 1821 and 1836, over the front door of the gaol, a detail from the watercolour by Cockburn. The small door that led onto the balcony was the last one the condemned ever went through. Note as well the plaque with the inscription, above, and the soldiers on guard, below. The device was erected in 1818 and taken down in 1844.

Sometimes, the courts could be frankly ridiculous. In April 1866, five boys between the ages of seven and twelve were put in gaol for two days for mischievously ringing doorbells ...

As for old prisoners, the record was jointly held by two unfortunate souls. Among those actually charged with a crime, the oldest was Joseph Lagueux, committed twice for vagrancy in the early 1850s, when he was 90-91 years old. He was even sentenced to hard labour, though whether the gaoler actually forced him to perform it, we don't know. But the very oldest occupant of the gaol was George Higgs. Higgs was a former soldier and a long-time resident of the Finlay Asylum for the destitute. In 1864, when he was ninety-two, he was briefly committed to the gaol as dangerously insane. He was released on Christmas Eve, and died two weeks later.

THE LAST WALK

One final group of prisoners deserve special mention: those who were executed. There were not many of them, but each execution was a dramatic public spectacle. In all, sixteen men were hanged during the half-century the gaol was open. In the eighteenth century, hangings mainly took place outside the city, on the Plains of Abraham, near where Martello Tower Number 2 stands today. But in a process that had already begun in England, nineteenth-century executions moved into town and to the gaol. Hangings were still carried out publicly, over the front door of the gaol, and large crowds gathered to witness each one. Initially, an ordinary gallows was used, which involved the executioner climbing up a ladder and pushing the condemned man off. This didn't satisfy the enterprising sheriff of Quebec, Philippe Aubert de Gaspé. In 1818, he arranged for an iron platform to be built over the entrance, with a special door leading out to it from a small room on the first floor and an iron beam above it for attaching the rope. Aubert de Gaspé hired a local locksmith, John Nixon, to devise some sort of contraption involving springs, levers, and chains, which activated a trap door in the balcony from inside the small room. This launched the condemned man into eternity; directly below the gaol's ominous inscription that tasked the prison with protecting the good from the bad.

The first men executed on Aubert de Gaspé's killing machine were Charles Alarie and Thomas Thomas, in 1818. Alarie's hanging went terribly wrong: the rope broke and he had to be strung up again. Indeed, the contraption didn't always work as it was meant to. The contraption didn't always work as it was meant to. Some of the men died in horrible struggles when their feet got caught in the iron railings or something else went wrong. This was also a period when more and more people were questioning the death penalty. Beccaria's ideas on the subject were finally beginning to get some traction! While the public continued to flock to executions, they no longer wanted to see people die a violent death. Sheriff Sewell responded by having a fence erected around the front door of the gaol for each execution. Spectators could watch the condemned man drop, but his death throes were hidden from their sight. By the end of the 1830s, even this became too much. After the hanging of a dozen Patriotes in Montreal in 1838 and 1839, Quebec seems to have gone sour on executions. None were held anywhere in the colony for the next fifteen years. In Quebec City, the iron balcony was taken down in 1844, following a petition from city residents (including Aubert de Gaspé himself!) who saw it as a relic of barbarity that was repugnant to humanity and horrific for the neighbourhood.

It was not until 1864 that another hanging took place in front of the gaol, when twenty-two-year-old John Meehan was hanged for the murder of Patrick Pearl, in the presence of yet another large crowd. This was the last truly public hanging in Quebec City, since hangings at the new prison on the Plains of Abraham took place within the prison's walls. When the gaol was transformed into a college in 1868, the contractor was explicitly instructed to destroy the execution door, the last remaining vestige of this barbaric practice.

Photograph of John Meehan, probably shortly before he was hanged. This was most likely taken in the gaol itself, as the clothes here correspond largely to the description of those he wore at his execution.

Prisoners executed in front of the Quebec gaol, 1812-1867

1814: Patrick Murphy* – murder of Marie-Anne Dussault
1815: James Welsh* – murder of Robert Stephens
1818: Charles Alarie – theft (from a vessel)
1818: Thomas Thomas – theft (from a vessel)
1821: John Mulkahey – murder of Moses McAllister
1823: William Pounden – murder of Agnes McKay
1826: John Hart – robbery (sacrilege)
1827: Benjamin Johnson – burglary
1827: William Ross – burglary
1827: Thomas (Robert) Ellice – burglary
1828: Pierre Ducharme – theft
1829: François Marois dit Malouin – murder of François-Xavier Guillemette
1829: Jean-Baptiste Desjardins – burglary
1834: William Shuter – murder of Living Lane
1836: Edward Develin – murder of Louise Caron
1864: John Meehan – murder of Patrick Pearl
* location not confirmed, but probably in front of the gaol

One other prisoner held at the Quebec Gaol, Jean-Baptiste Monarque, was executed in 1827 for burglary, but he was hanged across the river at Lévis.

Gaol staff

To watch over all of these diverse prisoners, the gaol needed staff. And lots of them. They are listed in the Appendix.

Sheriffs

The official who was ultimately responsible for the gaol was the sheriff, a high-ranking public servant who mostly dealt with civil cases. He was also responsible, on the criminal side, for summoning juries, organizing executions and corporal punishment, and looking after the gaol. Five different sheriffs were in office between 1812 and 1867. The most famous was no doubt Philippe Aubert de Gaspé, but the most important by far was William Smith Sewell, who was sheriff from 1822 until his death in 1866.

Sewell was a member of one of Quebec City's most prominent English-speaking families. His father, Jonathan Sewell, a prominent Massachusetts Loyalist (Tory) who had fled the American Revolution and settled in Quebec, was the colony's chief justice, and incidentally, the first vice-president of the Literary and Historical Society of Quebec, in 1824, and its president in 1830-1831. Jonathan Sewell used his influence to make sure his many sons were well placed in the colonial bureaucracy and the professions. Although William Smith Sewell had gotten his job through nepotism, he ended up being a relatively conscientious sheriff, at least as far as the gaol is concerned. As we saw, he was constantly pointing out the gaol's flaws, and seeking more money so that he could keep the building in repair and hire competent staff. He was also very interested in prison reform. At the same time, there was simply not enough money available to make any serious improvements to the building, a fact which Sewell found constantly frustrating.

William Smith Sewell in about 1865, a year or so before his death. Aside from his work as sheriff, Sewell was also a painter and a poet.

Gaolers

As a member of Quebec city's elites, the sheriff, of course, didn't run the gaol day-to-day. That was the job of the gaoler, who was appointed by the sheriff and paid a salary by government. Six different men served as gaolers between 1812 and 1867. All anglophones, they nevertheless came from a variety of backgrounds and were of variable quality, though as the salary went up over the years, so too did the worth of the gaolers.

The first gaoler to oversee the new gaol, George Stanley, was a former shoemaker from Trois-Rivières. He had thought the job would be easy, and when it turned out to be harder than he expected, and with less pay, he resigned in 1813. His successor, William Reed, was a former gaoler who had been dismissed from office in 1811, but who agreed to take on the job again. He lasted until he died in 1817. Next was George Henderson, a former Irish sergeant major in the British Army. He held on until he was dismissed in 1828. Henderson was himself somewhat dishonest. He was accused of taking advantage of his office by selling liquor to prisoners; renting out special rooms and furniture to prisoners who could pay; fraternizing with some prisoners and allowing them to have women prisoners in their cells; and even using prisoners to go out into the city on errands for him and for the other prisoners. Another former British soldier, John Jefferys, followed Henderson from 1828 to 1839. He seems to have had much greater personal integrity than his predecessor, but was swept up in political turmoil during the rebellions of 1837-1838. He ended up being briefly imprisoned in his own gaol for contempt of court, when he refused to release one of the Patriote prisoners. After he died, the position went to James Maclaren, yet another English immigrant. Perhaps fittingly, Maclaren had previously run Quebec City's Infant School, a charitable institution whose president was none other than the wife of Jonathan Sewell. The Sewells were everywhere, it seems! Maclaren, like Jeffreys, seems to have behaved with integrity. But he too got caught up briefly in the political fray. In 1855, he obeyed a court order to release a political prisoner, was censured for it by the Legislative Assembly and temporarily dismissed. He died tragically two years later in 1857 in the fire that destroyed the steamboat *Montreal*, on the Saint Lawrence River near Quebec City. He was replaced by his own son, William Mark Maclaren, who had grown up in the gaol, remained gaoler through to the end, and moved on to become gaoler of the new prison on the Plains of Abraham until his death in 1895.

A dynasty of gaolers – the Hills and the Reeds

One of the first gaolers of the new Quebec City gaol after its opening was William Reed. Reed was the last member of a dynasty of gaolers who served for over thirty-five years, since John Hill became gaoler in 1780. John's son, John Samuel Hill, followed him as gaoler in 1804-1805; after he died suddenly at the age of twenty, the position passed to Reed, John Hill's son-in-law, who had married his daughter Abigail. Reed was dismissed from office 1811 for neglect of duty, but after three more gaolers passed through in quick succession, he was hired back again in 1813, this time at the new gaol, only to die suddenly in 1817. Abigail Reed was the common thread. Born in the late 1770s, she had helped out with the gaol since the late 1780s, as daughter, as sister, and as wife of the successive gaolers. She had no doubt lived in all three gaol buildings: the Royal Redoubt, the Artillery Barracks, and finally the new gaol.

Turnkeys

All of the gaolers lived in the gaol with their families, and there are occasional references to wives, sons, and daughters helping out, especially in the earlier period. However, with the rapidly increasing number of prisoners, the gaolers needed professional help. Already in the 1810s, they began to hire what were called "turnkeys," that is, assistant gaolers. At first, the gaoler was expected to pay for these assistants out of his own salary, but in 1813 he was granted a small allowance to hire two turnkeys. There was an outside turnkey, who stayed at the front and received prisoners as they entered; and an inside turnkey, who occupied a room in the front of the gaol on one of the top floors. From the late 1820s, a third gaol official was added, the "superintendent of work," responsible for supervising prisoners put to hard labour.

Like the gaolers, almost all of these assistants were anglophones. While many stayed only a short time, some were in office for long years. Edward Turner, for instance, worked as a turnkey for two decades between 1847 and 1867. At least until the 1850s, the pay was very low, so the men who were hired were not all of the highest integrity. As the sheriff stated in 1830, the small amount allowed for hiring turnkeys did not allow the gaoler to get "men of sufficient character and intelligence to perform the duties of Turnkey as they ought to be performed." In short, some turnkeys were as dishonest as some of the criminals. Patrick Kelly, for example, apparently offered to let prisoners escape if they paid him £3, while Francis Roberts regularly sold liquor illegally to prisoners. Both were eventually dismissed. But not all the turnkeys were of this type. Patrick Henchey later became a tavern keeper, a caterer, and a hotel owner, and was elected to City Council; when he died in 1895, the newspapers described him as one of Quebec City's best-known and most respected citizens.

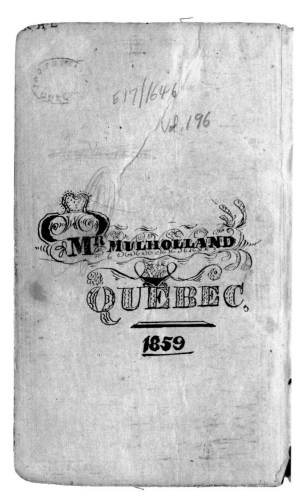

Turnkeys, and especially the superintendant of work, had to be literate, so that they could keep accounts of prisoners' work. This is the frontispiece from a little register of prisoners' activities kept by Richard Mulholland in 1859-1860. It suggests a sense of artistry that one might not expect from a gaol turnkey – or perhaps it was drawn for him by a prisoner ...

Matrons

The women prisoners needed watchers of their own, especially when they moved into the women's prison in 1829. Very soon, matrons were appointed to live in the women's prison and act as turnkeys. Most often, these matrons were the wives of the superintendents of work, who lived with them in the women's prison. This was the case for Tillotson and Lucy Hall; Thomas and Elizabeth Cooke; Samuel Church and his wife (we don't know her first name); George and Anne Wakeham; George and Sarah Gale; Charles and Margaret Boyle; and, in a variation on the theme, Anne Mullholland, her son Richard, and his wife Elizabeth. But being a married couple did not guarantee either probity or good behaviour. One 1837 petition from several women prisoners complained that the Cookes were drunkards who regularly got into fights and had to be separated by the women prisoners. Elizabeth Cooke also apparently paid so little heed to her job that instead of measuring the height of female prisoners as they came in, as she was supposed to do, she simply noted almost all of them as being 5'2" tall. The Cookes' successors, the Churches, were not much better. In 1842, the sheriff accused them of making money from the knitting, sewing, spinning, and washing that women prisoners were doing as hard labour. He also expressed his shock at a rumour about town that they had held a ball in the women's prison! It seems that the Cookes and the Churches were not that much different from many of the prisoners under their supervision.

Gaol guards

Last but not least among the regular staff were the gaol guards. Right from the beginning, colonial officials realized that the gaol wasn't very secure, and that prisoners could also communicate easily with people outside. In 1814, when American prisoners of war in

This undated photograph, probably from the 1860s, may show a turnkey (on the left) and a gaol guard (on the right) in the gaol yard. Behind may be a building used as a workshed. The dilapidated state of the building is clear.

the gaol were making frequent escape attempts, the British army posted sentries outside the gaol. This proved useful when a sentry foiled an escape attempt by five Americans, who had cut a bar in one of the windows and had begun to lower themselves down into the street. After the last American POWs were released in early 1815, the military guard was withdrawn from the gaol, but complaints from grand juries brought them back again by 1817.

The military guard usually consisted of a sergeant, a corporal, and a half-dozen or a dozen privates. The gaol guards were housed in one of the small rooms beside the entrance, and there were usually two or three on duty at any given time, standing outside or doing the rounds of the outside of the building to detect and deter escape attempts and stop prisoners exchanging with people in the street. They could also be called inside to help out with especially rowdy prisoners.

The military didn't much like having to guard the gaol, since they were essentially providing a free service to civil government. They justified it by the fact that there were always a few soldiers locked up among the prisoners. But army commanders regularly threatened to reduce the guard or even withdraw it completely, and complained as well about the small room made available to them. The separate guardhouse built in the back of the gaol yard in 1845 wasn't sufficient to address these complaints, and in 1852, over the objections of the sheriff, the military guards were withdrawn altogether. They were replaced by a new force of a dozen civil gaol guards, led by two sergeants. The new guards were armed with carbines and swords, and wore a plain uniform. Each night, half of them slept in the guardhouse and patrolled the outside of the gaol in two-hour shifts, while the other half were free to go to their homes in town. It seems to have been quite a professional and efficient force: many guards stayed on right through to 1867, and escapes diminished dramatically in the years following its establishment. But as we'll see, even they couldn't prevent prisoners interacting with the street.

Executioners

One other key gaol figure was the public executioner, or hangman. Hired by the sheriff, the hangman carried out the execution of prisoners condemned to death and was also responsible for meting out corporal punishment ordered by the courts, such as whippings or being put in the pillory. While hangings took place in front of the new gaol, other corporal punishments usually took place on the public market place not far from the gaol, although on some occasions, women were condemned to be whipped in private in the gaol itself.

Quebec City's hangmen were not directly part of the gaol staff, but right from the beginning of British rule, they had lived in the prisons, sometimes with their wives. One hangman even committed suicide in the gaol in the Artillery Barracks in 1810. The Quebec hangmen after 1812 are shadowy figures, but it seems that they continued to live in the new gaol, possibly right up until changes in the criminal law in the early 1840s meant that their services were no longer regularly needed. We know only three of them. One was "Cole," hangman in 1816-1817; this was perhaps Peter Cole, a Black former soldier who had been imprisoned on a charge of theft but then found not guilty. The second was Henry Beatson, another former soldier, who was hangman in the early 1820s. Finally, the man who may have been Quebec City's last hangman travelled to Montreal in 1838 to execute the rebels condemned for treason after the Rebellions of 1837-1838.

Doctors and clergymen

If the gaolers, turnkeys, and guards were there mainly to keep prisoners under control, and hangmen punished some of them, others were more exclusively concerned with the prisoners' welfare. The gaol was in no way a healthy place, and prisoners were constantly getting sick. Nobody wanted prisoners to die of illness while in the gaol; that wasn't its purpose. John Howard had insisted at length on the importance of prison hygiene. From 1814 onwards, the government hired a doctor to look after the prisoners. These doctors did not work full time at the gaol, and all had their own private practices. Still, for their substantial salary (initially £200 per year), they had to visit the gaol almost every day. The first doctor, Thomas Fargues, held the position for almost thirty-five years, until 1847. He was one of Quebec City's most respected medical men. Succeeding him was Joseph Morrin, the founder of Morrin College, who had been helping Fargues out since 1835. He was named gaol physician in 1847, and remained in office until his death in 1861. Fargues and Morrin were no doubt leading physicians of their time, and both seem to have cared genuinely for the sick prisoners. They could do little to cure infectious diseases, but they could advocate for good hygiene and could also "prescribe" extra food and drink for sick patients, along with a limited range of medicines. When we see Fargues ordering that prisoners be fed milk, beef soup, steaks, mutton, wine, tea, sugar, rice, extra bread, and even sausages and the occasional chicken, when they would otherwise be living on bread and water, it's hard not to think that the gaol physicians did make some prisoners' lives more comfortable. On at least one occasion, Fargues even intervened to stop a prisoner from being put in the pillory, on medical grounds.

Spiritual health was seen by prison reformers like John Howard as just as important as physical health. While the gaol had no permanent chaplain, both Anglican and Catholic clergymen visited regularly, and performed services in the chapel, which was just a converted cell-block that at times had to be used to confine prisoners. Unlike the doctors, the gaol clergymen were not paid for by government, which largely washed its hands of the prisoners' religious needs. In 1862, the Catholic priest and the Anglican minister then in charge of tending to the prisoners asked Sheriff Sewell to provide religious paraphernalia, such as surplices, a crucifix, Bibles, and prayer books. Sewell forwarded the request to the provincial government, and received a terse but telling reply: "The Executive has no funds at its disposal, to make provisions for payment for administering to the spiritual wants of prisoners." At best, gaol officials ensured that the ministers had a captive audience, since all prisoners were obliged to attend either Catholic or Anglican services. This was backed up with punishment: when the women in one ward refused to go to chapel in 1863 and again in 1864, the gaoler withheld their soup for a week.

Philanthropists and nuns

The gaol and its prisoners also attracted the attention of social reformers. In 1829, an association was founded with the express purpose of bettering the condition of prisoners in gaol. Presided by the Anglican Bishop of Quebec, its leaders included a large part of the local Anglican hierarchy, along with Sheriff Sewell as vice-president and three of his brothers as members.

The Quebec Jail Association, as it was known, had grand ideals. Like many similar organizations elsewhere in the British Empire, its members sought to promote "education, industry, and moral improvement" among prisoners. They proposed setting up schools in the gaol, sought to ensure that men and women sentenced to hard labour had tools and material to work with, pushed for better separation of the prisoners, and worked with gaol officials to impose a uniform code of discipline. One of their first actions was to hire the first matron for the women's prison. They also pressured the gaoler into giving up selling extra food to prisoners, on the principle that all prisoners should be treated equally, while at the same time distributing clothing to prisoners in need.

After these initial successes, however, the Association entered into decline. It was harder and harder to find money, and appeals for support to the Assembly and the colonial governor failed. Some of their most costly efforts, such as hiring a school-master for the gaol, brought little payback: much to the dismay of the well-meaning reformers, very few prisoners attended classes. This no doubt had something to do with the disconnect between these middle- and upper-class do-gooders and the real needs of the prisoners, a disconnect perhaps best summed up by an advertisement they published in 1831, thanking an anonymous donor for a number of books for the prisoners (see illustration). By 1834, they had been forced to close the schools, and after making a final report to Lord Durham in 1838, as part of his general inquiry into the state of Lower Canada, the Association itself appears to have become moribund.

A decade later, another charitable organization, this time Catholic, also sought to help prisoners in the gaol. This was the Soeurs du Bon-Pasteur, a female religious order set up in 1850 in part as a result of the efforts of George Manly Muir, with the express purpose of taking care of "fallen woman" such as those who cycled regularly through the gaol. They set up a house of refuge for ex-prisoners, and regularly visited prisoners in the gaol. Their efforts were part of a larger trend in Quebec, where Catholic institutions increasingly turned their attention to providing social services for needy. But again, like the Jail Association, the nuns' impact was limited. Between 1850 and 1867, the Asile du Bon-Pasteur housed about two hundred ex-prisoners. During that same time, more than two thousand women were committed to the gaol itself, on 10,000 separate occasions. For all their good intentions, the nuns' work was a drop in the bucket. Nor do they seem to have had any particular effect on how the gaol was run: gaol officials never mention the nuns in their correspondence or their records.

Jurymen and prison inspectors

One of the biggest impediments prison reformers faced in their efforts to "improve" the gaol was that no one was really paying much attention to it, and when they did, their complaints were ignored. For example, as we have seen, members of the grand juries that sat in the city's courts regularly visited the gaol. Every few months, grand jurymen would troop across to the gaol from the courthouse just up the street. They'd look in the cells, talk to the prisoners, smell the air, and then go back to the courthouse to write up what were very often scathing reports. These "presentments," as they were called, repeated over and over again what terrible shape the gaol was in and how much it needed to be reformed. The sheriffs were usually happy to have these complaints, as they provided ammunition for their constant demands to government for more money and resources. But little changed. Grand juries got frustrated that their repeated comments were basically ignored. Sheriffs as well. Matters seemed to be stuck.

Inspection mania

In the mid-nineteenth century, a new mania swept through the land: inspection. Inspection was meant to provide "scientific" information to governments so that they could make "rational" decisions. Everything was inspected: schools, hospitals, agriculture, industries, even the population itself (by census); and of course, prisons.

A first overall report on the state of the prisons in Lower Canada was prepared in 1852 by Dr. Wolfred Nelson, a former Patriote. Nelson denounced the state of prisons in the colony, and called for sweeping changes. He praised the administration of the Quebec gaol, but declared that the construction of the building itself was "extremely defective in every particular." In the late 1850s, the government set up a permanent board of inspectors of asylums, prisons, and other institutions, one of whose main jobs was to visit every prison in the colony several times a year and make reports and recommendations. The prison inspectors set eagerly to their task, and produced voluminous reports each year. The old Quebec gaol was one of their black sheep. A new prison was slowly being built on the Plains of Abraham, but in the interim, the old gaol was just wretched. As inspector Joseph-Charles Taché bluntly stated in 1860, "The inspection of the prison, like the present Gaol at Quebec, is unavailing. It is a mere Temple of Cloacina and a school of iniquity. With such materials, nothing can be effected, and we must await, though with impatience, the new buildings which will supply the means of the better organization."

The prison inspectors also had broader aims. They drafted a whole series of recommendations for transforming the colony's prisons. Reform and education should be the main goal of imprisonment, rather than punishment. Strict discipline should be enforced, but not by using harsh measures. Hard labour should be imposed consistently whenever the courts sentenced prisoners to it. Prisoners should all wear the same uniforms. Detailed new diets were worked out, based on scientific principles. A single set of rules and regulations was put together that was to be enforced in every prison across the colony. The idea was to move from the existing local gaols, unregulated and backwards, to rationalized, centrally controlled penal institutions.

In many ways, their observations and complaints were not so different from those advanced by prison reformers almost a century earlier. And as we will see, in similar fashion, while this push for prison reform did bring about some changes, the grand goals of the prison inspectors never came to fruition, least of all in older prisons like the Quebec gaol.

*   *   *

Above all, the people in the gaol were a wide and very diverse group. They weren't in any way a cross-section of Quebec society. Instead, they formed something of a society of their own. And like any society, the gaol had its own rules and power relations.

71

QUEBEC JAIL ASSOCIATION.

THE thanks of the COMMITTEE are returned to an unknown contributer, for the following Books, intended for the reading of the Prisoners, viz :—

Cook's Voyages, 2 vols.
Zimmerman on Solitude, 1 vol.
Lyric Poems on sacred subjects, 1 vol.
Voyages to the North Pole and Greenland, 4 vols.
Life of Nelson, 1 vol.
Solitude Sweetened, 1 vol.
Romeyne's Life of Faith, 1 vol.
Young's Night Thoughts, 1 vol.
By order of the Committee,
J. CHARLTON FISHER,
Quebec, June 27, 1831.   Hon. Secy.

An 1831 newspaper notice from the Quebec Jail Association thanking an anonymous donor for a series of books for the prisoners. Titles such as *Zimmerman on Solitude, Voyages to the North Pole and Greenland*, and *Solitude Sweetened* were hardly appropriate for prisoners locked up in gaol and might be taken as an elaborate joke, but the members of the gaol association were undoubtedly earnest in their philanthropy.

GAOL SOCIETY

Many well-meaning, middle-class prison reformers despaired of the Quebec gaol. They had such wonderful plans to reform prisoners and reduce crime, by imposing their vision on the people locked up in the gaol. But neither the people nor the gaol itself cooperated. There was a clash between two views of gaol society. Nineteenth-century prison reform emphasized discipline and regularity. But prisoners had different ideas, and the nature of the building, along with the nature of the prisoners themselves, allowed them to resist in part the regimented life thrust upon them.

THE IMPACT OF THE BUILDING

As we saw, the Quebec gaol as built was far from John Howard's ideals. This had a huge impact on gaol society. To many observers as well, even after the gaol was completed, it drifted further and further away from those ideals.

Already in 1814, less than two years after the gaol had opened, a grand jury report on the gaol painted a less than stellar picture. While the grand jurors allowed that the building was in tolerably good order, they noted that certain rooms were "too much crowded with Prisoners of every promiscuous description, such as madmen, vagabonds, Felons &c. all mixt together to the annoyance of each other." John Howard must have turned in his grave! In the part of the gaol building used as a house of correction (at that time, the top floor), they found from twelve to fourteen women in one room, "most of whom bore the appearance of abject wretchedness, being dirty, nearly naked, and several said to be sickly and diseased." The gaoler pleaded that he could do no better, as he had not the means.

In 1836, Sheriff Sewell was more direct. In a report to the Imperial government, he noted:

> The building is in a very dilapidated state, and has been reported to be very insecure by each successive Grand Jury which has visited it during the last ten years. It is built on the old plan, having no lockup sleeping apartments, and no means exist of affording the officers any secret inspection over the Inmates. The wards are large, and from its generally crowded state, and the facility of communication among prisoners, classification is very imperfect, and during the summer months, when all the prisoners have the use of the airing yard, none virtually exists.

Three decades later, in 1866, little had changed. The very last grand jury report on the gaol before it closed down declared bluntly that "the gaol is a disgrace to the district. To describe the dilapidated state of the old building, its low ceilings, with scarcely any ventilation; its crowded state, &c. would only be repeating the representations of former Grand Juries."

Overall, from the 1810s to the 1860s, the same complaints came back over and over again, whether from the sheriff, the gaoler, the grand juries, prison inspectors, or the newspapers. The building was too small. It was badly ventilated and it smelled. It was falling into ruin, and constantly in need of repair. There were too many prisoners. There was no classification and separation of the prisoners, so that the bad were corrupting the good. There were no separate exercise yards. There were no lock-up sleeping cells, and the construction of the wards made supervision impossible. Prisoners could easily pass things in and out the windows from the streets, and escapes were far too easy.

We could just stop here, like most historians have done: detail the gaol's shortcomings, and skip forwards to its closing in 1867. But it's much more interesting to look at how prisoners and gaol officials adapted to living and working in this less than ideal environment.

The gaol as it stood when first constructed, in a model of Quebec City by Jean-Baptiste Duberger and Colonel John By. Right from the beginning, the building was surrounded by houses on all sides.

INSOLUBLE PROBLEMS

Some of the problems seemed simply insoluble. First, the gaol was smack in the middle of town. In 1809, when the *Quebec Mercury* learned that the Presbyterian church was to be built right next to the new gaol, instead of beside the courthouse, it descended to doggerel: "Lo! sanctity, to save, can nought avail – The pious kirk is sent from court to jail." When a Methodist church was built just to the north, the gaol had churches on two of its four sides. As the city grew, it grew around the gaol. By the 1860s the gaol was completely surrounded by houses and other buildings.

Much of the gaol was also built directly on the surrounding streets. The main, central wards, used for housing most prisoners, only gave onto the yard, but anyone in the hospital ward, the chapel ward, the debtors' ward, the small rooms in front, even the "Black Hole," had direct access to the street. One prisoner even boasted to a visiting grand jury that there was no place in the gaol he could be put where he couldn't communicate with people in the street. The same was true for the women's prison, which had streets on two sides.

In both the main building and the women's prison, prisoners could thus easily speak through the windows to people in the street below. At night, when the gaol guard was distracted, they could lower down cords and haul up alcohol, tobacco, tools such as saws, weapons, even firearms. In return, prisoners sent out the blankets and clothes, which were provided them by the gaol staff. In 1849, the sheriff complained that this practice was so wide spread that blankets had been discovered in a city brothel that still had the words "Gaol and House of Correction" painted on them. The gaol accounts are full of purchases of clothes and blankets to replace those that had been lost. Various stratagems were attempted to stop this communications channel. Double bars were installed on the inside and the outside of the windows, and iron shutters that were to be closed at night. But prisoners always found a way. They were as determined to keep up their contacts with the outside world as gaol officials and prison reformers were to limit their access to it. In this particular struggle for control, the prisoners had the upper hand.

A photograph of the gaol building (visible just over the top of Saint Andrew's Presbyterian Church in the centre) a few years after it closed, in about 1870. The neo-gothic building in the middle right of the photograph is the Methodist church just across the street from the gaol, where the congregation was disturbed by imprisoned women shouting and swearing.

At any rate, unlike in the strict penitentiary systems that were being developed at the time in the United States, prisoners in Quebec's common gaol, even those who strictly followed the rules, were not entirely forbidden contact with the outside world. Prisoners who had not yet been convicted, as well as debtors, were allowed to have visitors at certain times of the day. Their lawyers could see them whenever they wanted (within reason). Since there were no special rooms set aside for visits, it seems that visitors were simply admitted directly into the wards, and left to their own devices with the prisoners. Prisoners were also allowed to send and receive letters, as long as these were opened and inspected by the gaoler, although as Sheriff Sewell stated in 1852, "situated as the Gaol is, this Rule is next to nugatory."

A LOVER'S LETTER

Prisoners could easily send letters directly out of the gaol without their first being read by the gaoler, using the windows, or sometimes other prisoners about to be released. For prisoners awaiting trial, this sort of private communication could be very important. One such letter has been preserved, sent by 20-year-old William Murphy to his lover, Christianne Allan, in January 1851. Murphy had been committed to gaol for larceny, and was awaiting trial. The letter was Murphy's attempt to get Allan to perjure herself and give him an alibi. It is transcribed below exactly as it appears on the page, with capitals only at the beginning of each line.

Dear Christianne,
Tis with pleasure i sit down to write
These few lines to you hoping to find
You in good health as this leaves me
At present My Dear if you will be
So kind as to come to see me to the
Gaol on teusday as i want to speak to
You verry particular My Dear the
Court begins on teusday and if you are
Coming to see come before 10 o'clock
My Dear i expect to be at liberty
In a few days as there is but verry
Little evidence against me and no
Solid proof <u>if you keep a still tongue</u>
<u>And say that i was with you that</u>
<u>Night</u> there is no fear of me My Dear
My Dear you must not think any
Thing about the words that [passed]

Between you and me and if you
Thought as much about me as i think
About you it would not have kept
You from coming to see me My Dear
We will make up for all this when
I get out of this bloody place.
Dear Chris there is many things
Running in my mind since you
Left off coming to see me i often think
Of old times when it was not like
This when a few words would not part
You and me My Dear give our best
Respects to Mr Knox and Mr and Mrs
Green and likewise the children and
To Mr Blair and family so no more
Till i see yourself your true lover
Till death
William Murphy

Unfortunately for Murphy, the letter was confiscated from the released prisoner who was smuggling it out for him. Murphy was convicted, and sentenced to three years in the penitentiary at Kingston. Ever resourceful, he turned to plan B: escape. First, he and four fellow prisoners broke up through the ceiling of the ward they were in, hoping to reach the garret. Placed in another, safer ward, they destroyed the bars of a window by levering them out with a bench, and had to be transferred again. Finally, they cut through the window bars of their third ward, lowered themselves down into the gaol yard, jumped over the wall, and ran away. This was the last major escape from the gaol. Murphy's luck ran out again, though: they were recaptured the next day, and he was sent to Kingston anyways, where he served out his full three-year term.

Keeping tabs

Another major problem that had no solution was keeping tabs on prisoners. One of Howard's key ideas was separate lock-up sleeping cells to prevent prisoners conspiring together at night. Baillairgé had indeed planned for this, and wooden doors with locks were installed on the cells in all the wards. Baillairgé went even further: following innovations then developing in Europe and in the United States, he intended for gaol officials to be able to carry out secret inspections of prisoners through small hatches or viewing-slots built into the walls of each cell in the central wards. This was to make sure that prisoners could be caught if they were doing things that were against the rules, or plotting escapes. As well, Baillairgé made sure that the entrance into each ward was a narrow passage, blocked off at the end with a pair of heavy doors, to make escapes more difficult.

In the end, none of these measures worked out, and some had exactly the opposite effect. Many of the lock-up cells had no windows, so that if the doors were closed, there was no ventilation. Also, heating came from a stove installed in the main room of each ward. In winter, if the cell doors were closed, the cells got too cold. As for the inspection hatches, prisoners quickly got in the habit of throwing things out through them, into the hallways and on to the main staircase, annoying the gaoler and the turnkeys. The hatches were also used to exchange contraband with prisoners walking along the passages. So the hatches were bricked up, and the doors of the sleeping cells left unlocked, and eventually removed altogether. The narrow entrance-passages and the heavy doors that creaked on their hinges also meant that prisoners always had ample warning of any approach from the outside.

Each ward thus became its own little world, surrounded by cells that simply served as bedrooms, and cut off from easy inspection by the turnkeys and the gaoler. Prisoners in the wards could essentially do what they wanted. They could saw away at window bars, manufacture wooden skeleton keys for the doors (a favourite pastime), or plot escapes. The most extreme example of this came in 1840. A counterfeit coining ring was able to operate right in the gaol itself, and it took several months before the sheriff and the gaoler were able to identify the prisoners involved. It takes guts to counterfeit coin right inside a gaol! But this also illustrates once again how the nature of the building meant that gaol society was not at all what prison reformers and gaol officials intended.

RULES AND REGULATIONS

This applied more generally to prison rules. Nineteenth-century prison reformers were convinced that strict discipline was the key to reforming prisoners. And discipline meant rules. While there were undoubtedly rules of a sort even in Quebec's earliest prisons, the first more formal set of regulations for the Quebec gaol appeared in 1829. The regulations were organized into forty articles and printed up on large sheets of paper. They covered everything from what should happen to prisoners when they arrived, through visiting hours and diet, to the duties of the gaoler and his turnkeys. In 1839, the new gaoler, James Maclaren, printed up his own set of what he called "Ward Regulations." Finally, in 1861, the newly established Board of prison inspectors adopted a province-wide set of prison rules, forty-seven in all, which replaced all previous regulations.

Reading the rules, one might get the impression that the gaol was a very tightly run place:

"No prisoner shall be suffered to loiter in the lobbies, kitchen or other public parts of the Gaol." (1829)

"No letter addressed to a prisoner shall be delivered, nor any letter or parcel from any prisoner be allowed to pass out of the Prison without the knowledge of the Gaoler." (1829)

"... all loud talking and indecent language is prohibited, as is also all secret conversation among prisoners." (1861)

WARD REGULATIONS.

1.—Every prisoner must conform to the Gaol Regulations, and conduct himself orderly and obediently to the Officers, who shall convey their directions to the prisoners in a mild and temperate manner, and any infringement of the Rules, or refractory conduct will be punished by solitary confinement in the Cells, on bread and water only, (in irons if necessary) in proportion to the offence.

2.—Every prisoner must keep his person clean, and wash his shirt at least once a week (Saturday) and any one found dirty when the Gaoler goes round to inspect at 8 o'clock on Sunday morning, will be punished. It is the duty of the Wardsman to see that every man in his ward is washed every morning, and report those who neglect to do so.

3.—Every prisoner that conducts himself in a proper manner will be allowed every indulgence that the Rules of the Gaol will permit.

4.—Complaints from any prisoner will be duly attended to by the Gaoler, to whom they must be made in the first instance—then to the Sheriff (if not attended to by the Gaoler) and finally to the Grand Jury at their periodical visits.

5.—Every prisoner is entitled to receive for his sustenance 1½ lbs. of Bread daily, 2 lbs. of boiled Potatoes, with salt, every second day, and 1 quart of prepared Gruel on the days the potatoes are not issued, and every Friday an allowance of Soap for washing.

Additional Rules for the Hard Labourers.

The Superintendent of work must be obeyed in all his lawful commands by the prisoners, who have the same redress in all cases where there is just cause of complaint as above detailed for the other prisoners, and will proceed therein accordingly.

The Junk to pick, or other work assigned is to be done by each prisoner in the best manner he is able, and no destruction, loss or waste of any article given him to work up, will be allowed—on the contrary, the value of any article destroyed, lost, wasted or otherwise made away with, or that is not forthcoming, or that cannot be satisfactorily accounted for, will be exacted from him by a stoppage of not more than half his allowance of bread per diem, until the said value is replaced, and that after he has been punished by solitary confinement.

As it is the desire of the Gaoler to relieve the irksome situation of every prisoner as far as circumstances will permit, he trusts that every one will see the necessity of conforming to the Rules.

The prisoners will be allowed the use of Books, both English and French, which will be exchanged once a week.

Instruction in reading and writing will be given to those who are desirous of learning.

As both the Roman Catholic and Protestant service is performed every Sunday, the prisoners must attend according to their respective Creeds.

JAMES MACLAREN,

GAOLER.

Quebec Gaol, 26th July, 1839.

James Maclaren's ward regulations from 1839. Unlike the 1829 regulations, these were published in French as well as English.

RULES AND REGULATIONS

For the Interior Order and Police of the **GAOL** at **QUEBEC**, drawn up, and homologated, according to the provisions of the Provincial Statute of the 9th Geo. IV. cap. 6, sec. xvi.

" And be it further enacted by the authority aforesaid, that the several Sheriffs having the custody of Goals in this Province, shall, from time to time, make general Rules and Regulations, and shall submit the same for revision and approval, to the Courts of King's Bench, for the Districts of Quebec, Montreal and Three Rivers respectively, if in Term, or to any two or more of the Judges of the said Courts respectively in vacation, and to the Judges of the Provincial Courts in the Inferior Districts of Gaspé and St. Francis respectively, whether in Term or Vacation, as the case may be, for the interior order and police of the Gaols, situate within their respective Districts or Inferior Districts, and for regulating the conduct of GAOLERS and other officers and ministers of justice in the keeping and governing of Gaols, and also for the safe custody, due care and sufficient protection of all Prisoners for Debt therein being ; and all GAOLERS and other officers and ministers of justice, concerned in the keeping and government of Gaols within the said District or Inferior District, severally and respectively, shall observe the said rules and regulations."

1. All prisoners shall on their first admission into the Gaol or House of Correction, be put into a separate Room, to be appropriated for their reception, where being thoroughly washed and cleaned, if requisite, they shall remain if possible until examined by the Physician ; to be then placed in their proper Ward.

2. Every article on the prisoner's person on admission, militating against the security of the prisoner or the discipline and regulations of the Gaol, shall be taken from such prisoner, and an entry thereof made against his or her name in a book to be provided for that purpose.

3. The Bedding for each Bedstead in the Gaol shall at all times consist of one Paillasse, the straw of which shall be renewed during the first week of every month, two Blankets, one Sheet and a Coverlet.

4. Prisoners shall be allowed the use of the Gaol Yard for air and exercise, under proper classification, as far as it is possible, but no prisoner shall be suffered to loiter in the lobbies, kitchen or other public parts of the Gaol.

5. No gaming shall be permitted among the prisoners and the Gaoler shall seize and destroy all dice, cards or other instruments of gaming.

6. The walls and ceilings of the Wards, Cells, Rooms and Passages used by the prisoners shall be lime-washed at least once in every month.

7. A proper supply of fresh water and wood shall be daily carried up by the prisoners into their respective Wards, before Ten o'Clock in the morning, by which hour the Bread for the day shall be given out.

8. The friends of prisoners committed for trial may be admitted on the Tuesdays and Saturdays of every week, between the hours of Eight in the morning and One o'Clock in the afternoon of those days, so that the same person be not admitted oftener than once in seven days.

9. The friends of convicted prisoners shall not be admitted at any time unless under the written authority of the Sheriff.

10. No person shall have admittance during the time the Gaol is closed, professional gentlemen and persons bringing written orders from the Sheriff only excepted.

11. No letter addressed to a prisoner shall be delivered, nor any letter or parcel from any prisoner be allowed to pass out of the Prison without the knowledge of the Gaoler.

12. All persons admitted to visit prisoners shall be searched by the Gaoler or Turnkeys (professional gentlemen excepted) to prevent the introduction of spirituous liquors, or of any tools that might be used to effect the escape of prisoners.

13. No person shall be admitted to visit *any* prisoner on a Sunday, unless by a written order from the Sheriff.

14. It shall be a rule with the Gaoler not to admit into the Gaol, as visitors, any person who has been under confinement there, unless under very special circumstances, or unless such person bring a written order from the Sheriff.

15. If any visitor or visitors to the prisoners shall at any time refuse to leave the Gaol when required or shall act improperly towards the Gaoler or Turnkeys, such visitor or visitors may be compelled to leave the Gaol and may be refused admittance at any future period.

16. Upon the death of any prisoner, notice thereof shall be given by the Gaoler to the Sheriff as well as to the Coroner, and in case of the serious illness or death of a prisoner, if practicable to a relative of the deceased.

17. The male and female prisoners shall be confined in the different parts of the gaol, so as to prevent them as far as possible from seeing, conversing or holding any intercourse with each other.

18. The prisoners of each sex shall be divided as far as possible into the following distinct classes, viz :—

Debtors, and persons confined for contempt of Court on Civil process.
Sailors committed under the Provincial Statutes, for desertion, &c.
Vagrants and persons committed for, or convicted of assaults.
Soldiers convicted of desertion and under orders for transportation.
Prisoners committed on charge or suspicion of misdemeanors.
Prisoners committed on charge or suspicion of Felony.
Prisoners convicted of misdemeanors.
Prisoners convicted of Felony.
Prisoners under sentence for execution.

19. Debtors shall have every accommodation which the present state of the Gaol will admit, and be separate at all times, if possible, from delinquents.

20. All the rules, relating to cleanliness and good order in the Gaol, shall be equally binding on the debtors as on other prisoners.

21. Each debtor shall be permitted to receive half a pint of spirits, one bottle of wine or two quarts of beer and no more *per diem*, and if any debtor shall be detected in procuring spirits, wine or beer, which is not *bonâ fide* for his own use, the Gaoler shall in future prevent admission of any of the above articles to such debtor, for such period as he shall think proper, not exceeding six weeks.

22. All debtors shall be required to attend Divine Service on Sundays, Christmas day and Good Friday, unless prevented by illness or other reasonable cause.

23. Debtors shall be liable to the same privations and punishments for disobedience of orders or infraction of the rules and regulations established for the good government of the Gaol, as other prisoners in the like case.

24. Each and every prisoner in the Gaol (entitled by law to receive the gaol allowance) shall receive one and a half pound of the best brown bread, being one day old, and two pounds of potatoes, or one quart of oatmeal gruel per diem, and it shall be the duty of the Gaoler to see that the said allowance be supplied to the prisoners of proper quality and weight.

25. No prisoner receiving the Gaol allowance shall be permitted to have any article of food brought to him in the prison, unless by permission of the Sheriff.

26. Prisoners under the Physician's care, shall be furnished with such diet and clothing as shall be ordered by him and no other.

27. The Gaoler shall exercise the authority delegated to him on all occasions, with temper and without favor, partiality or personal resentment, he shall not strike any prisoner unless in self-defence, and he shall require and enforce humanity and good temper towards the prisoners from his several subordinate officers.

28. The Gaoler shall keep a regular account of every expense of the gaol in a book to be provided for the purpose, and a correct inventory of the fixtures and moveable effects belonging to His Majesty's government, specifying the manner in which the latter may have been disposed of.

29. The Gaoler shall, as far as may be practicable, visit every Ward, and see every prisoner, (and if in irons shall examine them) and shall inspect every cell at least once in every twenty-four hours ; and if he shall discover any of the prisoners to be in a bad state of health, he shall report the same to the Physician without delay.

30. The Gaoler shall on no account punish any prisoner either directly or indirectly for any complaint made by such prisoner to the Sheriff or others.

31. It shall be the duty of the Gaoler to appoint in each of the Wards one of the prisoners to be Wardsman or Wardswoman, whose duty it shall be (and who shall be answerable) that the said Ward be kept clean, that no part of the building be disfigured nor the bedding destroyed, and who shall likewise see that the privies of the Wards be kept clean, and for this duty he or she shall receive double allowance.

32. The several Wards of the gaol shall be opened from Lady-day to Michælmas not later than six o'clock in the morning, and from Michælmas to Lady-day not later than eight o'clock in the morning.

33. The Gaoler, on the first opening of the gaol, shall see that the beds are regularly and neatly folded up and the bedsteads raised, and that each prisoner be as clean in his person as circumstances will permit, the Ward swept clean, or scoured if it be scouring day, and all dirt, filth, ashes, &c. removed out of the Ward, and the gaoler shall not suffer any prisoner to leave the Ward until this be done.

34. The Gaoler is to beware of giving up any prisoner on the verbal order of any Magistrate, he is to require a written order for whatever purpose, or for how short time soever, such prisoner may be wanted.

35. The Gaoler shall report every morning to the sitting Magistrate the committals for delinquencies during the night, by the verbal order of a Magistrate or by the Watch, and if there be not lodged with the Gaoler within four hours after he makes such report, a legal written Warrant against the offender or order for his detention, the Gaoler shall then liberate all such person or persons from prison ; but this rule shall not extend to such person or persons as shall be charged as above mentioned with any felony or felonies.

36. The Gaoler shall on no account, except by order of the Physician, furnish any prisoner or prisoners with any spirituous liquors, and he shall use every means in his power to prevent spirituous liquors from being brought into the gaol, the allowance of debtors only excepted.

37. The Gaoler shall not permit either of the turnkeys, directly or indirectly, to sell any article of provision or clothing, or other description of goods, to the prisoners, nor receive from the prisoners, under any pretence whatever, any sum of money.

38. For the purpose of order in the gaol, and to prevent insubordination, riot or insolence, the Gaoler is invested with the power to put all offenders in such cases into the cells or black hole, and in irons (if necessary,) until the next day, when he shall make report thereof to the Sheriff ; but the Gaoler is on no account to exercise this power further without such report.

39. The Gaoler shall keep a journal, in which he shall record all punishments inflicted by his authority, or by order of the Sheriff, stating the name of the prisoners by whom the offence was committed, the time when the punishment was inflicted, and the nature of it.

40. Divine Service being generally performed every Sabbath, by a clergyman of the church of England, and the Mass by a Priest of the church of Rome, the gaoler shall enforce the attendance of all Protestants at the former service and of all Roman Catholics at the latter.

Submitted for Homologation.

W. S. SEWELL, Sheriff.

Approved and Homologated the 20th day of April, 1829.

J. SEWELL, Chief Justice,
J. KERR, J. B. R.
J. T. TASCHEREAU, J. B. R.

Also a very clean place:

> "The walls and ceilings of the Wards, Cells, Rooms and Passages ... shall be lime-washed at least once every month." (1829)

> "Every prisoner must keep his person clean, and wash his shirt at least once a week (Saturday) and any one found dirty ... will be punished." (1839)

> "The cells, day rooms, passages, kitchens, and other places, the furniture of every kind, the bedding and the clothing, shall be kept in a proper state of cleanliness." (1861)

And a very moral place:

> "No gaming shall be permitted among the prisoners and the Gaoler shall seize and destroy all dice, cards or other instruments of gaming." (1829)

> "No spirituous or fermented liquors shall be allowed the prisoners, unless where specially prescribed by the Medical Officers." (1861)

If only discipline was as easy as making regulations ... Life in the gaol was quite different from the rigid discipline laid out in the gaol regulations. The regulations might well ban alcohol, but prisoners could get it smuggled it in anyways, or even at some points buy it directly (and illegally) from the gaoler or the turnkeys. Visiting hours might be limited, but if prisoners could speak to their friends through the windows, what did the rules really mean? And as for banning games, or preventing private conversations between prisoners, that was simply impossible. Even today, the worn floorboards of the surviving cellblocks have several examples of gaming boards scratched directly into the surface.

Many of the rules proved impossible to enforce. The 1839 ward rules seem to have become so unimportant by the 1850s that the gaoler was using his remaining printed copies as packing paper! As for the 1861 prison inspectors' rules, almost half weren't fully followed in the Quebec gaol, despite repeated insistence by the inspectors. For example, the prison inspectors were dead set on all convicted prisoners wearing standardized prison uniforms. Given the budgetary constraints of running a large gaol like that of Quebec, this was simply impossible. Instead, gaolers continued a practice that had been followed almost since the opening of the gaol: prisoners who lacked proper clothing would be given gaol clothes, but the rest could keep their own. This broke down any uniformity of outward appearance.

 The 1829 rules and regulations for the gaol. They were printed in English only on a huge sheet of paper 21 by 26 inches.

NOT ALL PRISONERS WERE CREATED EQUAL

At any rate, equality of treatment was a pipe dream in the complex society of the Quebec gaol. Depending on why they were put in gaol in the first place, prisoners' experiences could vary dramatically. At the top were state prisoners, such as the American officers imprisoned during the War of 1812 or the Patriotes imprisoned in 1837-1839. They were usually kept in separate rooms, furnished with comforts such as tables, chairs and rugs. They also had a much better diet than ordinary prisoners and were exempt from hard labour.

Next were debtors. If they or their families could afford it, they could live as comfortably as was possible in the gaol. They had their own ward, Debtors' Hall, which was never crowded. Some also had access to the smaller individual rooms in the front of the gaol, with decent furniture, though the exact means of getting such a room remain unclear (as noted, up to 1829, they rented them from the gaoler). They could get food and clothes brought in by their friends and had special rules for matters such as visiting hours, alcohol, and tobacco.

Deserting and disobedient sailors came next. They were crammed into the wards like everyone else, with sometimes up to sixty or more in a space designed for twelve or fourteen. But by law, their captains had to pay to provide basic necessities for them. Up to 1842, the amount was one shilling and sixpence per day. This was enough to give them not only food like fresh beef, butter, bread, milk, tea and sugar, but also extras such as tobacco and soap. After 1842, though, the allowance dropped by half. Military prisoners also had special rations paid for by government, which included milk.

Ordinary prisoners had none of this. They had to make do with the crowded wards and with the meagre gaol diet, unless they could get food smuggled in to them by their friends or, up to the late 1820s, had enough money to buy extra food from the gaoler. In 1822, Aubert de Gaspé had iron bedsteads and mattresses installed in all of the sleeping cells, but prisoners had to sleep two or even three to a bed. If they were sentenced to hard labour, prisoners also might have to spend hours every day doing chores such as picking oakum, which was untwisting the fibres of old rope, used for making caulking for the wooden ships that were Quebec City's specialty. If they were women, they might also be set to spinning and sewing. Women were never committed as state prisoners, debtors or sailors; their lot was the same as ordinary prisoners, even if they did have their own separate building. The worst off were prisoners sentenced to death, especially before the 1840s. They were kept in chains, in dank cells, for fear of their escaping from the insecure gaol.

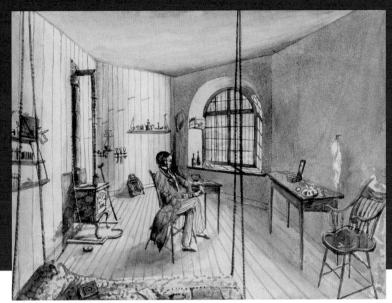

Robert Shore Milnes Bouchette, one of the Patriotes imprisoned in Montreal, in his cell in the new Montreal prison (Au-Pied-du-Courant) in 1837 or 1838. Similar sorts of furnished cells were probably provided to elite prisoners incarcerated in the Quebec gaol.

Experienced prisoners and ward leaders

There were other ways in which prisoners distinguished themselves from each other. One was how experienced they were. The Quebec gaol prisoners, unlike those in a penitentiary, were usually in gaol for relatively short terms. Up to 1841, the average stay in gaol was about fifty days, although some prisoners were in for much longer. After 1841, when Quebec prisoners could be sent to the provincial penitentiary in Kingston, no prisoners in the gaol had sentences longer than two years. The average stay in gaol dropped to about thirty days. But right through the period, many prisoners came back to gaol multiple times, as we saw. These repeat prisoners formed what gaol officials and prison reformers called "old offenders," seen as hardened criminals who were especially dangerous in that they trained up novice criminals in crime. Since all prisoners were crowded together in the same wards, without any systematic classification, this turned the gaol, according to Sheriff Sewell and Jefferys the gaoler, into "a seminary of vice rather than a school of reform" and "a nursery for the perpetration of crime."

From another perspective, some of these old offenders appear to have acted as leaders in gaol society. In his account of the Chambers gang, François-Réal Angers described two of these leaders, Édouard Dumas and Charles Charland. While his account is fictionalized, the descriptions he gives correspond fairly accurately to what we know about them from gaol records.

Both Dumas and Charland were in their twenties. Both spent more than three quarters of their lives between 1828 and 1840 in the Quebec gaol. They were committed for offenses ranging from vagrancy, through theft, to highway robbery and burglary. Angers described Dumas as a skilled and careful thief, who always managed to avoid the risk of "dancing in the air," in other words, execution. According to Angers, his fellow prisoners called him Captain Dumas, and he was the leader of the professional thieves.

He even kept a journal of his exploits, and took charge of initiating young criminals into the ways of crime. He also set up mock courts to train prisoners on how to act when they were brought to trial.

As for Charland, whom Angers said was a hunchback, he was the leader of his ward. He took it upon himself to make sure that younger prisoners confined with him got the clothing they needed (in part so it could be traded with the outside for tobacco and rum), and it was he who acted as spokesman for his ward when dealing with turnkeys and the gaoler. Eventually, however, Dumas and Charland slipped up. In 1839, they were jointly convicted of burglary, and sentenced to death. They were pardoned on condition of being transported for life to Australia.

This informal leadership structure in gaol society was encouraged by the way the gaol was divided into wards, and the necessity of getting prisoners to participate directly in running the gaol. In 1821, a grand jury suggested that each ward should name its own leader. "If it were possible in every room to select, with the consent of the prisoners, some from among themselves who would maintain order, cleanliness and good behaviour, their authority ought to be firmly supported by the gaoler, and their regulations enforced allowing them some reward in proportion to their success." This was recognition that the gaol officials had little authority over the wards, which was held instead by prisoners like Dumas. The system was eventually adopted, and from the late 1820s, each ward had its own wardsman or wardswoman, or "ward captain." This is certainly the position that Charland held, and perhaps Dumas as well. According to the 1829 gaol regulations, the wardsman or wardswoman was only responsible for making sure that prisoners kept the ward clean. The 1839 ward regulations added the responsibility of making sure that every prisoner washed regularly, and reporting those who didn't. But as Charland's case suggests, the ward captains had a more general leadership role, and made sure that all ran smoothly in the ward. As a reward, they received an extra ration of bread, which could presumably be traded with other prisoners for various services or, perhaps, illicit goods.

Other opportunities

Just as in prisons today, prisoners also had other opportunities to get ahead. Trusted prisoners could earn extra money or food by working as nurses for the sick or, if they were men, by cutting firewood or even by cleaning the drains of the privies (which were constantly stopping up). In the 1860s, extra bread was even given to a "Captain of the Bathroom & Barber," evidently a prisoner who helped others keep clean and cut their hair. Some gaolers exploited this system for their own benefit. We already saw that George Henderson sent trusted prisoners out of the gaol to do his errands. But even more upright gaolers, such as James Maclaren, seem to have used prisoners as servants in their apartments. At some periods, prisoners could also make money by doing extra hard labour tasks, such as picking oakum, over and above what was imposed by their sentence.

While some prisoners were paid to look after the sick and the insane, others took on this role voluntarily. Prisoners also helped each other out in other ways. Some literate prisoners, especially debtors, seem to have acted as scribes for the many illiterate prisoners. Most notably, they might help draw up petitions for poor people who couldn't afford their own lawyer: for example, petitions for reduction in sentence or even for the commutation of a death sentence.

Frictions

But relations between prisoners were not always smooth. Prisoners stole from each other quite regularly, and some were known as notorious thieves, ready to steal anything from their fellows. Stealing bread was a favourite pastime, but other valuables might also be targeted. The gaolers even offered a kind of deposit service for prisoners who wanted their money or valuables kept safe while they were in the gaol.

Prisoners also got into violent fights, some of them quite brutal. They hit each other with fists and bits of old rope, banged each other's heads against walls, or threw buckets of water and quarts of hot tea on each other. Women were no better than men in this respect, with some of the worst fights happening in the overcrowded women's prison. In 1846, for example, Rosa Drum, Adelaide Lemay and Mary Ann Leonard attacked Susan Taylor, with Lemay and Leonard holding her down while Drum and Lemay repeatedly struck her with sticks used to beat oakum, wounding her severely. While we don't know exactly why this attack occurred, some fights were probably meant to reinforce the pecking order within a ward. Drum and Lemay had been in and out many times, and Leonard was just setting out on the same career. In contrast, this was Taylor's first time in gaol. Perhaps this was Drum and Lemay's way of establishing their authority over the newcomer.

None of this is much different from how prisons operate today. The gaol was a miniature society, with its own rules, its own social order, its own rulers, its own ruled. We can only guess at the contours of this society from the hints that come across now again in official sources, and there are many blank areas. For instance, there is almost no mention of any form of sexuality in the gaol records, apart from occasional complaints about debtors being allowed to have women in their rooms. At best, occasional reports mentioned in vague terms that the lack of separate, individual sleeping cells encouraged vice and immorality. In only one instance, in 1865, was there a case where a male prisoner was accused more specifically by his fellows of attempting to commit "an unnatural offence." Studies of other similar institutions elsewhere show us that sexual activity among prisoners was very common. In the Quebec gaol, though, with no secret inspection possible in the wards, what went on in the wards stayed in the wards.

THE LIMITS OF FREEDOM

But was this freedom? If it was, it was very limited. Regardless of what they could or could not do within their wards, prisoners were prisoners, and their lives were constrained in many ways.

Food

One very obvious constraint concerned that most basic of needs: food. While the food available to prisoners varied considerably according to their status, for ordinary prisoners, it was the basic gaol diet that mattered. And this was entirely subject to decisions made by gaol officials and by government.

Up to 1829, the only food that prisoners got in the gaol was one pound and a half of bread per day, usually brown. At about two thousand calories, this was just enough to survive on, but was severely deficient in nutrients. There were many ways that prisoners could supplement this diet. Friends and family could bring them food. They could be declared sick by the doctor and receive additional food. If they had money, they could buy extra food directly from the gaoler, who kept a small store in the gaol.

All of this was upended in 1829 when the new gaol regulations, and pressure from the Jail Association, radically modified the way food worked in the gaol. The bread allowance was supplemented by two pounds of potatoes or one quart of oatmeal gruel per day. At the same time, all food brought in from the outside was banned, at least for ordinary prisoners. The gaoler and the turnkeys were forced to give up selling food to the prisoners. Prisoners could of course get contraband food through the windows, but this was hardly worth it when alcohol, tobacco, and the like made the risk of running contraband much more worthwhile. They could also get extra food by being sick, by acting as nurses, wood choppers, drain cleaners, and so on. But the loss of food brought in by visitors still meant that for the ordinary prisoner, the diet got a great deal less interesting.

Rule changes shifted the gaol diet again in the early 1860s. The regulations adopted by the prison inspectors in 1861 divided prisoners into four different classes, each with their own diet. Prisoners condemned to hard labour were to get more food than those who were not, and those who worked longer were also to get more. As well, men were to get more food than women. The bread, potatoes, and oatmeal were now supplemented by soup with boiled meat in it. And debtors were no longer allowed to have their own food. The complicated dietary system laid out by the inspectors was too much for Quebec gaol officials, and they simplified it down to two basic classes: those who were at hard labour, and those who were not. But apart from that, they followed the new instructions. The gaol diet had become richer, but at the same time more uniformly applied. Again, some prisoners no doubt found ways around these restrictions, but it was impossible to smuggle in more than small quantities of food. Here, prisoners had much less freedom, because the food supply really was under the control of gaol officials.

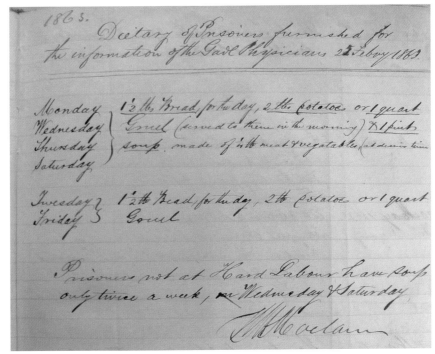

Diet of the prisoners in 1863, as described by the gaoler William Mark Maclaren.

Health, sickness and death

Health was another issue over which prisoners and gaol officials had little control. Anyone visiting the gaol would be convinced that it was an unhealthy place. After all, one of the first things to hit visitors was the smell. Quite frankly, the gaol stank. Grand jury after grand jury remarked on the stench in their presentments. This was understandable. For one thing, Baillairgé's elaborate plans for ventilated privies didn't work that well. They were no doubt better than the "necessary tubs" of the previous gaols, but the building still reeked of human waste. As well, the changing seasons brought their own special smells. In the summer months, the building was usually overcrowded with sweating prisoners, who often had only limited facilities to wash. In the winter, there were often fewer prisoners, but the windows had to be kept closed to keep out the cold, limiting ventilation. As well, the wood stoves that heated the wards produced lots of smoke. It got so bad that in 1838, the gaoler even hired a "smoak doctor" to fix the problem. It is unlikely that he had any effect. Prisoners also added their own smoke to the environment. Up until 1861, they were allowed to use tobacco, and smoked copiously, knocking their clay pipes out between the wooden floorboards.

All of this made the atmosphere in the gaol less than pleasant. As one newspaper declared in 1860,

> ... it is almost better to hang a man at once than to poison him by inches. On a fine, cool, summer's morning with a strong breeze blowing, a stranger may visit the Quebec Gaol, and, keeping to the windows where at such a time the fresh air of heaven kindly will enter, may think it a tolerable abode. But if he should repeat his visit on a calm July afternoon, when the thermometer runs up nearly to the hundreds, or on a January night when all the windows or rather air holes are closed, he would never afterwards forget the lesson he would learn as to the forgetful way in which a number of human beings will vitiate a given limited quantity of air.

At this time, smells were associated with disease. Germs had not yet been discovered, and many people, including most doctors, were convinced that disease arose from "miasmas," or emanations in the air. An 1827 grand jury denounced the gaol's "want of order and of cleanliness which maintains a foul air capable of engendering Disease dangerous to the unfortunate persons dwelling therein." Of course, sick prisoners did smell, adding yet another layer of odour to the atmosphere. But smells alone did not make people sick. In fact, considering the number of prisoners crowded together, their general poverty, and the limited opportunities for hygiene, the gaol was relatively free of major disease, and especially of fatal illness. In 1832, 1834, 1847, and 1849, major cholera and typhus epidemics ravaged Quebec City, killing thousands of residents. While there were a few cases in the gaol, there was no major outbreak.

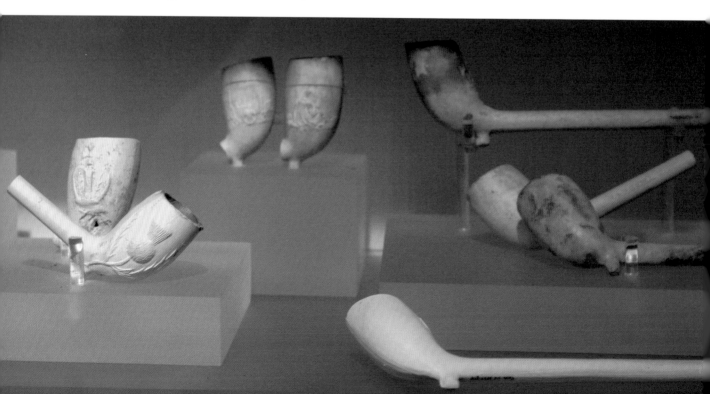

Part of this was because of the gaol's rudimentary hygiene measures, which gradually improved over time. The wards were regularly swept and washed down and were periodically whitewashed. The gaolers' accounts are full of purchases of brooms and mops. Right from the beginning, there was running water available on each floor, fed from a reservoir in the attic, so that prisoners could easily fill up buckets for their wards. In earlier decades, water continued to be brought in barrels from the river, but as of 1855, the gaol was hooked up to the city's new water supply. In 1820, a bath was purchased for prisoners' use, and from the late 1820s, they were supplied with soap. Prisoners whose clothes were in tatters were provided with new ones. Sick prisoners got medical attention, such as it was at the time. With the gaol doctor on regular call, they probably got better medical attention than most poor people in Quebec City could afford. More importantly, those who were very sick were removed from the regular wards and kept in the separate hospital ward. From the 1840s, prisoners sick with serious contagious diseases such as typhus were even taken out of the gaol altogether, and confined instead in the Marine Hospital, which specialized in such cases.

At the same time, vermin and rats abounded, and the gaoler regularly bought rat poison and rat traps and hired tinsmiths to block rat-holes with tin. Compared to what middle-class prisoners were used to at home, the whole thing must have seemed awful. Etienne Parent, one of the Patriotes incarcerated in the late 1830s, was so affected by the damp of his cell that he partially lost his hearing. But for ordinary prisoners, sanitary and health conditions in the gaol were probably not much worse than what they faced outside, and got better over time.

Death visited the Quebec gaol more often than it did the city's population as a whole, however. Overall, out of the 30,000 or so different prisoners who were admitted, about 280 died in the gaol. This might not seem like many, but most prisoners were not in gaol for long. If we calculate the actual gaol death rate, as if prisoners had stayed a whole year, it works out to two to three times the yearly adult death rate for the city as a whole. The gaol death rate fell by about half by the 1860s, probably due to improved medical knowledge. Still, woe betide the prisoner who died in gaol friendless, with no one to claim their body. From 1843 onwards, their corpse might be handed over to the medical profession for dissection. This is what happened to Maria Alexander's body in 1861. She had not even been committed as a prisoner, but was instead brought to the gaol with delirium tremens, and then died.

Clay pipes found during archaeological digs at the Morrin Centre. The one with the anchor probably belonged to a sailor.

Hard labour

Hard labour was another part of gaol life that showed there were limits to prisoners' "freedoms." In the 1810s and 1820s, while some prisoners were put to work picking oakum, there were problems with getting enough "junk," or old rope, for prisoners to pick. This meant that very often, prisoners sentenced to hard labour didn't actually work, and this part of their sentence was merely symbolic. One solution adopted in England was to set up "stepping mills," contraptions which required prisoners sentenced to hard labour to step on an endless treadmill or wheel. The force was used to break rocks, grind grain or pound old rope. In the early 1820s, the idea gained favour in Lower Canada. Gaol officials in Quebec erected a small building in the back of the gaol yard to house a stepping mill for breaking rocks. However, cost overruns meant that the project was never finished, and the building was instead transformed into the women's prison in 1829.

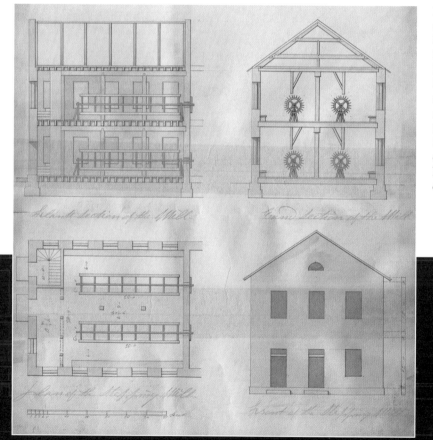

Plan of the proposed stepping mill for Montreal. The Quebec City device would have been very similar. Prisoners were meant to step endlessly on the outer rungs of the cylinders illustrated at the bottom left, which would provide energy for various tasks. Neither stepping mill was ever completed.

Nevertheless, the hard labour system grew increasingly more effective. The turning point was once again 1829, the same year the new gaol regulations were adopted, the new diet put in place and the Jail Association founded. With the new "superintendent of work," whose main job was to make sure that hard labour got done, prisoners could no longer avoid their sentence. Initially, they were meant to work ten hours per day, from seven in the morning until six at night, with one hour for lunch. After a failed experiment with setting prisoners to breaking rocks, it was picking oakum that once again became the mainstay of hard labour in the gaol, along with sewing, knitting and spinning for women. Sometimes, prisoners were also set to cleaning horsehair for upholsterers. Set hours of work were soon replaced by set tasks: prisoners picking oakum, for example, had to pick either ten pounds of wet or six pounds of dry oakum per day. This led to all kinds of clever schemes, most notably prisoners who soaked their dry oakum in water so as to make it weigh more. Still, by the 1860s, the Quebec gaol was the only one in the province making a consistent profit from the sale of the product of the prisoners' labour. Symbolically, some prisoners were even put to work helping finish their new prison on the Plains of Abraham. The system had won, although it still faced resistance.

OAKUM,

FOR SALE at the House of Correction, 2 tons Oakum at 30s. per Cwt.——By order of the Commissioners.
Apply to GEORGE STANLEY, at the New Prison, or to BENJAMIN TREMAIN, one of the Commissioners, No. 5, St. Peter Street.   N. B. Any person having Oakum to pick, and any Slop work, or coarse sewing, may have it done on reasonable terms, by application as above.
Quebec, 20th May, 1813.

ÉTOUPE.—A vendre à la Maison de Correction, 2 tonneaux d Etoupe à 30s par quintal.
Par Ordre des Commissaires.
S'adresser à   GEO. STANLEY,
à la Nouvelle Prison, ou à
BENJ. TREMAIN, un des Commissaires,
No. 5, Rue St. Pierre.
N. B. Les personnes qui ont de l'étoupe à échiffer ou des hardes à faire ou d'autres gros ouvrages de couture pourront les avoir faits à des conditions raisonnables, en s'adressant comme ci-dessus.—20 Mai, 1813.

NOTICE.

THE highest price given for Junk and all kinds of old Rope. Oakum constantly on hand for sale. Apply to the undersigned,
J. MACLAREN,
Gaoler and Keeper of the House of Correction.
Quebec, 27th August, 1840.   2 m 2

Newspaper advertisements for selling oakum (picked-apart old ropes, used for caulking wooden ships), in 1813 and in 1840, by the respective gaolers, George Stanley and James Maclaren. Stanley was also advertising the labour of female prisoners for sewing. All of the profits gained from these sales were supposed to go towards financing the operations of the house of correction, for example, paying for food and clothes for the prisoners.

RESISTANCE

Soaking oakum to make it heavier was just one example of how prisoners tried to resist gaol authorities. They gave false names when they were committed. They shouted and sang in their wards. They broke window panes, refused to pick their oakum, swore at the guards, and threw water and ice at the gaol guards outside. Some even tried to set fire to the gaol, hoping to escape in the confusion. Military prisoners were a particularly difficult bunch, as they tended to band together, and some were strong enough to break down the doors of cells and even, in one case, break off leg irons.

But generally, the resistance put up by prisoners was pretty mild. Nobody ever killed or wounded a gaoler or turnkey, even though prisoners had access to knives and even swords. There was never a full-fledged riot in the gaol, let alone an incident where prisoners took control of the entire building. At most, the prisoners in one ward might resist the turnkeys.

That didn't stop some particularly creative forms of collective resistance. In 1864, for example, there was a kind of hunger strike among the women prisoners in one ward. When they felt that their gruel was of poor quality, they refused to eat their soup, launching what the gaoler called the "soup movement."

This sword-blade was found hidden under the floorboards of the cells during recent renovations of the Morrin Centre.

Escape

The ultimate form of resistance was to escape. Escape was a constant preoccupation for gaol officials, and especially the sheriff and the gaoler. Both were held responsible if a prisoner escaped. If that prisoner was a debtor, in theory the sheriff then became personally responsible for the debt. Sheriffs and gaolers complained continually about how insecure the building was and how easy it was for prisoners to escape. And there were indeed numerous escape attempts, many of them successful. Between 1812 and 1850, over a hundred prisoners managed to escape from the gaol, and only about half were ever recaptured. Even in 1850 and 1851, a dozen prisoners broke out in two different incidents. Interestingly, escape was an almost entirely masculine pursuit. Despite the fact that there were many women in gaol against their wishes, only two women ever escaped, Mary-Ann Cashan and Catherine Rogue, who got away in 1837. It didn't help Cashan much, because she died in the gaol about a year later. Catherine Rogue was never heard of again.

Prisoners tried to escape down through the privies and then along the drains, which led out to the Saint Charles River. In 1815, one enterprising prisoner, François Daigle (charged with stealing an ox), was found in the privy drains with his mattress, bottles, and provisions. Prisoners sawed away at window bars so that they could break out into the street or the gaol yard. They sawed up through the ceilings of the privies, hoping to get into the attic and then lower themselves down with ropes made of sheets. They broke through walls. They used wooden keys to open the primitive locks. One prisoner, Joseph Hamel, simply ran off from the front of the gaol in 1830 when an inexperienced turnkey asked him to help unload a barrel of water. Another, Abraham Hainse, ran off in the same way in 1847 when he was helping clear snow. Recaptured, he escaped again a few months later, and was never found. In 1836, a group of five prisoners even broke out through François Baillairgé's *oeil de bouc*, the round window under the peak of the roof. They lowered themselves down to the ground on a rope, going right past the iron balcony from which one of them, Francis McCoy, was supposed to be hanged. They were caught as they came down. Less than three weeks later, McCoy escaped again. He was recaptured once more, only to escape a third time several months later, this time for good. For him, it really was "third time lucky."

The creation of the civil gaol guard in 1852 seems to have put a stop to this. In their nightly report books, the guards frequently noted having detected and foiled escape attempts. In the last fifteen years of the gaol, between 1852 and 1867, there was only one successful escape from the gaol itself. In 1865, André Ouellette escaped through the privy of the hospital ward, into the yard, and over the wall. In contrast, in the first ten years of the new prison on the Plains of Abraham, there were sixteen successful escapes, including eight prisoners who were never retaken. It seems as if the new, improved prison was less secure than the old gaol! Indeed, just a few days after the move to the new prison, the guards were reporting that one prisoner had managed to open the door of his ward with a spoon ...

DISCIPLINE

Resistance and escape did not go unpunished. Gaolers and turnkeys were forbidden from using corporal punishment such as whipping, which could only be imposed by the courts as part of a sentence, and which was usually carried out not in the gaol, but on the public marketplace. Still, gaol officials had other means of punishing refractory prisoners. The two most common forms of punishment were to be put in irons (which meant having a heavy chain and perhaps a ball attached to one's leg) and to be put in solitary confinement in the "punishment cells" in the "Black Hole" (which still exists in the building today). Just like in the eighteenth century, blacksmiths' accounts from the

The first escape

The first escape we know of from the Quebec gaol was by three American officers who were being held as prisoners of war in 1813. One of them, Isaac Roach, kept a journal of his exploits, in which he described their escape in great detail. They had first tried to tunnel down under the gaol, only to realize that the solid rock made this impossible. On their next try, they escaped upwards. As officers, they were given special treatment, including the run of the building and the right to have a carpet in their room. They cut this up into strips, and made a rope. They used an almanac to choose a moonless moment, and got their washerwoman, a *Canadienne* from Beauport, to arrange for someone to ferry them across the Saint Lawrence so that they could escape southwards. They then got the gaoler (William Reed) drunk on the brandy that formed part of their provisions. They used their carpet rope to let themselves down from one of the windows in the north garret, evaded the guard, and ran off. Though they were eventually captured and brought back, this showed that the gaol was in no way secure, especially when prisoners were not locked up in their wards.

1810s and early 1820s show frequent use of irons for prisoners, although how many of these were for disciplinary reasons is impossible to know. However, increasing concern for prisoners' health and well-being, as well as William Smith Sewell's personal beliefs, led to both of these means of punishment being significantly reduced. Sewell was inspired by prison reform movements, which condemned harsh discipline. Under his guidance, ironing was replaced by handcuffs, which were used very sparingly. By 1832, Sewell was also refusing to let the gaoler use the cells in the Black Hole for long-term solitary confinement: "being on the ground floor [they] are not properly ventilated, fractious prisoners cannot be left in solitary confinement for a time sufficient to subdue their tempers without the risk of injury to their health being incurred."

By the 1850s, the gaoler was even forbidden from confining anyone in the punishment cells overnight, which defeated their purpose. However, other more subtle forms of punishment were substituted. Prisoners might have their right to see visitors taken away. Extra food beyond the basic bread allowance might be stopped, including gruel, potatoes, and soup, leaving the prisoners to eat what their predecessors had eaten decades before: bread and water. When tobacco was still allowed in the gaol, an entire ward might be prohibited from smoking.

Riveted iron ring used to restrain prisoners, found during archaeological digs at the Morrin Centre. This would have been attached to a prisoner's ankle and to a chain attached to a large ring in the floor.

CRUEL AND DESPOTIC CONDUCT

"The subject of discipline is the next in the category. An experience of thirty years and a trial of both systems, that of the severe and the lenient enables me to give a decided preference to the latter, hence while it is necessary that Gaolers and other officers of prisons, should have the means of compelling offenders to obey all lawful commands, they should be restricted from all cruel or despotic conduct and every species of arbitrary punishment should be put out of their power, all use of the lash strictly prohibited, the use of irons abolished, with the exception perhaps, of handcuff, and generally every punishment which tends to degrade a man in his own eyes, or that of his fellow prisoners; all swearing and improper language to prisoners, and indeed all unnecessary conversation, should be forbidden, and a gentle and mild demeanor strongly recommended. Indeed I would conceive it to be the duty of Inspectors to make it a matter of serious consideration with the Government, whether an officer, who cannot maintain discipline without an excess of punishment, is fit for the situation he holds, and to me it would be fitting to give the highest encomiums to those who maintain the best discipline with the least punishment. I may say in passing that such a state is not unattainable, nowhere does a man feel harshness so keenly as in Gaol, and nowhere is kindness more appreciable and appreciated. If therefore all prisoners are treated with consideration and gentleness, and with strict justice and impartiality, it follows as a consequence, that their conduct will be proportionally quiet and orderly."
- William Smith Sewell on prison discipline, 1852

Initially, punishments seem to have been confined to the most serious cases, such as escape attempts. By the 1850s and 1860s, minor punishments were being doled out for increasingly minor offenses. Prisoners were punished for fighting with others, for refusing to work, for not cleaning out their wards, for using insulting language towards gaol officials, for singing too loudly, and for food-fights. One prisoner, Daniel Sinis, was even put in the punishment cells in 1865 for talking back to the gaoler at roll call. Instead of just replying "Yes Sir" when his name was called, he declared that he would much prefer to be called "Mr. Sinis" rather than just plain "Sinis." Here again, what might seem like progress for the prisoners (fewer harsh punishments) was actually the beginning of a more intrusive form of controlling their behaviour. The gaol was finally moving towards what the prison reformers had always wanted: a disciplinary institution of total control.

*   *   *

But by then, it was too late for the old building. A new prison was being built, and the old gaol was about to be closed down.

EPILOGUE: THE END OF THE GAOL

As we saw, within a decade of its being built, the Quebec gaol was already condemned as obsolete. A new wave of prison reform was sweeping the Anglo-American world. In the new prisons, the emphasis was on reforming prisoners through even stricter discipline, using the penitentiary model. In penitentiaries, prisoners were locked up in individual cells in solitary confinement, and if they came together to work or eat, they were forbidden from even talking. Prisoners were under constant surveillance, wore uniforms, and every aspect of their life was strictly regimented. This was a far cry from the semi-freedom of society in the Quebec gaol.

Calls to supplement or to replace the Quebec gaol with a new, better-designed one were made as early as 1829. A grand jury, denouncing once again the existing building, called on the legislature to set up a penitentiary and house of correction quite apart from the existing gaol, a call that was taken up as well by the Jail Association. A contest was launched for the best design, but in the end, it was Montreal that got a new prison in 1836, at Au-Pied-du-Courant (completed just in time to be used for incarcerating the 1837-1838 rebels). By the late 1830s, even the colony's Board of Works, which was responsible for public buildings, was calling for a new gaol, though not until other institutions had been built first. Through the 1840s, various plans were discussed and various sites were examined. William Smith Sewell himself submitted a detailed report on the principles that should be adopted. But it was not until the 1850s that planning for the new prison really got off the ground.

In 1855, the Board of Works decided that it was no longer worth repairing the old gaol, and opened another architectural contest to replace it. This time, funding was found, an architect was hired (yet another Baillairgé, this time François' nephew Charles), and the process launched. Ironically, the construction of the new prison, on the Plains of

Abraham, suffered from many of the same problems that had plagued the Quebec gaol a half-century earlier. The military objected to the proposed site, and construction was delayed until 1861. Once started, it was supposed to be completed rapidly. The old gaol was sold to Morrin College, on condition that they only take possession once the new prison was completed. This also took far longer than expected. There were cost overruns; the contractors worked very slowly; Baillairgé left the project before it was finished; and the final product was only part of what he had planned. It was not until 1867 that the new building was ready. On May 31 and June 1, one month before Canadian Confederation, a procession of carts and "vehicles of all description," including a horse-drawn omnibus, took the prisoners from the old gaol to the new prison. Two months later, the building was transferred to Morrin College. The Morrin Centre had definitively turned the page on its criminal past.

One of the early proposals for a new prison on the Plains of Abraham, in 1856. This would have been a very large and expensive structure indeed.

An engraving of the new prison on the Plains of Abraham shortly after opening. The new building was not all it was supposed to be. There were frequent escapes, and even items like tobacco passed in through basement windows. Only one of the two planned wings was ever finished.

The "Black Hole," before and after renovation. It currently houses an exhibit on the history of the Quebec gaol. In the centre, what was apparently the last pillory used in Quebec City.

Timeline

1712-1717	Royal Redoubt erected
1744-1747	Royal Redoubt used to house American POWs
1760	Royal Redoubt likely used as a civil prison by British
April 1787	Gaol moved from Royal Redoubt to Artillery Barracks
1802	Grand jury presentment denounces Artillery Barracks gaol
1803	House of Assembly committee recommends new gaol
1805	Gaols Act passed
1807	Gaols Act confirmed
1807	Gaol commissioners appointed
1808	Old gaol (Royal Redoubt) demolished
1808	Construction of new gaol begins
1809	Cornerstone laid
November 1812	Prisoners moved to new gaol
1813-1815	American POWs in gaol
1814	First gaol physician appointed
1814	First execution in front of gaol
1818	Drop erected
1829	Women's prison opens
1829	New gaol rules
1829	Quebec Jail Association established
1844	Drop taken down
1845	Construction of guardhouse
1849	Gaol lit by gas
1851	Last major escape from gaol
1852	Civil gaol guard established
1855	Gaol hooked up to city waterworks
1859	Board of Inspectors of Asylums, Prisons, &c. established
1861	General regulations for common gaols
1861	Construction of new prison on Plains of Abraham begins
1861	Old gaol sold to Morrin College
1864	Last execution at gaol
1865	Last escape from gaol
June 1867	Prisoners transferred to new prison on Plains of Abraham
August 1867	Building transferred to Morrin College
1868	Morrin College and LHSQ in old gaol

APPENDIX: QUEBEC GAOL PERSONNEL, 1812-1867

Most of those in office in 1867 continued in their positions in the new prison on the Plains of Abraham

Sheriffs			
James Shepherd	1812-1816	Thomas Ainslie Young	1824-1827
Philippe Aubert de Gaspé	1816-1822	Charles Alleyn	1866-1867
William Smith Sewell	1822-1866		

Gaolers			
George Stanley	1812-1813	John Jefferys	1828-1839
William Reed	1813-1817	James Maclaren	1839-1857
George Henderson	1817-1828	William Mark Maclaren	1857-1867

Turnkeys and superintendents of work			
J-B Laurent	1812	Samuel Broadbank*	1839
George Thompson	1819	Robert Jefferie	1839-1840
Robert Kidd	1825	Patrick Henchey	1839-1846
Bernard Moreau	1828	Samuel Church*	1840-1844
John Musset*	1829-1831	Patrick Shine	1840-1847
Tillotson Hall*	1829-1832	George Wakeham*	1844-1845
Patrick William Kelly*	1829-1833	George Gale*	1845-1847
Edward Allen	1831	Francis Roberts	1846-1848
Thomas Cooke*	1831-1837	Edward Turner	1847-1867
John Wallace	1832	Charles Roberts	1848-1850
James Schultz	1833-1835	William Browning*	1848-1863
Butler Kidd Morris	1835-1838	Charles Boyle	1850-1853
Daniel McCarthy	1836	Richard Mulholland*	1853-1867
William Morrison	1838	Wesley Browning	1863-1866
Thomas Glackern	1839	* = superintendent of work	

Matrons * = married to a turnkey or a superintendant of work			
Lucy Hall* (née Eddy)	1829-1832	Sarah Gale* (née Valiant)	1845-1852
Anne Elizabeth Schultz* (née Bourke)	1832-1833	Margaret Boyle* (née Stewart)	1852-1853
Elizabeth Cooke* (née Boyling)	1833-1840	Anne Mulholland	1853-1859
?? Church*	1840-1844	Catherine Mulholland	1861-1863
Anne Wakeham* (née Davidson)	1844-1845	Eliza Ann Mulholland* (née Sadleir)	1863-1867

Gaol guards (the names of the military guards prior to 1852 are essentially unknown)			
Patrick Deegan	1852	George Morisette	1852-1867
Henry Kerwin	1852-1853	Henry Morton	1852-1867
William Leonard	1852-1854	James A. Staton	1852-1867
Patrick O'Regan	1852-1854	Honoré Tessier	1853-1867
Charles Turner	1852-1857	Fenton Kerwin	1854-1861
William Deegan	1852-1867	Robert Modler	1854-1867
William Gunn	1852-1867	Alexander McGinnis	1857-1867
Samuel Brown Jennings	1852-1867	Alexander Powell	1861-1867
Jean-Baptiste (John) Lapointe	1852-1867	William McCabe	1867
Thomas Moisan	1852-1867		

Physicians			
Thomas Fargues	1814-1847	Jean-Étienne Landry	1862-1863
Joseph Morrin	1835-1861	Pierre O. Tessier	1863-1867
Vincent Martin	1839-1840	Olivier Robitaille	1863-1867
Charles Frémont	1859-1863		

A NOTE ON SOURCES

We are very lucky in that there is a wealth of information concerning the Quebec gaol, far more, for example, than for its equivalent in Montreal. In preparing this text, I consulted all of the sources described below, though some of the primary sources only in part.

Detailed references for the text are available at www.morrin.org/morrinbook.

Primary sources

Bibliothèque et Archives nationales du Québec in Quebec City has the records of the common gaol itself, within those of the Ministry of Justice. They include the registers of prisoners committed to the gaol, which are available online, and administrative documents such as the gaol accounts, lists of deaths, punishments and escapes, and the gaoler's notes and correspondence. There are also the records of the criminal courts and especially the Sessions of the Peace (from 1800) and the Court of King's/Queen's Bench. They provide documents such as calendars (lists) of prisoners, grand jury presentments, criminal complaints involving the gaolers and coroners' inquests into deaths in the gaol. Other documents of interest include notarial contracts for putting up and repairing the gaol, the sheriff's accounts and a number of photographs, maps and plans showing the building.

There are also important records at Library and Archives Canada in Ottawa. The public accounts up to 1841 include records of everything from the minute details of building and repairs, through payments for food and clothing for prisoners, to the expenses of punishments and executions. The records of the Civil and Provincial secretaries include the letters, petitions and so on sent in by prisoners, by sheriffs, by gaolers, on any number of subjects and the official responses to them. Other useful sources include the records of the Department of Public Works, which was in charge of repairing the gaol from the late 1830s onwards; the so-called "Blue Books of Statistics", which contain very detailed descriptions of the gaol from 1828 onwards; the records of the Executive Council (the colonial cabinet); and British military records (the "C" series), which provide information on gaol guards and prisoners of war. There are also a number of maps and plans of the gaol, though, frustratingly, no complete floor plans. Indeed, none of the plans originally prepared by Baillairgé seem to have survived, although the wooden model was apparently still in the attic of a house in the rue Ferland in 1891. The document often referred to as Baillairgé's plan of the first floor is actually a sketch of the foundations for use by the masons.

There are also sources of interest in other archival centres, such as the Archives de la Ville de Québec, the Centre de documentation de l'Amérique française of the Musées de la civilisation and even the National Archives in London, England!

Newspapers are a useful complement: especially the *Quebec Gazette* (1764-1867), the *Quebec Mercury* (1805-1867), *Le Canadien* (1806-1810, 1831-1867) and the *Morning Chronicle* (1847-1867). They contain things like descriptions of escapes and of executions, published versions of grand jury presentments and articles, letters and editorials regarding the gaol and its occupants.

The journals of Quebec's different legislatures contain things like petitions, public accounts, the reports of prison inspectors and of the Department of Public Works and investigations by parliamentary committees. They help fill in gaps in the archival record, though alone, they give a very partial view of the gaol's history. The main ones of use are those of the House of Assembly of Lower Canada (1792-1836) and of the Legislative Assembly of the Province of Canada (1841-1867). The gaol is also mentioned in various laws passed by the colony's legislatures.

Finally, there are a few other published sources of use, such as the six annual reports of the Quebec Jail Association (1830-1837, the second and sixth surviving only in the *Quebec Mercury*).

SECONDARY SOURCES

The Quebec gaol and its predecessors have actually been written about quite extensively (in over 70 different texts), though often erroneously. The earliest "historical" piece I know of was in George Hawkins' 1834 *The Picture of Quebec*, which not only described the gaol building, but also gave a brief history of prisons in Quebec City since the French régime. Other historical overviews followed. There have been local historians such as James MacPherson LeMoine and George Gale; academic historians such as Jean-Marie Fecteau and myself; and studies by architectural historians, archaeologists, museologists and Morrin Centre researchers, connected with the various heritage projects that have developed around the building since the 1970s. Many repeat each other (including errors!) and not all add significant new information. There are also several unpublished dossiers or reports on the gaol and its predecessors which provide the fruits of previous historical and archaeological research. Finally, there are also books on prisons outside of Quebec which provide useful context. Among all of these sources, the most useful are:

Published works and theses

Cellard, André. *Punishment, Imprisonment and Reform in Canada, From New France to the Present.* Ottawa: Canadian Historical Association, 2000.

Dufresne, Martin. «La justice pénale et la définition du crime à Québec, 1830-1860». Ph.D., University of Ottawa, 1997.

Evans, Robin. *The Fabrication of Virtue: English Prison Architecture, 1750-1840.* Cambridge: Cambridge University Press, 2010.

Fecteau, Jean-Marie. *Un nouvel ordre des choses: la pauvreté, le crime, l'État au Québec, de la fin du XVIIIᵉ siècle à 1840.* Montréal: VLB, 1989.

Fyson, Donald. *Magistrates, Police, and People: Everyday Criminal Justice in Quebec and Lower Canada, 1764-1837.* Toronto: Osgoode Society for Canadian Legal History / University of Toronto Press, 2006.

Gale, George. *Historic Tales of Old Quebec.* 2nd edtition. Quebec: Telegraph Printing, 1923.

Gray, Colleen Allyn. «Captives in Canada, 1744-1763». M.A., McGill University, 1993.

Hawkins, Alfred. *Hawkins's Picture of Quebec; With Historical Recollections.* Quebec: Neilson & Cowan, 1834.

Karel, David, Luc Noppen and Claude Thibault. *François Baillairgé et son œuvre (1759-1830).* Québec: Groupe de recherche en art du Québec de l'Université Laval / Musée du Québec, 1975.

LeMoine, J.M. *Picturesque Quebec: A Sequel to Quebec Past and Present.* Montreal: Dawson, 1882.

LeMoine, J.M. *Quebec Past and Present: A History of Quebec, 1608-1876.* Quebec: Augustin Côté, 1876.

Mimeault, Martin. *La prison des plaines d'Abraham.* Sillery: Septentrion, 2007.

Morris, Norval and David J. Rothman (eds). *The Oxford History of the Prison: The Practice of Punishment in Western Society.* New York: Oxford University Press, 1995.

Moussette, Marcel. *Le site du Palais de l'intendant à Québec: genèse et structuration d'un lieu urbain.* Sillery: Septentrion, 1994.

Noppen, Luc, Claude Paulette and Michel Tremblay. *Québec, trois siècles d'architecture.* Québec: Libre expression, 1989.

Oliver, Peter. *'Terror to Evil-Doers': Prisons and Punishment in Nineteenth-Century Ontario.* Toronto: University of Toronto Press, 1998.

Proulx, Jean-Philippe. «Examen du plan d'une maison de travail, de plaisir et de correction à Québec conçu par François Baillairgé». M.A., Université Laval, 2004.

Rivet, François. «La vision de l'ordre en milieu urbain chez les élites locales de Québec et Montréal: le discours des grands jurys, 1820-1860». M.A., Université du Québec à Montréal, 2004.

Wallot, Jean-Pierre. «La querelle des prisons dans les Bas-Canada (1805-1807)». In *Un Québec qui bougeait: trame socio-politique au tournant du XIXe siècle* (Montréal: Boréal Express, 1973).

Unpublished research reports

Bouchard, Frigon, Lafond et Associés. *Rapport de conservation Ancienne prison de Québec/Morrin College.* Ville de Québec, Service de l'urbanisme, 1991.

Écossais, chaussée des - Morrin Collège (Dossier ÉCOSS.44). Ville de Québec, Service de l'urbanisme.

Gobeil-Trudeau, Madeleine *et al.* under the direction of Luc Noppen. *Dossier d'inventaire architectural de Morrin College ou Ancienne Prison de Québec.* Québec, Ministère des affaires culturelles, 1978.

Laperrière, Stéphanie. *Dossier de recherche prison de Québec.* Literary & Historical Society of Quebec, 2005.

Morrin College, Dossier Historique. Québec, Ministère des affaires culturelles, 1979.

Moss, William (ed). *Recherches archéologiques sur le site de l'ancienne prison de Québec / Morrin College.* Ville de Québec, 1996.

Centre historique Joseph-Morrin Historical Centre, Document complémentaire. Muséoconseil, 1995.

Veilleux, Christine. *Daily Life in the Common Gaol of Quebec, 1813-1867.* Literary & Historical Society of Quebec, 2002.

A PRESBYTERIAN STRONGHOLD IN CATHOLIC QUEBEC: MORRIN COLLEGE (SINCE 1862)

Patrick Donovan

INTRODUCTION

Morrin College, Quebec City's first English-language institute of higher education, existed between 1862 and 1902. It was founded by Dr. Joseph Morrin, prominent physician and former city mayor. The College first occupied rooms in the Masonic Temple on rue des Jardins, moving to its permanent home in the remodelled Quebec gaol in 1868.

Although officially nondenominational, Morrin College had a strong Presbyterian identity. The school's founder and Principal for thirty of its forty years was the Reverend John Cook of Saint Andrew's Presbyterian Church. It attracted some Protestants of other denominations but few Roman Catholics.

The college had three faculties. The Faculty of Arts, affiliated to McGill University, was its heart. Forty-six students graduated with a Bachelor of Arts (B.A.) degree from the college, including the first female graduates in Quebec City. The Faculty of Divinity trained twenty-four Presbyterian ministers. A short-lived Faculty of Law also existed, and many well-attended evening lectures were given.

Morrin College struggled from the beginning. In addition to persistent financial problems, the declining Anglo-Protestant population of Quebec City became too small to justify its continued existence, prompting its closure in 1902.

Nevertheless, Morrin College still exists as a charitable trust. In addition to supporting Quebec City's Protestant schools and students, College authorities preserved and maintained their former building for most of the twentieth century. Rooms were rented out on favourable terms to the Literary and Historical Society of Quebec and other community organizations. Without continued support from the Morrin College board, the living heritage treasure that is Morrin Centre would not exist today.

William Smith, c1851
Chief Justice William Smith was a
Presbyterian Loyalist from colonial New
York. He hoped to start a
nondenominatonal bilingual university in
eighteenth-century Quebec City.

BEFORE MORRIN COLLEGE

EDUCATION AND SECTARIANISM IN LOWER CANADA

In 1800, Lower Canada's education system was rudimentary. The few schools around
were either private one-person operations or larger institutions run by the clergy. They
received little support from the state. Most parents educated their children themselves.
Less than a third of Quebec City's population could read, and illiteracy was even more
widespread in the countryside. This was not fertile ground for the development of higher
education. The few who aspired to become doctors or lawyers usually sought out senior
figures of the colony to obtain apprenticeships or clerkships.

Some civil servants tried to develop a state-funded education system but were constantly
blocked by religious authorities. In 1789, Chief Justice William Smith presented a plan
for a system capped by a bilingual non-denominational university in Quebec City. To
avoid religious friction, Smith insisted that no theology courses be given. The Catholic
bishop of Quebec Jean-François Hubert opposed the scheme, fearing it would create
irreligious people who lived according to the laws of nature. The bishop also worried
about Smith's open desire for the anglicization of the colony. Since Church authorities
ran a seminary in Quebec City and a series of private schools, they had no interest in a
rival scheme. The plan was eventually shelved.

Anglicans also bogged down the state's educational efforts by seeking to impose a
dominant role for themselves. When Anglican bishop Jacob Mountain arrived in Quebec
City in 1793, he felt that other religious groups had too much power, especially Catholics.
This was not the case in England: non-Anglicans were barred from Oxford and Cambridge
until the late 1850s, and Mountain saw no reason why Anglicans shouldn't dominate
education in British North America. The Royal Institution for the Advancement of
Learning was founded in 1801 to oversee the development of a public school system,
and was for a long time dominated by Anglican interests. This led to sectarian

conflicts that hindered its growth and, consequently, the development of education. At the university level, Anglicans fought hard to make McGill into an Anglican institution until the 1850s. They also founded their own college in 1843, Bishop's College in Lennoxville, open exclusively to Anglicans.

By the mid-1800s, Anglicans had softened up and were more likely to join forces with Protestants, whereas Catholics hardened in their resolve for separate denominational education. Educational legislation initially encouraged an integrated system while providing loopholes for religious schools as a compromise. With every new education act, public money for sectarian schools increased. The educational system came to be split into Protestant and Catholic sectors, a denominationalism eventually enshrined in law.

Boundaries separating Catholics and Protestants were at their strongest in the second half of the nineteenth century. The rise of Ultramontanism meant that many Catholics looked to the clergy and Rome for guidance. The number of pious associations increased, cementing Catholics into a closer and more exclusive group. The firebrand Bishop Bourget of Montreal excommunicated those who argued against the authority of the Church or belonged to literary clubs with anti-religious books. Quebec's Protestant minority felt threatened by this increasingly intrusive Catholic clergy who authorized what books could be read and what subjects could be taught. Protestants came to see themselves as a bulwark of liberalism. John William Dawson, the Presbyterian principal of McGill, expressed this as follows:

> I fear that the claims of duty tie me to this place, where an important handful of Protestant people are holding an advanced front in the midst of Ultramontanism, and where but for the utmost effort of all willing to help, the cause of liberal education and science is likely to be overwhelmed, and with it all reasonable chance of the permanent success of our Canadian Dominion, for unless the gospel and the light of our Modern Civilization can overcome popery in French Canada our whole system will break up.

The situation was not as polarized in Quebec City as in Montreal. The bishops were more moderate, the literary societies more likely to censor themselves, and the Protestant minority less antagonistic towards Catholics. Nevertheless, the city was not immune to broader currents and influences in North America, and religious groups still retreated behind boundaries, though perhaps more quietly.

This was the context that gave birth to Morrin College. By 1860, a state-sponsored system of denominational schools existed throughout the province that prepared students for university education. Protestant students in Montreal and the Eastern Townships had access to Protestant-run universities, McGill and Bishop's respectively. However, the only university in Quebec City was Laval University, a French-language Catholic institution under the authority of the archbishop. Reverend John Cook, the first principal of Morrin College, argued that a new university was necessary because "a large number do not have

Seal of Morrin College, early 1860s
The seal of Morrin College shows a chevron with three fleur-de lis on the top left, a goddess seated in front of Cap Diamant on the top right, and an open book with a pyramid and oil lamp on the bottom.

the means to attend Colleges at a distance" and that Laval "being exclusively Catholic, and its instructions given almost entirely in the French language, can never be extensively useful to the Protestant and English-speaking youth of the city." But was the English-speaking Protestant population of Quebec City large enough to support a college of its own?

QUEBEC CITY ON THE CUSP OF DECLINE

Quebec City was not always as Francophone as it is today. In the early decades of the nineteenth century, Quebec was the capital of British North America, the major port of entry for English-speaking migrants, and the most populous city in the colony. By 1860, the English-speaking population had reached a high of nearly forty percent, many involved in the city's important shipbuilding and lumber trades. Whereas the French-speaking population formed a largely unified group, at least culturally, English-speakers were fragmented into different ethno-religious communities. Most were Irish Catholics, who had their own institutions and were likely to shun a Protestant school. However, 16.5 percent of the population in 1861 was non-Catholic, representing over 13,000 people.

Was this enough to justify a college? The other Anglo-Protestant colleges in the province had a larger pool of students to draw from. There were over twice as many Protestants on the island of Montreal in 1861. As for Bishop's in Lennoxville, over fifty percent of the population in Sherbrooke and its adjacent counties was Protestant, totalling more than 35,000 people. Even in 1862, Cook recognized that Morrin College was a gamble, saying that:

> Any marked success in the attendance of a large number of students is not to be anticipated. The number of our population does not admit of it . . . It is impossible not to feel that it is an experiment which we are now making — and that it may not prove successful.

Although the gamble may seem ill considered in retrospect, there was no reason to suspect that Quebec's Protestant population was on the cusp of decline at this time. Protestant numbers had been increasing with every decade, and College founders probably expected they would continue to do so. Quebec was still the second biggest city in British North America. Morrin College seemed like a worthy gamble.

Joseph Morrin, by Henry Daniel Thielcke, 1854
Joseph Morrin, by Théophile Hamel, 1859
These two portraits of Joseph Morrin date from the same
period but seem to depict two different people. The first,
by artist H.D. Thielcke, is probably the least accurate. It
was commissioned as a charitable gesture by Dr. Morrin
to help a starving artist. Contemporaries complained
that *"il n'est pas tout à fait ressemblant."* The second is
one of numerous portraits of Morrin by accomplished
artist Théophile Hamel, who was known to represent
his models accurately.

BUILDING A COLLEGE

ACCOUCHEUR OF ARISTOCRATS

Joseph Morrin rose from a modest background to an impressive medical career. Born in Scotland, Morrin immigrated to Quebec City with his parents at age four. Since there were no medical schools in Lower Canada at the time, he worked as an apprentice to James Cockburn, an English surgeon and pharmacist in the city. He was barely eighteen when he got his first medical job on a military vessel carrying soldiers wounded in the War of 1812. When the ship docked in Britain, Morrin stayed to study medicine at the University of Edinburgh. Although he did not complete his degree, he was eventually granted a license to practice in Quebec City and did so for the next forty-two years.

Medicine as it was practiced at this time would be considered unusual today. Basic notions like the theory of germs, hygiene, and antiseptics were only accepted after Morrin's retirement. Some doctors treated cholera by bloodletting and opium, while others recommended ingesting mercury. For a young girl with a case of worms, one Quebec doctor prescribed brandy every ten minutes, a castor oil suppository, and the application of twelve leeches – she died the next morning. Anesthesia did not exist, so surgeons had to be quick, frequently getting their patients drunk to ease the suffering.

While Dr. Morrin usually left surgery up to others, he was reputed as a physician and especially as an *accoucheur* (obstetrician). One of his peers claimed he was "*le favori des dames de la haute aristocratie*" ("the favourite of aristocratic ladies") but Morrin did not reserve his treatments for the elite. He was also the official doctor at the Quebec prison, where he experimented with new treatments such as the use of magnetism, or hypnosis.

Medical practice was not an especially lucrative field at the time, and Morrin supplemented his earnings elsewhere while fighting for a better recognition of the profession. He was the first president of the Quebec Medical Society. He helped found the Marine Hospital (later the Marine and Emigrant Hospital), which looked after transient sailors and the city's poorest patients. He was also the first president of the Quebec School of Medicine in 1848, which became the medical faculty at Université Laval. Morrin served two terms as mayor of Quebec, reorganizing the police force, setting up wooden sidewalks, and fighting to have Quebec remain the colony's capital. He was also one of the founding members of the Literary and Historical Society of Quebec, serving as the second honorary librarian in 1831.

In 1845, Morrin was one of the three founders of the city's first psychiatric hospital. Prisoners in the Quebec City and Montreal jails incarcerated for "being of unsound mind," along with insane people housed elsewhere, were put to work in the bucolic fields of Beauport. The founders hoped this would cure their afflictions. Some patients improved, but idealism soon gave way to harsh realities: seventy-five percent of the patients were incurable, tuberculosis was rampant in the asylum, and the facilities were inadequate to deal with the more aggressive cases.

First home of the Beauport Asylum, c1870
This 1642 building was the seigniorial mansion of Robert Giffard, first surgeon at the Hôtel Dieu hospital. It was seized by American rebels in 1775 and rented out to the Beauport asylum from 1845 to 1849. The mansion was destroyed in a fire in 1879.

Despite all its failures, the asylum was a lucrative investment for Morrin and his colleagues. They were criticized for treating it like a cash cow at the expense of staff and inmates. They received regular grants from the government and kept expenses to a minimum: there was only one guard per twenty-three inmates inside the asylum, whereas most asylums had more. Guards were expected to work twelve hour days, perform many odd jobs, and earned half as much as their counterparts in Canada West. Near the end of his life, Morrin was able to sell his quarter interest in the asylum for the impressive sum of $32,000.

Some of Morrin's other earnings also lead us to question his integrity. For instance, towards the end of his life, he found it increasingly difficult to do his job as gaol physician. At the same time, this was a very lucrative patronage position. So, instead of giving up the position and the salary that went with it, Morrin got his protégé, William Marsden, to do the job instead. This was a violation of Morrin's agreement with the government to do the job in person, and irritated local officials such as the sheriff and the gaoler, who resented taking directions from Marsden. Morrin also tried to make sure that Marsden succeeded him as gaol physician, bypassing more senior physicians. In the end, the central government found out what was going on, reprimanded Morrin, and appointed someone else.

Last Wishes

In 1860, Morrin entrusted $42,591.05 to three colleagues for a "permanent memorial of his regard for the city of Quebec." His Deed of Trust specified that the money be used for founding "a University or College for the instruction of youth . . . in the higher branches of learning, and especially for young men for the Ministry, for the Church of Scotland." The College was incorporated by an act that received royal assent on May 18, 1861.

Although the financial value of Morrin's gift was similar to the endowments that launched McGill and Bishop's, the latter two also came with land. James McGill's trust included a forty-six-acre estate in what later became downtown Montreal. When parts of this land were sold to housing developers, the McGill endowment grew considerably. Bishop's was also gifted the land on which the campus was built. Morrin's trustees had to buy the building and land for the college, and total costs after renovations ate up more than half the initial endowment.

The trustees were aware that they did not have enough money to start a college. In his inaugural address, Principal Cook said that they had considered delaying the opening until Morrin's gift "accumulated to a sum more adequate to the wants of a Collegiate institution." In the end, they went ahead, hoping to attract additional donations.

Some people felt Morrin had never intended to leave money for a school at all. Many sources say he suffered from "mental and bodily decrepitude" in later years. Morrin's eldest son said that, "interested and designing parties" had taken advantage of his father's "enfeebled state of mind," and that he had not intended to found a sectarian college. Dr. Olivier Robitaille, who considered Morrin "*un second père,*" also thought his mentor had been manipulated. He said Morrin had always wanted to leave money for a maternity home and had been far too invested in Université Laval to found a rival institution. Furthermore, he added that "*mon bon patron serait mort dans le giron de l'église catholique s'il n'eut pas comme seconde épouse une dame très fanatique qui refusa même la porte à notre curé son ami.*" ("My patron would have died a Catholic if his second wife had not been a very fanatical lady who refused to open the door for his friend our priest.")

These claims remain debatable. For one, Morrin's son could have been interested in invalidating the will for his own personal gain. Robitaille was not impartial either, being the owner of a conservative ultramontane newspaper. As mentioned above, broader societal changes were driving wedges between Catholics and Protestants in the mid-1800s. At the same time, evangelicalism had also revived Protestant practice, leading to a stronger sense of religious identification. While Morrin had been invested in Université Laval at one point, he was likely swept up by this tendency. His declining health may have intensified his religious practice. One of his contemporaries stated that, in later years, "morning and evening, he was regularly to be found at Saint Andrew's Church, of which he was an attached and zealous member." It is convenient to blame Morrin's second wife or his enfeebled mind for these changes, but society as a whole was becoming more divided along religious lines.

Joseph Morrin died in 1861, and never lived to see the College come to fruition. His dream was now in the hands of the College trustees.

THE REVERED PRINCIPAL

Of all the trustees in Morrin's deed, Reverend John Cook influenced the College most. He was chairman of the Board of Governors and principal of Morrin College until his death in 1892, which represents thirty of the school's forty years as an educational institution.

Born in 1805, Reverend Cook spent the first decades of his life in Scotland. He studied theology in Glasgow and Edinburgh before reluctantly accepting a call from Saint Andrew's in Quebec City at age thirty-one.

Cook grew to love the city, where his moderate approach appealed to the congregation. Cook spent some time in Kingston as principal of Queen's University but couldn't wait to get back to Quebec, where he found the people more congenial. Kingston was an Orange Order stronghold at the time, known as "the Derry of Canada." The ethnic and religious tensions were palpable. Even the Prince of Wales refused to land there during his 1860 visit, preferring to avoid the throng of fifteen thousand anti-Catholic Orangemen in full regalia gathered on the docks to welcome him. A completely different atmosphere prevailed in Quebec City. Owing to its overwhelmingly Catholic majority, it was not favoured by Protestant extremists. Cook himself was a moderate, praised by the French-language press as an enemy of fanaticism who worked "to maintain between the two nationalities that spirit of good will which distinguishes the population of Quebec City." His preaching was also moderate, with contemporaries describing his sermons as "calm and reasonable, neither feverishly evangelical nor laxly liberal."

Moderates make good moderators, and Cook became a pivotal figure in Canadian Presbyterianism for his ability at reconciling different groups. When Cook arrived in the colony, Presbyterians were splintered into four major churches. Cook was at the

Reverend John Cook, late 19th c.
At the end of his life, Cook's reputation among Presbyterians outshone that of the little-known college he managed in Quebec City.

Saint Andrew's Church and Manse
Inaugurated in 1810, Saint Andrew's Church remains the heart of Quebec's Presbyterian community. The Manse was built in 1837, soon after Reverend Cook's arrival.

forefront of initiatives to unite them. In 1875, the Presbyterian Church in Canada was created, uniting most Presbyterians into one church. In recognition for his work, Cook was elected first moderator of this new church. Other honours followed, such as being named the first chancellor of Queen's University in 1877.

Cook's longstanding involvement with education made him an excellent choice as principal. Soon after his arrival in the colony, he became a trustee of the Royal Institution for the Advancement of Learning. Although the institution's grammar schools didn't last, the Royal Institution managed McGill University and continues to do so today. Cook helped found Queen's University in 1840 and the High School of Quebec around 1842. He was also a key player on the province-wide Protestant Committee of the Council of Public Instruction.

MASONIC HANDSHAKES

During its first three years, Morrin College developed many partnerships to strengthen its position. Through these affiliations, the school gained a building to hold its classes, a library, and enhanced its reputation.

The earliest partners of Morrin College were the Freemasons. In May 1861, Morrin College loaned $12,000 to the Masonic Hall Association for a permanent temple. In exchange, the Freemasons provided the College with temporary quarters in this new building.

The Freemasons were part of the same Protestant minority as the administrators of Morrin College. The exact origins of this discreet fraternal order remain obscure. Since the Catholic Church perceived them as a devious group, their membership in Quebec City was composed almost exclusively of English-speaking Protestants. Links were further facilitated by the fact that College trustee James Dean, Jr. was also the "Right Worshipful Provincial Grand Master of English Free Masons."

Masonic Hall, first home of Morrin College
The four-storey classically inspired building of cut limestone is topped with a mansard roof. A pediment flanked by two chimneys contains the three symbols of masonry engraved in stone: the volume of sacred law, the compass, and the square. Freemasons continue to hold their rites on the fourth floor of this building today, financing their operations by renting out the lower floors.

114

Masonic Temple Banquet Room
The inauguration of Morrin College took place on November 6, 1862 in this "spacious Gothic chamber, in the upper part of the hall." The room was crowded. Latecomers stood at the back. A portrait of Joseph Morrin hung above the pedestal. Nineteen students in academic dress stepped up to the platform and signed the collegiate roll before two inaugural speeches were read. Today, this is used as an informal banquet room for the Masonic lodges that hold their ceremonies in the adjacent ritual room.

It took two years to build the Masonic Hall. The Freemasons bought land on the corner of Des Jardins and Saint Louis streets in April 1861. The cornerstone was laid following a parade and ceremony that attracted about four hundred Masons in August 1861. The lower floors were completed by the fall of 1862, allowing Morrin College to begin courses.

LITERARY LEANINGS

The College's longstanding association with the Literary and Historical Society of Quebec also dates from this time. The Society was looking for "more accessible and comfortable" rooms than the cramped quarters it occupied on the upper floors of a bank. In 1862, Morrin College agreed to share its leased quarters in Masonic Hall. The deal stipulated that the Society had to spend a minimum of £60 yearly on books, half of which were to be selected by College authorities. Moreover, Morrin College professors, students, and governors would have free access to the library and museum. In exchange, the Society got rent-free rooms.

Unfortunately, the agreement came too late. Ten days after it was signed, fire raged through the Society's quarters. The *Quebec Mercury* of October 28, 1862 states that "with the exception of a small part of the library and old manuscripts . . . and a few more volumes thrown ruthlessly out of the windows on the heads of the people in the street, . . . the entire contents of the third and fourth stories fell a prey to the flames." Thankfully, the loss was almost entirely covered by insurance and an outpouring of sympathy led to a significant increase in membership.

Within a few years, the library had outgrown its former size and was a valuable asset for Morrin College. By 1866, it had 8,500 books, more than double the number it had owned before the fire. In relative terms, McGill and Bishop's only had 5,000 books in their libraries at the time. Morrin College could therefore boast of a respectable college library for the time.

Quebec City's Answer to McGill

Although McGill had officially been in existence for over forty years when Morrin College was founded, it had not built its reputation overnight. In 1844, twenty-three years after its foundation, McGill had only nine students and was considered no better than "a third-rate grammar school" by its own governing body. A decade later, McGill's new principal John William Dawson referred to it as "two blocks of unfinished and partly ruined buildings, standing amidst a wilderness of excavators' and masons' rubbish, overgrown with weeds and bushes."

Dawson changed McGill. Enrolment doubled in the five years after his arrival, applied sciences and commercial courses were added to the curriculum, and endowed chairs in Language and Literature were established. By 1864, it had grown to a respected institution with twenty-six professors and 233 students.

A new institution like Morrin College could struggle like McGill for decades, or it could ride on McGill's coattails by becoming an affiliated school. In the 1850s, Dawson introduced an affiliation scheme. Students in affiliated institutions were subject to the same three exams as McGill students: the Matriculation at entrance, the Intermediate after the second year and the Degree at the close of their fourth year. The teaching curriculum at affiliated schools was also subject to approval and tended to be broadly similar to McGill's.

John William Dawson, 1859
Instead of the British-born clergymen that ran most universities in Canada, McGill's board chose this dashing young scientist from Nova Scotia. He changed McGill from a struggling college to a reputable university in less than a decade. He also oversaw its affiliation with Morrin College.

Soon after the inauguration of Morrin College, Reverend Cook made a request to affiliate with McGill. Representatives inspected the institution. After months of negotiations, affiliation with the Faculties of Arts and Law was granted in 1864.

Morrin College was a notch above the other schools affiliated with McGill during the nineteenth century. It was the only school to have "first class" affiliation, which meant that more than one faculty was recognized. Furthermore, the other affiliated schools outside Montreal, namely Saint Francis College in Richmond (affiliated 1858-1900), and Stanstead College (affiliated 1889-1907), were essentially high schools that had expanded their programs to offer one or two years of university-level education. Morrin College was different in that it offered a full four-year Arts program and no secondary-level education. Students could graduate with a McGill degree without ever leaving Quebec City.

PEACHY PREMISES

Even before settling into Masonic Hall, the board was already on the lookout for a permanent building. Quebec's overcrowded jail was up for sale and seemed like a perfect fit. College authorities purchased it on October 16, 1861 for $12,000. This was to be paid in six instalments once the new jail was completed and all prisoners transferred. The trustees had no reason to suspect it would take six years before this would take place. Morrin College only moved to its new quarters in June 1868.

Architect Joseph-Ferdinand Peachy was hired to turn the old jail into a college. Despite his British surname, Peachy's family had been in Quebec City for four generations, he spoke French as a first language, and was known to his contemporaries as "Piché." He designed about thirty Catholic churches in Quebec, including some of the most beautiful ones in the city, namely the Séminaire Chapel, Saint-Sauveur, and Saint-Jean-Baptiste. These buildings blended many styles, decorated with the wild ornamental flourishes typical of late nineteenth-century architecture. Morrin College belongs to Peachy's earliest work, revealing the more restrained neoclassical influence of Charles Baillairgé, his teacher and eventual business partner between 1853 and 1866.

When the old prison was renovated to house the College, a larger entranceway topped with a triangular pediment was installed, many windows were enlarged, and the Doric pilasters in the central part of the building were extended to street level.

Changes to the interior, which had been full of poky little cells, were even more dramatic. Cell partitions and ceilings were removed to open up imposing spaces, including two spacious rooms at the extremities of each wing. The College Hall and library reading room were Peachy's most impressive additions to the building, with their modern use of decorative cast-iron. This new use for iron had become popular in the previous two decades, notably through the Bibliothèque Sainte-Geneviève in Paris

117

Université Laval's Convocation Hall, 1860
Joseph-Ferdinand Peachy probably worked on the design of this room at the beginning of his internship with architect Charles Baillairgé. Like Morrin College Hall and the Society's library, it has cast iron columns supporting an ornate balcony, a lightly vaulted ceiling, and chandeliers hanging from decorative rosettes.

Morrin College, c1890
Numerous changes were made to the building's exterior in 1868. All references to the prison were removed: the inscription above the doorway, the door to the condemned cell, the prison bars, and the privy towers behind the building. The front door was given a more imposing classical appearance. The plaster covering the exterior walls was removed. A small stone wall topped with a decorative wrought-iron fence was built in front of the two side wings.

Morrin College Hall
This room initially hosted lectures, convocation ceremonies, student debates, concerts and elegant dinners.

(1842-50), London's Crystal Palace (1851), and buildings in New York's SoHo. Cast iron was used for the first time in Quebec City by Charles Baillairgé for Université Laval's Convocation Hall (1854-57); in fact, this was most likely Peachy's direct inspiration for Morrin College.

SECONDARY STRUGGLES

While Morrin College succeeded in affiliating with many institutions, its relations with the High School of Quebec were less successful. The High School petitioned against the College's incorporation in 1861 and refused all aid from the College afterwards. This relationship did not live up to Dr. Morrin's hopes.

Morrin College needed to take a proactive role in secondary education to ensure a pool of students for its own institution. Potential students were expected to have a basic knowledge of Greek and Latin to pass the McGill entrance exams. In Quebec City, this meant working closely with the High School, the only English-language Protestant school that offered a proper preparatory classical education.

Other universities had incorporated local high schools into their institutions or created new feeder schools. McGill had integrated the High School of Montreal, which became the "High School department of McGill College" in 1852. Bishop's created the Bishop's College School a few years later. Université Laval and the Séminaire de Québec were largely under one administration. It was only natural that Morrin College tried to do the same.

The High School of Quebec needed all the support it could get. In 1863, 135 pupils were crammed into "a building most unsuitable for the purpose" that had been "originally intended for a coachman's house, its rooms . . . low and ill ventilated." It had the most poorly stocked library and the highest tuition fees of all the classical high schools in the province. Nonetheless, it was also one of the rare schools largely under lay control, and certainly the only Protestant high school in Lower Canada where Roman Catholics accounted for nearly fifteen percent of the students.

Joseph Morrin had been aware of the High School's needs. His deed requested that "ample accommodation . . . be provided in the College building for the High School of Quebec, free of all charge, on condition that the said High School shall be subject to the College Government." However, his deed also specified that replacements on the College Board of Governors had to be Presbyterians. Although the High School needed the money, it could not agree to these terms. During a meeting in January 1862, the High School board said that:

> If the High School were given up to the management of Morrin College, all the members of which must by law belong to one religious body, a cry of sectarianism would be raised which whether well or ill founded would prove injurious to the institution and probably give rise to rival institutions, such as cannot advantageously exist in so small a community as is formed by the English-speaking population of Quebec.

In the end, the High School raised money for a new building on its own. Morrin College authorities sat on the High School's board and shared teaching staff to ensure that both institutions worked together. This arrangement worked for a few decades, but broke down in the 1880s.

High School of Quebec, 1904
In 1865, a large neo-gothic building facing the Citadel was built to house the High School of Quebec. It remained in this building until 1941, when it merged with other institutions to become Quebec High School on avenue Belvédère, which exists to this day.

THE MORRIN COLLEGE SCHOOL

In 1886, Morrin College created its own secondary school. Reverend Cook's resignation from the High School board in the early 1880s may have distanced the two institutions. Moreover, the local school inspector argued that the High School's reputation had declined. Despite the larger premises, the High School remained chronically underfunded throughout the nineteenth century and briefly came under the control of the public school system in 1886, a shift that may have worried Morrin College authorities. Whatever the reasons, the College clearly felt that the High School could no longer prepare students adequately for the McGill matriculation exams.

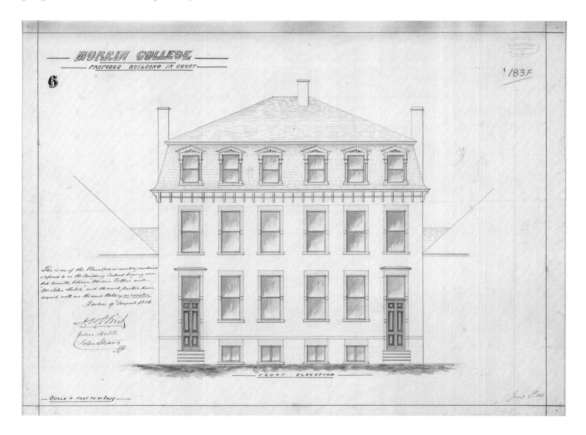

Architectural Drawing of Morrin College School, Harry Staveley, 1886
Harry Staveley designed the Morrin College School building. His architecture displays some whimsical flourishes typical of the Victorian era but is generally more sober, symmetrical, and less obviously French than that of his contemporaries. With the Morrin College School, Staveley showed more restraint than usual, producing a classical and fairly generic mansard-roofed city building with little ornamentation. The school filled a hole behind the college that had once been the women's prison yard.

6 This new venture took a large chunk out of the College's finances, costing approximately $7,000. The College raised $2,500 in new money from Montreal railway magnate and first CPR president Sir George Stephen.

The school did not last long. School attendance was limited to forty pupils. The first year opened successfully with thirty-five students. The following year attracted twenty-four. There was no third year. In 1888, the school was converted to apartments and two Morrin College professors moved in.

Sources do not mention why the school closed down. The school inspector's report for 1886-87 says that the death of Professor Miller, "one of the best classical scholars on the continent," had been a severe blow to its operations. The High School also seemed to be doing better under public management, which may have appeased the College board's fears.

In retrospect, the whole venture seems foolish. In her 1950 sociological analysis of Morrin College, Laura Bancroft writes that the Morrin College School was the most unrealistic move in the history of the College: "The amount of money expended on it could well have been used to support the existing Protestant High Schools and bring them up to the standards rightly stressed by the Professorial Staff of Morrin." This type of non-sectarian approach would have to wait until the college shut down for good.

This is one of the Plans (six in number) mentioned & referred to in the Building Contract bearing even date herewith, between Morrin College and Mr John Hatch, and the said parties have signed with me the said Notary in caritur

Quebec 9 August 1886

FRONT ELEVA

SCALE 4 FEET TO AN INCH

CURRICULAR AND EXTRACURRICULAR PURSUITS

Morrin College offered many programs and an interesting student life outside class. The heart of the college, as in most universities of the day, was its Faculty of Arts. Morrin College also had a Faculty of Divinity that trained Presbyterian ministers, a short-lived Faculty of Law, and well-attended evening lectures for a general audience. From the 1880s onward, extracurricular activities were available, including a school newsletter, glee club, and Alma Mater Society.

BACHELOR OF ARTS: THEN AND NOW

The Faculty of Arts was open to all students regardless of faith. Forty-six students graduated with a Bachelor of Arts (B.A.) in the four decades of the institution's lifetime.

The Morrin College B.A. program differed from those at universities today. Nowadays, students can major in fields as diverse as accounting, anthropology or viticulture. The mid-nineteenth-century B.A. was a general course of study with no specific major. The study of classical languages and cultures was the heart of this curriculum, and students were expected to have learned the basics of Greek and Latin grammar in high school. The course also included philosophy, literature, history, mathematics, and physics. The natural sciences, chemistry, and modern languages took on a greater importance later in the century.

Today's undergraduate degrees are often specialized in one branch of learning, many of them preparing students for a particular profession. The B.A. of 1860 had loftier ambitions: it was a broad Liberal Arts degree that aimed to prepare students for life. According to Principal Cook, a classical education,

> ... though not intended to prepare for any particular line of life, . . . cannot fail to improve and enlarge the minds of those who go through it, or to give, even in the peculiar studies and the subsequent exercise of any of the learned professions an infinite advantage over those whose course of instruction has been less extended.

Humanists like Cook adhered to the Renaissance principle that the language and literature of antiquity were the intellectual capital of the educated gentleman. They believed that stylistic elegance in English was best acquired through Greek or Latin. Cook also believed an Arts degree led to greater Christian piety and restraint, being "especially desirable and important at the season of life . . . when the passions are beginning to exercise a dangerous influence and to claim an unlicensed indulgence."

First Year Exam at Morrin College, 1863
Although Plato's *Republic* is still studied at university today, most students are not expected to understand the original Greek text or to explain "euphonic laws of inflection."

Morrin College.

SESSIONAL EXAMINATION: 1863.

FIRST YEAR.

PLAT. REIP. I. c. I-XIV.

I. Translate (1) literally, (2) freely, one of the two following passages :—

(π) Plat. Reip. p. 330, D. ἀλλά μοι ἔτι τοσόνδε εἰπέ . . . . συμβάλλεται.

(β) ib. p. 333, E. οὐκ ἄν οὖν, ὦ φίλε, ... βλάπτειν δὲ τοὺς ἐχθρούς.

II. Analyse the structure of the sentences in the first of the above passages.

III. Parse the following words :

(π) ἅ, ἄν, ᾗ, ἐν ἕν, ᾗ, ᾗ, ᾗ, ᾗ, ᾗ, ᾗ, ἤν, ἤν, ἤν, ῶ, ῷ, ὧν, ὧν.

(β) δραμόντα. ἑωράκη. ἥμεν. πυθοίμην. ἀποφυγών. κτησάμενοι. ὦσι. ἐνεγκοι. ἀποδόσθαι. ὥρα. ἐγνωκώς.

IV. State and explain the euphonic laws of inflection of which each of the following words contains an illustration.

περιμενοῦμεν. ἴστε. ἀμείνων. ἔχουσι. ἀνδρός.

V. State and explain the principles of Greek syntax of which each of the following sentences is an illustration.

(α) καί μου ὄπισθεν ὁ παῖς λαβόμενος τοῦ ἱματίου. . . .

(β) εἰ μὲν γὰρ ἐγὼ ἔτι ἐν δυνάμει ἦν τοῦ ῥᾳδίως πορεύεσθαι πρὸς τὸ ἄστυ, οὐδὲν ἄν σε ἔδει δεῦρο ἰέναι. . . .

(γ) τοῖς ἐχθροῖς ἀποδοτέον, ὅ τι ἄν τύχῃ ὀφειλόμενον ;

(δ) καί μοι δοκῶ εἰ μὴ πρότερος ἑωράκη, αὐτὸν ἢ ἐκεῖνος ἐμέ, ἄφωνος ἄν γενέσθαι.

VI. Compare by instances from this book the conversational idioms of Greek and English.

VII. State the drift of the arguments of this book, and show their relation to the rest of the Republic.

VIII. In what respects may the influence of the circumstances (1) of Plato's personal history, (2) of his age, (3) of his country, be especially traced in the Republic.

Times were changing, and some felt that too much stock was placed in learning dead languages. They argued for a more practical university education. With the industrial revolution in full swing, they called for more applied science courses to meet the needs of the contemporary workplace.

As a result, the conservative classical curriculum was modernized with a dose of practical liberalism. In Britain, the University of Edinburgh led this change, challenging the medieval Oxford-Cambridge models. In Quebec, McGill embodied this new Scottish model. John William Dawson introduced modern languages and natural history to the Arts curriculum. He also brought in career-oriented diplomas in engineering, hailed as a progressive change by business leaders. Although classical languages were still an important part of the Arts curriculum, the upper years included more practical science and modern languages. By the twentieth century, French and German had largely replaced Greek in many universities.

George Irvine, Dean of Morrin College's Faculty of Law, 1868. Irvine was described by a contemporary journalist in the following questionably flattering terms: "A circle of hair of reddish hue surrounds his head, the crown of which, rendered bald from study and severe labor, preserves a brilliant ivory polish. His long and narrow face, hemmed in with a pair of light whiskers . . . give him the appearance not unlike that of a condor or vulture."

Not all were happy with these changes. The *Quebec Mercury* criticized McGill in 1856, stating that "diffuseness tends to weaken not strengthen the powers of the mind." Laval and Bishop's resisted pressure to change their traditional Arts curriculum for many decades. McGill benefited from the funding and political pressure of industrialists, encouraging Dawson to develop courses that would serve the country's industrial development. Some felt he was selling out to capitalist interests. This debate between utilitarians and humanists is still relevant today; while few want to bring back compulsory Greek and Latin, many still worry about gearing education too closely to the needs of the job market, forming overspecialized workers without the broad humanistic culture that fosters lateral thinking.

Although Morrin College was affiliated with McGill, its curriculum took a more traditional path that initially eschewed modern languages and natural sciences. In the 1860s, Arts students at McGill were required to study French or German for two years but Cook felt that these subjects did not belong in an Arts course: "modern languages should be acquired before, or after, such a course." Cook was not as overtly dismissive of the natural sciences. Nevertheless, he still claimed that these subjects "are liable to be daily altered by new discoveries" whereas the Classics were immutable. This may explain why Morrin College did not offer any instruction to full-time students in these fields during the early years, preferring to focus on more traditional disciplines.

Morrin's curriculum evolved with the times. Introductory night classes for part-time students in chemistry, French, and German began to appear by the early 1870s. By the mid-1880s French, German, and many of the natural sciences were an integral part of the full-time Arts curriculum. The teaching of these subjects became more specialized with time: in 1889 there was only one year of elementary chemistry in the Arts curriculum; by 1899 students could take up to three years of chemistry with advanced laboratory work. Nevertheless, the College's financial condition and size meant that it could never have as many professors or course offerings as McGill.

125

The Phantom Faculty

Morrin College's Faculty of Law affiliated with McGill in October 1864, a few months after the Faculty of Arts. Things were off to a promising start. A session of courses had taken place in the spring. Seven students were enrolled in the three-year program leading to a Bachelor of Civil Law (B.C.L.) degree. The faculty was staffed by three professors. George Irvine, MP for Megantic and later solicitor general of Quebec, was named faculty dean.

Unfortunately, the faculty fizzled out after two years, never producing any graduates. This may have been due to lack of interest or because of the cost involved in maintaining a larger professorial staff. Nevertheless, affiliation was never formally revoked by McGill. The faculty continued to exist on paper, with McGill calendars claiming that Morrin College was affiliated in Arts and Law until the very end.

The Divine Elect

A Faculty of Divinity was established early on to prepare young men for the Presbyterian ministry. It attracted a handful of students per year at most, and none at all in certain years. Twenty-four students qualified as ministers of the Presbyterian Church between 1862 and 1900. Students in Divinity had privileges: bursaries, exemption from admission fees, and priority access to the few dorm rooms available on the upper floors of the College. At the end of their studies, approximately two thirds of the graduates migrated outside the province. They preached in Ontario, Nova Scotia, Manitoba, British Columbia, North Carolina, New York, Arizona, and Minnesota.

In the early years of Morrin College, Presbyterians were splintered into several groups. The most important schism took place in Scotland when the "Free Church" separated from the "Old Kirk" in 1843. The same split took place in Canada a year later. The Free Church pushed for greater local control in an institution dominated by the Scottish state and its wealthy establishment. They questioned the State's right to dictate to the Church in spiritual matters. Free Church members had more missionary zeal and stood on the frontline of the fight against "slavery, intemperance, popery, and Sabbath-breaking." In contrast, Old Kirk members were closer to the establishment, more self-effacing, polite, and conformist.

Morrin College was affiliated with the conservative Old Kirk. For a few years, it was the only college offering a theological course for Presbyterians in the province. The nearest alternative was five hundred kilometres upriver at Queen's in Kingston. It was only in 1867 that Montreal's Presbyterian College, affiliated with the Free Church, began offering classes.

The union of Presbyterian churches in 1875 threatened Morrin's theological program. The initial idea was to merge the theological faculties in Quebec City, Montreal, and Kingston into one Montreal institution that Dr. Cook was invited to lead. In the end, perhaps because of Cook's attachment to Quebec City, all schools remained and were recognized by the new Presbyterian Church in Canada.

The theological program involved a basic education in Arts followed by specialized courses such as Church History, detailed analysis of the Bible, and Apologetics (the art of defending faith through reason). In addition to Greek and Latin, students were also expected to learn Hebrew to better read the Old Testament.

In the summer, students were assigned a home mission field and set loose. The lack of supervision meant they could either learn a great deal, or form bad habits that would last a lifetime. At age seventeen, Morrin College student George Pidgeon went to Lanark county, Ontario. He prepared a sermon every Sunday and embarked on a tour of three preaching points in the county. In the days before cars, the round of itinerant visits could mean frequent nights away from home.

At the end of the course, students obtained a license to preach in the Presbyterian Church. Eventually, in 1882, the Quebec legislature recognized Morrin College's ability to grant proper degrees. Morrin College could confer the degree of Bachelor of Divinity (B.D.), which required an extra year of study beyond the ordinary course. The school could also deliver honorary Doctor of Divinity (D.D.) degrees to outstanding religious scholars. Since degrees in Arts were delivered in Montreal by McGill, these were the only degrees that Morrin College could legally confer in Quebec City. Thus the first convocation ceremony in the history of the College took place in College Hall in 1885, where they awarded a D.D. to former student John Bennett of Almonte, Ontario.

EXTENSION LECTURES

Morrin College also provided evening classes for a general audience. These gave working men the "facilities for pursuing the higher branches of education during moments of leisure." Many evening classes were also open to women in the 1870s. Some classes were co-ed while others, such as James Douglas' series of twenty lectures on "Domestic Chemistry" in 1873, were strictly "for ladies."

Popular adult education at universities was a relatively new phenomenon. At McGill, Dawson began a course of public lectures in 1855 on "zoology, natural philosophy, chemical engineering, paleontology, and the chemistry of life." A program of adult education was also introduced at Laval in 1859, with T.S. Hunt giving evening lectures in chemistry and T.H. Hamel in physics.

Table of Metalloids and Metals, late 19th c.
This ancestor to the modern periodic table of elements was once displayed in the chemistry and physics laboratory. It lists thirteen metalloids and fifty-two metals. Most of the metalloids here are now considered non-metals. Some of the metals listed (Ilmenium, Norium and Pelopium) were later invalidated.

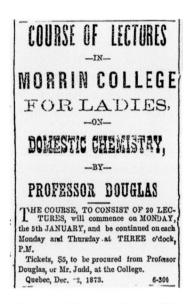

Ad for Domestic Chemistry Class, 1873.
Domestic Chemistry used everyday objects to explain elementary chemistry. Teapots were frequently used as a starting point. The notion of "infusion" could be explained from a chemical standpoint. Since tea was frequently adulterated by merchants, simple experiments allowed well-informed housewives to analyze what they were buying. In *The Scientific Phenomenon of Domestic Life*, published in 1847, the author explains how to best add sugar to tea, namely by holding a sugar-filled spoon at the surface of the cup to make the most of circulating currents so the sugar is "constantly in contact with a fresh portion of unsweetened tea."

Henry Hopper Miles, 1867
In 1873, Henry H. Miles participated as a guest lecturer in the Morrin College ladies' evening courses. This devout yet irascible Anglican had recently arrived in Quebec City after decades of teaching at Bishop's University. In addition to writing history books, Miles is remembered for initiating the Literary and Historical Society of Quebec's petition that launched the Public Archives of Canada.

Evening classes at Morrin College were typically introductory courses in chemistry, physical geography, or modern languages. In later years, classes in technical drawing were added. In his 1868 course of lectures on chemistry, James Douglas began by explaining the difference between "solid, liquid and gaseous" matter and dispelled "the formerly erroneous notion that water, air and fire were simple elements" by introducing the sixty-five elements known at the time.

These evening classes were more popular than the degree courses. Although there were only nine full-time Arts students in 1873-74, 126 students were registered in the evening classes.

Dainty Fingers and Hairpins

On March 10, 1873, George Mercer Dawson wrote to his mother about an incident that had occurred in the Morrin College ladies' chemistry course. This is an abridged version of his original letter:

> I heard a capital story concerning the ladies' lectures the other day but fear I cannot do it justice in writing. Dr. Miles, who seems to consider all the subjects under the sun as belonging to physical geography, was giving the other day the geology and chemistry of the course. He was engaged in demonstrating the composition of water, and for that purpose wished to obtain a piece of potassium. The potassium however, in big or awkward shaped pieces, absolutely refused to leave the narrow-necked bottle into which he fished in vain in the fussy way so peculiarly his own.
>
> The ladies of course sympathized deeply in his trouble and embarrassment. After watching his movements earnestly for some time, they at last found a spokeswoman in Mrs. Cassells, who ventured the suggestion of a hair-pin, and at the same time proffered a small one. The learned doctor, no doubt blessing female sagacity, accepted the implement, but soon found it of no avail.
>
> The anxiety of the class now rose to such a pitch that Nina Wotherspoon felt moved to withdraw an immense hair-pin (described to me as at least six inches long) from her hair, and offer it as a sacrifice to science. At this moment one eye of each member of the class was fixed on N.W's "back hair" and the other on Dr. Miles. How great the disappointment when this was found to be of no use.
>
> At last Mrs. Miles, feeling that now at last the time for action had arrived, extended her hand for the bottle. Regardless of a holy horror which she entertains for all chemicals whatsoever, she with a Spartan resolution and a steady hand drew forth a fragment of the desired mineral.

Student Life

Before drunken "frosh weeks" and initiations became the norm, a college student was expected to behave respectably both in and out of class. In the early days of Université Laval, students were not allowed to go to taverns, gambling houses, or even to the theatre and the city's liberal reading rooms. There was a 10 p.m. curfew for those staying in residence. This was not only true of Catholic universities. Similar rules existed at Oxford and Cambridge. Rules at Morrin College were not as specific, but a student was required to attend "the religious services of the denomination to which he belongs, and to maintain without as well as within the walls of the College, a good moral character." School regulations added that students were expected to be in "Academic dress while in or about the College building." Despite all these rules, the College still encouraged some fun activities from the late 1870s onward.

The College Debating Society was formed in 1878. Debating societies began in eighteenth-century Scotland and were carried to the rest of the British Isles and the United States by the early nineteenth century. They were intended as a training ground for gentlemen, showing students how to criticize each other's thoughts without resorting to foul play. The group met on Friday evenings in College Hall, and debates were open to the public. Students would debate questions such as "Which is the happier, the barbarous or the civilized man?" and the crowd would then be asked to vote. To the question "Which is the more honourable profession, Law or Medicine?" the crowd voted in favour of medicine—something to make the College founder proud!

A Glee Club was established "to concern itself with the study and practice of music" and often sang at the weekly Debating Society meetings. They also organized musical nights, such as the one in December 1891 when "the Convocation Hall was filled to the doors by a large and select audience." The program included choruses by the students, recitations by the lady students, "a banjo solo by Mr. Genge and an artistically rendered violin solo by Miss McWilliam." Reverend Macadam then launched into a promotional spiel for the college and "commented, amid loud applause, on the high moral tone prevailing among the students."

The College produced a newspaper between 1882 and 1884, *The Morrin College Review*. Only one known issue, dated March 15, 1883, remains today. The issue contains a plea for free libraries in Quebec City, a description of unique boats on skates that crossed the frozen Saint Lawrence, and some gossip about a second year student with a love interest in Lévis. There is even some cringe-worthy Presbyterian humour:

Q: Why was Abel the first Scotchman?

A: Because he was the first man who got kilt.

Extracurricular sports were not a feature at Morrin College. Although many colleges had sports teams by the late nineteenth century, Morrin College never had enough full-time students for a sports team. The only time physical activities are mentioned in any of the sources is in the final college calendar from 1899-00, which states that students can access the YMCA gymnasium and the QAAA (Quebec Amateur Athletic Association) grounds and skating rink at special rates.

An Alma Mater Society sought to foster a fraternal spirit among students and alumni. John Theodore Ross founded this group around 1883. This shows that a college spirit was emerging, no doubt influenced by the extracurricular activities above that strengthened the student community. The Society hosted regular dinners and activities in the building.

Sketch of John T. Ross by Arthur Racey, 1921
John T. Ross was heir to one of the wealthiest merchant families in Quebec and director of the Quebec Bank/Royal Bank for fifty-seven years. He founded the Alma Mater Society upon graduating with a B.A. in 1883 and carried the college spirit with him for life, serving as chairman of the Morrin College board from 1925 until his death in 1954.

PROFESSORS

Morrin College had four to nine professors in Arts during most years. Many also taught Divinity courses. Although the board of governors had to be exclusively Presbyterian, college professors could come from any Christian denomination. Nevertheless, approximately two-thirds of the professors were Presbyterian. The other third were mostly Anglican. Nearly sixty percent of the professors were ordained ministers, most of them Presbyterians.

A few exceptions stand out. Martin Miller, a Roman Catholic from Germany, taught French and German from 1874 to 1885. He was replaced by Reverend Charles Tanner, a French-speaking Presbyterian graduate from Morrin College's Faculty of Theology.

The situation at other universities in Quebec was similar. Most schools tended to be dominated by one religious denomination with a minority of professors from other denominations. Laval was largely Catholic with a few Protestant professors. McGill was more liberal than the others, having a lay principal and a Jewish professor among its staff, but Protestants still dominated.

SCHOLARSHIP AND ITS DISCONTENTS

In addition to teaching, university professors today are also expected to engage in original research, but this was not always the case. There was a time when professors did not have to "publish or perish." The first modern university uniting teaching and research was Von Humboldt's *Universität zu Berlin*, founded in 1810. This did not emerge in Canada until much later. Canadian universities taught students basic research methods, but the advancement of science was the business of learned societies. Towards the end of the century, government departments became the dominant forces in scientific research. It was only after World War I that universities took on a larger role.

The German model took a long time to reach Canada because professors were overworked and lacked proper research facilities. Dawson describes his workload at McGill as "about twenty lectures weekly, besides the care of the management and interests of the institution and frequent efforts for its extension and enlargement." This was the day of the "one-man department," and professors did not have the stimulation of graduate students or other professionals. In Quebec, McGill attracted more private funding than other universities and was the first to make the gradual shift towards research. The appointment of Ernest Rutherford as a Professor of Physics in 1897 is an early indicator of this shift, leading to discoveries that earned him the Nobel Prize and solidified McGill's reputation.

THE PASSIONATE CLASSICIST

Although many professors came and went, the College had two pillars in its first thirty years: Principal Cook and Reverend George Weir. They met at Queen's University. As Cook grew older, Weir took on a greater role in the management of College affairs. Educated at the University of Aberdeen, Weir was a brilliant classical scholar who mastered Greek, Latin, and Hebrew, while also teaching logic and philosophy.

Weir was a passionate teacher with a strong temper. George Pidgeon, who studied at Morrin College in 1887, described him as "a perfectionist who drilled his classes in paradigms and would almost leap over his desk in anger when a mistake was made. He was also a warm-hearted teacher who succeeded in conveying to students his own enthusiasm for his subject." Pidgeon said the other professors at Morrin College paled in comparison. Although Pidgeon transferred to McGill to complete his studies, he said no single teacher in Montreal had impressed him as much as Weir. Ethel Gale, one of the first full-time female students at Morrin College, had similar recollections:

> One recalls with delight the hours in his lecture room, how, after our halting recitations were over, Dr. Weir would take the period in hand. First there would come his sonorous reading of the Greek or Latin text, then the rendering of the lesson in his own incomparable English. Sometimes there would be a sudden descent from the platform and the perplexed student would find himself overshadowed by a gowned form, his work scrutinized by a compassionate, if critical, eye, and his violations of style indicated by an infallible forefinger.

The Sinner and the Sociopath

Before settling into a quiet life at Morrin College, George Weir spent a decade clashing with the authorities at Queen's.

Weir was twenty-three years old when recruited in Scotland by Queen's. He was considered able and passionate, even if impatient and ambitious. He arrived in Kingston with his sister, who worked briefly as his housekeeper before returning to Scotland. He initially got along well with Reverend James George, the school's vice-principal and professor of moral philosophy.

But the two men soon clashed. This began in 1857 when Queen's board received a letter attacking the vice-principal for mismanaging Queen's preparatory High School. Weir stood up for the letter's author. Soon after, Weir opposed George when he tried to get reappointed as vice-principal. By this point, the two men were no longer speaking to each other.

The feud rose from a simmer to a boil. When Weir returned to Scotland in 1861, he found his sister raising a six-year-old son who bore an uncanny resemblance to his archenemy. His sister admitted that Reverend George was the father. Weir was furious. His first thought was to kill the Reverend, but he later decided to disgrace him before the board. George called the accusations "a hellish plot." When the board ordered an investigation, George resigned due to ill health, putting an end to the questioning. The allegations were never proven but had become the talk of the town. Weir encouraged this talk. He wrote a mock-heroic poem of sixteen cantos that dragged the "immoral professor" of moral philosophy through mud. The university tried to silence him for letting "personal feeling prevail over university discipline."

Reverend George left Kingston in 1862, but this did not put an end to Weir's crusade. He found a new enemy in Principal Leitch, with whom he clashed over the management of school affairs. The Principal accused him of "a monomania expressed in singling out certain parties as the object of persecution, while to all others he may have the strongest feelings of kindness and good will." Nevertheless, Weir was not the only professor to have issues with Leitch. Many resigned or were dismissed, and students tended to be on Weir's side. The farewell party of one professor turned into "a scene of riot and confusion." Weir was blamed for this and fired. He sued the school for wrongful dismissal, won the first round, but lost the appeal.

Dr. Cook was a good friend of Weir's and a critic of Principal Leitch. He felt that Weir's "removal from Queen's was utterly without just cause or reason." He was also angry that the investigation of the vice-principal's alleged affair with Weir's sister had been dropped. Cook was confident in Weir's abilities and hired him soon after his dismissal.

God gives us almost every day
new troubles experience to educate + test us.
Always yours sincerely
Edwin Hatch

Edwin Hatch, 1880s
The first classics professor at Morrin College was an important biblical scholar and poet. His most famous poem is the hymn "Breathe on me, Breath of God," the late Princess Diana's favourite.

TODAY MORRIN COLLEGE, TOMORROW THE WORLD

A few professors began their careers at Morrin College and went on to achieve international renown. Three stand out: Oxford Bible scholar Edwin Hatch, copper mining magnate James Douglas, Jr., and Victorian Renaissance man George Mercer Dawson.

Edwin Hatch was born in the English Midlands and obtained a B.A. from Oxford University. Hatch moved to Quebec City in the 1860s where he married, became rector of the High School, and was the first professor of classics and moral philosophy at Morrin College. After five years in the city, Hatch returned to Oxford and became vice-principal of St Mary's Hall.

He began writing about early Christian history in the 1880s. Most of his books on the subject are recognized as key texts today. Hatch's greatest work is undoubtedly the *Concordance to the Septuagint*, written with H.A. Redpath. This series of thick tomes remains an indispensable reference to Bible scholars. Every word in the Greek Old Testament is listed, followed by its Hebrew equivalent, the verses these words appear in, and the context of each verse.

Quebec-born James Douglas, Jr. was trained as a Presbyterian minister, but found his true calling in rocks and minerals. After years of theological studies, Douglas said, "my faith in Christ was stronger but my faith in denominational Christianity was so weak that I could not sign the Confession of Faith." Instead of preaching, he began offering evening courses in chemistry from 1868 onward. He was not paid for the first few years, teaching "purely for the love of it," and only received a salary after 1873. In 1869, Douglas developed a patent for the "Hunt and Douglas" process of extracting copper from its ore with Thomas Sterry Hunt of Laval University.

Douglas's patents attracted attention in the United States. He was recruited by Phelps Dodge, a company founded to trade American cotton for British copper, tin, and other metals. The company produced thousands of miles of copper wire, including the wire used for the first transcontinental telegraph line. Eventually, Phelps Dodge became interested in mining its own copper. They sent Douglas to Arizona to investigate opportunities, leading to the creation of the Copper Queen Mine, which became one of the top copper-producing mines in the world. Douglas became influential in Arizona. The Mexican border town of Douglas, Arizona was named after him. He eventually became president of Phelps Dodge, which grew to become one of the most important American mining companies.

In later years, Douglas devoted himself to philanthropy and history. He wrote several books on Canadian history and established the first chair in Canadian and Colonial History at Queen's in 1910. He spent the last years of his life as Chancellor of Queen's, bailing it out of a financial crisis with nearly a million dollars from his own pocket. Douglas also financed the Douglas Hospital in Montreal, the Douglas Library at Queen's, and Douglas Hall at McGill. Interest from his donations to the Literary and Historical Society of Quebec continue to cover most of the monthly book purchases.

George Mercer Dawson is an exceptional figure in Canadian history. The son of McGill's rector was afflicted with a childhood disease that stunted his growth and left him with chronic back pain and fever. Despite this condition, he accomplished a remarkable amount in his short life. Before age twenty-five, he had surveyed the forty-ninth parallel from the Lake of the Woods to the Rockies with the International Boundary Commission. At twenty-six, he was appointed Paleontologist and Chief Geologist of the Canadian Geological Commission, obtaining a PhD from Princeton a few years later. He did surveying work in British Columbia that led to gold discoveries along the Klondike. The gold rush capital of Dawson City, which was the largest Canadian city west of Winnipeg in the late 1890s, was named in his honour while Dawson was still in his forties. If that isn't enough, Dawson is also considered the father of Canadian anthropology for his insightful writings and photographs of First Nations peoples in the West.

All great lives start somewhere, and Dawson's first job was as Chemistry lecturer at Morrin College. He delivered twenty evening lectures to a general audience who paid five dollars for the course. The *Morning Chronicle* reported that College Hall was packed for his first lecture: "The style of the lecturer is pleasing, and he presents his facts in a clear and interesting manner." Dawson himself felt less certain, stating that he read "rather fast and not a little confused towards the end but [hoped] to improve in these respects over time." In the end, Dawson felt he was not cut out for a life of teaching. He spent most of his time in Quebec City "in a chronic state of misery" over the prospect of losing his chances of surveying British Columbia: "When I think of anybody else getting the appointment to go to survey that splendid country with splendid scenery, it puts me in the blues for a day."

George Mercer Dawson, 1885
Dawson began his career as a chemistry lecturer at Morrin College before mapping the West, lending his name to the Klondike capital of Dawson City, and becoming the father of Canadian anthropology.

FULL-TIME STUDENTS

Although Morrin College was managed by Presbyterians, its Arts program was open to all. This was not true of all universities. Bishop's required students to attend Anglican services and take divinity courses. Oxford and Cambridge required some students to refute Roman Catholic practices as superstitious and idolatrous until 1871. Principal Cook emphasized that Morrin College professors would not introduce content injurious to any religious denomination in Arts classes.

Nevertheless, students were inevitably drawn from the social networks of its governing body. Approximately fifty-eight percent of the students who graduated in Arts were Presbyterian. Nearly a quarter were Anglican. The rest consisted of a few Methodists, Congregationalists, Lutherans, and one lone Roman Catholic.

This composition mirrors the social boundaries of the day. The majority of the city's English-speakers in the late nineteenth-century were Catholic, yet the Church actively discouraged them from attending Protestant institutions. The lone Catholic graduate of Morrin College, Edith Sloane, had more leeway because her family bridged the religious divide—the boys were raised according to their father's Methodism whereas the girls followed their mother's Catholicism. This was rare: fewer than two percent of Catholics in Quebec City married outside their religion in the second half of the nineteenth century. In addition to reflecting this Catholic-Protestant divide, the student composition also reflected a lesser divide between Protestants from the established Churches of Scotland and England, and so-called "dissenters" from the newer evangelical denominations.

By today's standards, Morrin College did not have many students. On average, the school attracted fourteen full-time students per year. Patterns fluctuated throughout the school's four decades, with the first and third decades drawing the most students. In 1872 and 1873, the College reached a low of two full-time students. A high of twenty-eight full-time students was reached in 1888. These numbers may seem small but are similar to the full-time Arts enrolment at Bishop's for the same period.

Morrin College Arts students were slightly younger than undergraduate students today. Students did not need prior schooling to take the admission exams, but needed to be at least fourteen and to know enough Greek, Latin, algebra, trigonometry, and English to pass the exams. Although at least three students began this early and graduated by eighteen, most students began around seventeen and graduated in their early twenties.

After Graduation

Although a B.A. did not lead to a particular profession, most male graduates ended up as clergymen, lawyers, doctors, or teachers. Law and religion were the most popular careers for Morrin College graduates, drawing nearly a third of the graduates each. The remaining third ended up in business (15.6 percent), medicine (12.5 percent), and teaching (9.25 percent). This is broadly comparable to patterns in other schools. A study over the same period for the University of Toronto shows that most B.A. graduates ended up as clergymen, lawyers, and teachers.

Morrin College graduates spread across the country. Approximately a third remained in Quebec City, some establishing a lasting legacy. Archibald Cook (class of 1869), the principal's son, practiced law in the city and served on the Morrin College board until his death in 1925; two generations later, Cynthia Cook Dooley lived on the Morrin College grounds and managed the Literary and Historical Society's library until 1997. Many college graduates took up jobs in the new capital, Ottawa, including Robert Cassels (class of 1866), first registrar of the Supreme Court, and Senator Albert J. Brown (class of 1883). Some were drawn to the new lands opening up in the west: Nathaniel Rolph (class of 1885) became an accountant for the C.P.R., quite literally following the railway lines westward before settling in British Columbia. However, it was in the field of religion that Morrin College graduates had the greatest impact.

Radical Reformers

The most well-known Morrin College graduate is probably Salem Bland, a pioneer of progressive religion and politics in Canada. Bland was the son of a Methodist preacher from Yorkshire who came to Quebec City in 1874. The teenager was introduced to the "common sense" school of Scottish philosophy at the College. He also attended religious revivals at the YMCA, providing him with a more emotional experience of Christianity.

Bland was an evangelical, serving as the informal head of the Canadian Social Gospel movement. Evangelicalism is now associated with the religious right, but most Victorians understood it as a series of progressive movements that tried to free the soul from the domination of Church and State. As a teacher, preacher, and editorial journalist, Bland became popular with young people. The Social Gospel movement sought to engage religion in the struggle for social justice. Bland rattled businessmen with newspaper columns that blamed labour unrest on an "unchristian way of doing business." He was a strong voice against fascism and helped found the leftist Co-operative Commonwealth Federation (CCF) in Ontario, which later became the New Democratic Party (NDP). Bland credited his teenage years in Quebec City as invigorating his faith and future religious practice.

George Pidgeon, another important religious reformer, also studied at Morrin College. Pidgeon went on to teach and preach in Montreal, Toronto, and Vancouver. He is best known for leading the Presbyterian Church into the union of 1925 that created the United Church of Canada. He was elected first moderator of this new church in recognition of his work. The United Church is now the largest Protestant denomination in Canada.

It may seem surprising that radical religious figures emerged from a traditional school like Morrin College, but they may have been influenced by John Cook's ecumenical vision. When the Presbyterian Church in Canada was created in 1875, Cook said, "I look for union in the future before which the present union, blessed and auspicious though we justly count it, shall appear slight and insignificant." The careers of Bland and Pidgeon certainly reflect this hope.

**Dr. Salem Bland,
by Lawren Harris, 1926**
Group of Seven painter Lawren Harris is best known for his mystical landscapes, but a different kind of mysticism permeates this portrait of Salem Bland, a Morrin College graduate who became a renowned leftist minister. There is something arresting in the minister's straight-ahead gaze, looking not at us but through us with an ambivalent mix of calmness and intensity.

Universitas McGill,

Monte Regio, in Provincia Canadensi: Omnibus ad quos hae Literae pervenerint Salutem.

NOS REGENTES, PRIMARIUS ET SOCII COLLEGII McGILL, TESTAMUR;

Editham Joannam Sloane

(Collegii Mervin)

per illud tempus quo apud nos commorata est, omnes disciplinas quae ad Artium
Facultatem hujus Universitatis pertinent, diligenter ac feliciter navasse, et praestitis
rite omnibus exercitiis ad hoc constitutis, Gradum

Baccalaureatus in Artibus

adeptam esse.

In cujus rei Testimonium, Sigillum Universitatis Literis hisce more
usitato subscriptis apponi fecimus.

Datae in Comitiis solennibus die Tricesimo Mensis Aprilis
Anno Domini, MDCCCLXXXIX

Actingilus Felix R. Robelson, Regens.

Prim. J. Gulielmus Dawson, LL.D. Primarius.

Decan. Alex.ᵈ Johnson, LL.D. Math. et Nat. Phil. Prof.

W. Cornal Gregoria Cornish, L.L.D. Litt. Hum. Prof.

Howe Markey M.A., D.C.L. LL.D. Off. Francicum Lit. Gal. Prof.

Murray J. Clark Murray, LL.D., Log. et Eth. Prof.

Harrington B.J. Harrington, B.A., Ph.D., Chem. et Min. Prof.

Prof. Moyse Charles E. Moyse, B.A. Ett. Ang. Prof.

Pendallos D. P. Penhallow, B.Sc. G.S.A.I. Ing. Phys. Prof.

Cornish at Daniel Cornish LL.M., B.D., Heurim Academico; Hebr. Ling. et Orient. Lit. Prof.

Eaton A. Eaton M.A. Ph.D. Ling. et Litt. Graec. et Lat. Prof. H.J.

P. Jones, M.d. Ling. et Litt. Germ. Praelector.

Jacobus W. Brakeenridge B.A.
Hony. Registrar

WOMEN AND EDUCATION

Before the 1880s, there were few options available to women seeking a university degree. Colleges in the American Midwest and South, such as Oberlin and Wesleyan, were the first to offer degrees to women in the 1830s and 1840s. In Canada, women could take university-level courses at some institutions, including Morrin College, but they did not have access to the full four-year B.A. program. Mount Allison University in Sackville, NB was the first to open its B.A. program to women in 1872, but it took another ten years for the first female B.A. in Canada to graduate from this school.

By 1890, most Anglo-Protestant universities in Canada had opened their B.A. programs to women. This trend started in the Maritimes and quickly spread to Quebec, Ontario, and Manitoba. The first woman to study in Morrin College's four-year program was Kate Pilkington in 1883, though she could not technically obtain a degree and only completed one year. Morrin officially opened its four-year program to women in 1885, one year after McGill. The first two women to earn a B.A. in Quebec City graduated from Morrin College in 1889. Seven of the College's forty-six B.A. graduates were women, representing over a third of the total in the school's last decade.

French-language universities in Quebec were late in admitting women. Laval granted its first certificate to a woman in 1904, but she was not invited to the convocation ceremony—the rector explained that Quebec's women "*sont assez intelligentes pour savoir qu'elles doivent être comme des fleurs qui n'exhalent leur parfum que dans l'ombre*" ("are intelligent enough to know that they must be like flowers, who only give off their perfume in the shade"). A special B.A. for women was eventually created, but it was only in 1945 that women had access to the same program as men. This gave Laval the distinction of being only slightly less backward than Cambridge, which only granted proper B.A. degrees to women in 1948.

Seen in this light, Morrin College must have appeared relatively progressive in Quebec City, especially as its Arts classes were co-ed. Even at McGill, women studied in a separate building. Principal Dawson believed this was necessary to preserve the emotional and spiritual refinement of womankind, which should not be coarsened by too much contact

Edith Sloane's diploma, 1889
Edith Sloane was in the first graduating class with women at Morrin College, receiving her degree in 1889. She was offered a teaching position in Nova Scotia but her family did not consider it suitable for a woman to go off on her own. She followed her family from Quebec to Ottawa, and later to Toronto, before finally settling in Winnipeg around 1912. In Winnipeg, Edith Sloane lived in a large home with her brothers, their wives, and children. She never married, was in charge of running the household, and provided early education to the children.

with men. Even if the governors of Morrin College had wanted to do the same, the school's small size made single sex classes impractical. The first year opened with two female students, hardly enough to warrant separate classes.

The women at Morrin College eventually petitioned the College for a room of their own. Former student Ethel Gale wrote that:

> … almost the only recognition of the women's department at Morrin, aside from our seats in the lecture rooms, and the particularly pleasant manner which the professors adopted towards us, was a small dressing room at the head of the staircase leading from the entrance to the Assembly Hall. Here a table and a deep window seat provided us with space for text books, note books, and such properties as would not hang on the hooks provided for our hats and coats, or gowns. The age of luxury had not yet arrived—or, perhaps, we were not sure enough of our status to make demands—and we seem to have been satisfied with these conditions. However, there did come a day when stirrings of a noble discontent were apparent and a group of women students assessed themselves for an amount sufficient to curtain the windows, supply a much desired mirror, and add to the room a few touches suggestive of feminine occupation.

A Woman's Place

By the twentieth century, many women had access to education but still faced discrimination in society and on the job market if they chose to educate themselves. Educated women were derided as unfeminine bluestockings. A university education was considered character forming for men, but impeded a woman's prospects for marriage—nobody liked an opinionated strong-minded woman.

The women who ignored such warnings faced fewer job prospects than men. Women with a B.A. usually ended up as teachers or housewives, but never both at the same time. Teaching was socially acceptable because it was seen as an extension of child care. Since an educated married woman was expected to stay at home, she had to give up teaching when she got married.

At least four of the seven female Morrin College graduates were professional teachers at some point in their lives, mostly at the primary and secondary levels. Ethel Gale (class of 1893) was the "lady principal" of Commissioners' High School in Quebec City for many years. Euphemia MacLeod (class of 1889) pursued her studies at McGill and became the first woman in the province to earn a Masters in Philosophy. She returned to Quebec City and taught at Morrin College during its last two years.

Euphemia MacLeod, M.A., 1919
One of the first two women to obtain a B.A. in Quebec City, Euphemia MacLeod worked as a teacher and published two books: *My Rose and Other Poems*, and *Seances with Carlyle*. Her poetry deals with nature, mythical warriors, World War I, and a concern for animal rights, all infused with a tinge of dour Calvinism. The latter is best seen in a poem called "Communion": "Drink this, 'tis the cup of Life's wine,— / Stress, failure and infinite pain: / Drink deep ;—and thy spirit shall find / Strength, courage, and God for the gain."

Breaking the Mould

"It is useless manufacturing articles for which there is no market," said Sir William Osler, professor at McGill's medical school, when asked about opening this school to women in the 1880s. "Quebec and Montreal have none, and in the smaller towns and villages of this country she would starve."

Despite these grim prospects, Margaret Ethel Fraser (class of 1894) was determined to study medicine. This meant leaving her hometown of Quebec City. Fraser studied at the **Ontario Medical College for Women** in Toronto, where she graduated in 1899.

Prospects for female doctors were better in the United States. Fraser eventually moved to Colorado, joined the staff of the Denver City Hospital, and worked for the Colorado State Board of Health.

Dr. Margaret Ethel Fraser, 1918
This Quebec City-born Morrin College graduate received the Medaille de la Reconnaissance française for her work as head of the American Women's Hospital in La Ferté-Milon, one of the hardest hit regions of France during World War I.

During the First World War, many women physicians were eager to contribute. Dr. Fraser was named head of the American Women's Hospital in a devastated part of France. The fact that she had spent the first twenty-two years of her life in Quebec City and spoke French probably helped. She was decorated by the French government for her work.

Aside from her medical work, Dr. Fraser remained committed to improving the condition of women and protecting the environment. She was a member of the American Association of University Women, worked for their scholarship fund, and attended several meetings of the International Federation of University Women in Geneva, Helsinki, and Copenhagen. She was also a co-founder of the Colorado Mountain Club and the only woman on its first board of directors—this group was instrumental in creating Colorado's Rocky Mountain National Park.

FROM COLLEGE TO CHARITABLE TRUST

In the 1891-92 school year, Principal Cook and Reverend Weir died. The loss of these two pillars signalled the beginning of a decade of change and uncertainty. Some attempts were made to launch the College anew, but a variety of factors forced the school to close down by the turn of the twentieth century. After 1902, Morrin College funds were redirected to scholarships and community development initiatives.

FINANCIAL CHALLENGES

In the 1890s, the College was not generating enough income to cover operations. The 1888 effort to raise a $150,000 endowment had not paid off. The College succeeded in getting a few thousand dollars here and there, but Quebec City's stagnant economy made it harder to find major donors than in Montreal, where McGill had raised well over two million dollars from industrialists by the 1890s. Furthermore, by restricting board membership to Presbyterians, the College may have cut itself off from many potential donors. Queen's had raised $150,000 when Principal George Monro Grant distanced the university from its Presbyterian roots.

The College received modest annual grants from the Protestant Committee of the Council of Public Instruction but these were gradually cut off in the 1890s. From 1873 onward, Morrin College received $1,500 to $2,000 per year. This was barely enough to cover the salaries of two professors, yet it still provoked outrage at other schools. High schools and small colleges received less, even though most had more students: "At McGill, money is employed to public advantage, but at Morrin it is nothing more than a personal gift," argued an editorialist from the Eastern Townships in 1886. He called Morrin College a "one-horse institution" that only obtained public funds because "the domineering genius of the [Protestant] committee is Dr. Cook." In 1893, Saint Francis College argued that they "sent out ten students to Morrin College's one" and received less. The Morrin College grant was reduced soon after. By the end of the century, public funding was based on the number of students who passed examinations, and Morrin College received next to nothing.

The one hope that College authorities clung to was money from the estate of James Gibb Ross, who had been one of the wealthiest merchants in Quebec City. Ross had made his fortune in dry goods, shipbuilding, lumber, and railways. When he died in 1888, he left an estate valued between five and ten million dollars. In his vague will, he bequeathed his property to his brother Frank Ross, who was to distribute half to charitable Protestant institutions in Scotland and Quebec City. Since the Rosses had donated money to Morrin College in the past, it was believed that more was on the way. After all, Frank Ross was on the College board and his nephew was head of the Alma Mater Society.

As it turned out, the Ross will generated bad blood between Frank Ross and Morrin College. When College governors wrote an official request for details of the trust, Ross was insulted: "I beg to notify you that I herewith withdraw any proposal of assistance I have made to the College and further that you will please remove my name as a Governor." The family soon launched a long battle to have the will invalidated. Principal Cook's son William defended the Protestant charities. Ross's attorneys argued that Morrin College was not a Protestant charity but a sectarian Presbyterian school.

As the trial dragged on, the new Saint Andrew's minister Reverend Andrew Tannahill Love struggled to keep the College going. He had taken over as interim Principal after Cook's death, remaining longer than intended because the College could not afford a new Principal. Student numbers nosedived from thirty-one to six. In 1894, professors were told to vacate their houses by May, signalling the end of the institution.

By this time, the Ross will case had reached the Supreme Court of Canada. It eventually declared the will valid and Morrin College a rightful benefactor in 1894. Newspapers proclaimed that, "if all that we hear is true, Morrin College will be brought to the surface as one of the leading educational institutions in the Dominion for Arts students."

Unfortunately, this was not to be. In the end, Morrin College received $120,000 (worth approximately $3,000,000 today). The terms of Ross's donation were more liberal than Morrin's original deed, allowing the College to become moderately less sectarian—one third of the board could now consist of "Protestants of other denominations." Although this substantial sum was nearly three times Joseph Morrin's initial bequest, it was far less than the "half million of dollars or upwards reasonably expected."

This nevertheless gave the College a new lease on life that came at just the right time. The Ross bequest allowed a new principal to be hired, teaching staff to be increased, repairs to be carried out, and loans to be paid off.

Morrin College, c1892
The only known surviving photo of Morrin College professors and students was taken soon after the death of Principal Cook under the interim principalship of Reverend A.T. Love (bottom row, first from right). Two female students are portrayed, a recent addition to the school.

SECOND WIND

In April 1896, the sixty-two-year-old Reverend Donald Macrae took over as principal of the College. He left his post as minister in Saint John, NB, which he had occupied for the previous twenty-two years. Macrae was a respected Presbyterian, having been elected moderator of the General Assembly of the Church in 1880 and holding an honorary doctorate from Queen's University. He was offered an annual salary of $2,000 and one of the houses behind the school "until the college attains a financial condition for a more liberal provision."

The staff was brought up to a record nine professors, many of whom also came from New Brunswick. William Crocket, Chief Superintendent of Education for New Brunswick, replaced Reverend Weir as professor of classics soon after the latter's death. William Gunn, who had studied in France and Germany, accompanied Principal Macrae from Saint John to teach modern languages. Alfred MacIntyre was appointed to physics and chemistry, having recently completed university studies in Germany, which stood at the cutting edge of science at the time. MacIntyre had been responsible for setting up Canada's first wood distillation plant in Saint John. He turned the College's rudimentary facilities into a functional laboratory.

Student numbers shot up to eighty-seven, and newspapers said the school had "renewed her youth." This didn't last. Only two students graduated under Macrae's principalship. Four years later, the College's second wind looked more like a last gasp.

Dr. Donald Macrae, c1891
Macrae was the last principal of Morrin College, serving from 1896 to 1900. He tried to launch the school anew while broader societal changes and internal struggles conspired against his efforts.

Former Chemistry and Physics Laboratory
Laboratory work was added to the Morrin College Arts curriculum as an option in the late 1880s, but it only took off ten years later under professor Alfred MacIntyre. In addition to teaching classes in the laboratory, MacIntyre also used it for his own work as an "analytical and consulting chemist and bacteriologist." Aside from the original blackboards, markings on the floor, and hanging lamps, few traces of this laboratory remained at the time of the building's restoration. The present reconstruction was based on period photographs of other late nineteenth-century school laboratories.

WINDING UP

Four major factors contributed to the school's closure: the gradual decline of Quebec City's Protestant population, continued financial difficulties, friction among the College staff, and changing standards in education.

Between 1861 and 1901, the Protestant population in the Quebec region fell, reducing the potential pool of students by more than half. In 1861, there were 13,848 non-Catholics in the region, representing 16.5 percent of the total population. Forty years later, there were 6,550 non-Catholics, or 5.6 percent of the population. In comparative terms, the non-Catholic population on the island of Montreal nearly tripled, with a pool of potential students fifty times larger than in the Quebec region—no wonder McGill was growing exponentially! Even rural Bishop's had nearly six times as many non-Catholics in its vicinity.

There were many reasons for the departure of Quebec City's Protestants, most of which are related to the city's economic decline. The development of transportation networks on a continental scale ended Quebec City's days as a major seaport: the dredging of the Saint Lawrence allowed ocean-going ships to bypass Quebec; Montreal became an important railway hub in the 1850s, while Quebec remained disconnected from the railway network until the 1870s. Moreover, the shipbuilding and timber trades that had fuelled the economy for the first half of the century collapsed. Tanneries, footwear manufacturers, and other small industries sought to revive the city, but these activities did not generate much capital and urban growth. Canada's capital moved to Ottawa in 1867, and many English-speaking civil servants followed. In the face of these economic and cultural changes, English-speaking Protestants were more likely to leave than the French-speaking inhabitants because they spoke the language of the North American majority and had fewer family ties in the region.

Even with the added money from the Ross bequest, Morrin College could not keep up. In 1897-98, revenue from interest, donations, and grants was just under $6,000. Expenses were $9,692, including $8,000 of salaries to teachers who considered themselves grossly underpaid. Morrin College had to eat into its endowment to survive, which was not a sustainable solution.

The College appealed to the Presbyterian Church in a tone filled with reproach and desperation, one of many yearly pleas for help:

> An institution fighting for its existence in the very citadel of a community specially antagonistic to Presbyterianism in all its aspects and relations, is surely entitled to a larger and more generously practical measure of recognition and aid than the Church has hitherto accorded.

A committee was eventually appointed to consider the situation. The Church was reluctant to help, arguing that most Presbyterian theological colleges elsewhere were better equipped and more likely to attract students.

Since public grants were related to the number of students passing exams, the College loosened its admissions requirements. Professors put in extra hours tutoring students "hoping that by the time of the intermediate exam they would make at least a pass mark." Unfortunately, this did not work. If anything, it contributed to a breakdown of relationships within the school.

In 1898 and 1899, the board spent its meetings dealing with bickering among the staff. In addition to constant requests for pay increases, it was the "differences between some of the professors and the principal" that must have been the most taxing.

An angry fifteen-page letter from Professor Crocket explains some of this tension. This letter came after a petition was launched by the principal's son asking for more class work: "The whole thing, gentlemen, is a farce," answered Crocket, "The class had twice as much Greek prose in a week as the corresponding class at McGill." Crocket said the principal's son had subjected him to:

> . . . the most gratuitous insults and every form of annoyance . . . In his own interests and in the interest of the College he should attend a larger institution where the superiority of numbers will put him in his proper place, and where he will have to be under control instead of controlling.

Crocket argued that the principal had enabled his son to cheat. First, he had bought him a key to Latin prose: "No teacher or professor permits such help to be in possession of any student when he knows it, and further the publisher is debarred from selling the book except under specified conditions." More importantly, there had been an incident around McGill examinations:

> I received the [examinations] from the Principal's young son carelessly rolled up in a ragged piece of brown paper tied around the middle with a piece of twine, open at the ends, just before the examination commenced . . . I hold that the Principal had no right to keep these in his house for two days . . . I also claim that I had the right to shew the students the form in which I had received them.

The son finished writing the exam early and the principal soon appeared "in a furiously excited state" and publicly berated Professor Crocket for insinuating that his son had cheated.

While these tensions were certainly not the main reason for the College's closure, they probably undermined the desire of board members to keep the school going.

Changing standards in education made it hard for Morrin College to remain competitive as improved transportation facilitated study in Montreal or elsewhere. Large universities introduced more options to their Arts programs, allowing students to tailor their studies to their own interests. By the late 1890s, McGill had added options in economics, political science, art, archaeology, Roman law, jurisprudence, constitutional law, history, anatomy, and physiology. This was intended to provide "a natural transition for professional students to work in the Faculties of Law, Medicine, and Applied Science."

McGill also had state-of-the-art laboratories that drew the likes of Ernest Rutherford, where he discovered the concept of radioactive half-life. Meanwhile, the Morrin College board refused Professor MacIntyre's request to purchase basic equipment in experimental physics due to a lack of funds.

In 1899, McGill revised its standards for affiliation to reflect this broader curriculum. The Morrin College board met on May 4, 1899 to discuss how they could meet these new standards: "After much discussion it was resolved that in view of the financial position and present prospects of the College, that notice be given to all the professors that after next session their services would no longer be required." Affiliation was revoked at the end of the year and everything looked set to shut down. Principal Macrae was given a severance package and returned to Saint John.

As news spread of the College's imminent closure, many gathered in support. Renowned local author Sir James MacPherson LeMoine wrote "A Plea for Morrin College." James Douglas, Jr. offered a thousand dollars a year for five years on condition that instruction be given at the College. These demonstrations convinced the board to continue.

The College trudged on without a principal or any affiliation for two more years. It offered disparate preparatory courses rather than a full-time B.A. program. Professors Gunn and Crocket stayed on. The well-known poet and Anglican minister F.G. Scott taught English literature. One hundred and two students enrolled in the first year, most of them attracted to Scott's English class and to Gunn's French and German lessons. Approximately fifty students enrolled in the second year, and classes in technical drawing were added. No professor appears on payroll after 1902, though the building was still occasionally used for courses and lectures.

From the first day of the College, Reverend Cook had wondered whether it was too ambitious for Quebec City's small Protestant community. The institution plodded on in the hope that the population would grow and money would come pouring in, but this did not happen. When McGill revoked its affiliation, this effectively put an end to the utopian ideal of an Anglo-Protestant College in a city that did not have the population or resources to support it. Although the College slogged on without an Arts faculty, it was actively looking for a new orientation in these transition years.

Soul Searching

What to do with over $100,000 and no College to spend it on? In June 1900, the rector of the High School proposed a scheme to concentrate Protestant education in one institution. College authorities liked this idea since they believed Joseph Morrin's original intention had been to leave his money for the High School, "an idea that had changed only at the last moment." They purchased new scientific equipment for the High School and gave it a $500 grant.

Sketch for a New Morrin College Building, 1902
This is one of the sketches prepared for a larger building that would have included the College, High School, and Literary and Historical Society. Separate entrances are included for each institution. Although the building seems wider, it is in fact the same width and just a little higher. Different sketches were completed by the Montreal firms of Cox & Amos, and Hutchison & Wood.

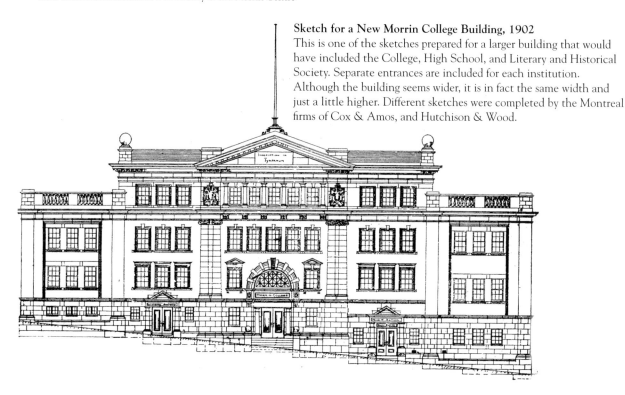

A more ambitious plan was then drawn up. It involved tearing down the College and replacing it with a new building meeting "modern requirements for the High School, for some College classes, with ample space reserved for the Literary and Historical Society." The board asked for tenders and sketches. In March 1903, the College was set on demolition. They gave the Society two months to empty its library.

The plan was shelved soon after for financial reasons. The initial estimate of $30,000 was revised to $60,000, a cost "too great to be entertained, more especially as the [High] School in its present financial condition requires permanent aid." Instead, Morrin College provided a $6,000 grant to help the High School improve and enlarge its existing building. They also promised an annual grant to support operations. With this decision in the fall of 1903, the College changed from a struggling educational institution to a charitable trust.

This new charitable vocation initially rattled the Presbyterian Church. In 1904, the Church sent a representative who urged the board to give all its money to Queen's University. This initiative failed, and Archibald Cook replied that the College had no legal obligation to the Church and that the money had originally been entrusted for educational work in Quebec City. He added that his father had continually repeated, "how discreditable he thought it was that the Church took so little interest in Morrin College and that it could not be persuaded to render it any assistance." The Church eventually gave its blessing to Morrin College's new orientation.

A FOUNDATION IN ALL BUT NAME

Although Morrin College continued to be known by its original name, it was a College without classes and a foundation in all but name. Board meetings were concerned with donations and bursaries, managing investments, and finding suitable occupants for their buildings. Many schools, organizations, and young students benefited from the College's generosity throughout the twentieth century.

Support for Institutions

The High School of Quebec received annual donations until 1937. These ranged between $1,650 and $2,500 per year. In 1941, this private school for boys merged with others in the region to become the co-ed public Quebec High School on avenue Belvédère, where it continues to this day.

The Literary and Historical Society also benefited from the College's new orientation. In fact, it would probably not exist today had the College not intervened to save it. The Society had been in a precarious financial position for most of the 1890s, yet College authorities remained lenient about rent. By 1904, Morrin College could afford to be more generous since it no longer had to run a school. The Society was given rent-free rooms, sporadic donations, and authorization to expand its library beyond the main reading room. Rent was charged from 1916 on, but remained a modest amount well below the actual cost of maintaining the building. From 1925 to 1948, Morrin College sponsored membership fees for all Protestant teachers wishing to join the Society. The College also financed a free joint lecture series with the Society in the early decades of the century. Topics were eclectic, ranging from the Biblical Abraham to the Panama Canal. Renowned Canadian writer Stephen Leacock gave several lectures in this series, including one on "The Outlook for Imperial Unity" in 1910.

Between 1922 and 1966, Saint John's Hall received annual donations of up to $2,500, becoming the main beneficiary of Morrin College funds for the mid-century period. This home welcomed teenagers from the Saguenay and the Lower North Shore, where Protestant schools only went up to grade ten. Located at the western end of rue Saint-Jean near de Salaberry, it housed around thirty children. After 1925, the United Church of Canada took over the home. Hubert Bauch, who lived there in the early 1960s, remembers that they informally referred to it as "The Home for Wayward Boys." The home closed in June 1967 due to declining support from the Church.

The Presbyterian and United Churches also received donations. At first, these were small amounts to support their Sunday schools in the Quebec City region. Saint Andrew's Church Sunday School met in College Hall until 1907, with newspaper accounts as far back as 1877 describing the "happy, smiling faces and sparkling eyes of the young people, as they sat around the tables loaded with good things" for their annual tea meeting. Since the late 1970s, funding has expanded beyond the Sunday schools; many Presbyterian and United churches in the eastern part of the province receive funding, with a large chunk going to Saint Andrew's and Chalmers-Wesley in Quebec City. They have since become the main beneficiaries of Morrin College's generosity, and continue to receive annual grants.

Support for Students

Bursaries to individual students began in 1911. At first they were given only to theological students. After 1922, available money was supplemented by interest from the estate of Quebec City merchant Robert Bruce. By the 1930s, bursaries were being given to any university student regardless of their subject of study provided they lived within the region and were members of the Presbyterian or United Churches. For a short while, bursaries were opened up to members of other churches, but this did not last. Membership in the Presbyterian or United Churches is still required today, but the geographical extent of support now includes communities east of Quebec on the North Shore and Lower Saint Lawrence. In the past, one to two dozen students benefited every year, with these numbers increasing in recent years.

Morrin College bursaries were not always widely publicized, and there were times when the board may have liked things this way. For instance, of the twenty-two students who received bursaries in 1967, five had the same surname as one of the wealthier board members. Nevertheless, some genuinely needy students also benefited from bursaries.

Former Saint John's Hall, 2016
Until 1967, this building on Rue Saint-Jean housed Saint John's Hall, a student residence that was the main beneficiary of Morrin College donations in the mid-twentieth century.

A Living Building

Although many journalists have played up the notion that Morrin College was a quasi-deserted romantic ruin in the twentieth century, this is not exactly true. The building was alive with celebrations, intellectual pursuits, artists, war relief efforts, and mischievous children. It was always more than a school and library. Outside the Society rooms, things slowed down gradually only after the 1960s, and ground to a halt in the 1990s.

ANNUAL CONVENTION OF THE ASSOCIATION AT MORRIN COLLEGE, QUEBEC.

Annual Meeting of the Protestant Teachers Association, 1879
Even at the time of the College, rooms were rented out to third parties or used for special events. Ladies traditionally had the better seats on the balcony. One of the papers read during this three-day meeting of Protestant teachers in 1879 was "A Plea for the Metric System" by Dr. J. Baker Edwards (metrication in Canada only began in 1970).

The largest events were held in College Hall. The famously eccentric Austrian world chess champion William Steinitz welcomed members of the Quebec Chess Club there in 1893. The Quebec Geographical Society hosted a talk by Captain Joseph-Elzéar Bernier about his planned expedition to the North Pole in 1898. Such activities continued long after the school's closure. In 1915, British writer Mary Hall talked about being the first woman to trek from Cape to Cairo "alone" (she was accompanied by up to forty African porters who carried her in a hammock when things got tiring, but it seems they did not count).

The Scottish festival of Saint Andrew's Day was also celebrated with annual dinners in College Hall. The room was decorated with the Saint Andrew's Society banner surrounded by bunting and fresh spruce. The dinner involved music, speeches, and toasts, which could get out of hand when too much whisky or wine was served. In 1882, the upper-class members of the Society circumvented this problem: "the Scotch people, by holding their dinner on the grand old principle of temperance, have inaugurated, as was truly said last evening, another Scotch reform." Unfortunately, temperance may have been the death knell of these dinners, as they soon fizzled out. The Saint Andrew's Society continued to have a room in the building well into the twentieth century before disbanding in 1977.

The College supported the war effort during both World Wars. In 1917, more Victory bonds were sold by a group of English-speaking volunteers in College Hall than by any other group in town. That same year, a fundraising lecture "illustrated with lantern views" allowed Dr. Stewart Ramsey to explain his experiences on the front. During World War II, the rear section of College Hall was used in the daytime to pack clothes for British air raid victims, and in the evening by the nursing section of Saint John's Ambulance Brigade.

Saint Andrew's Society Banner, 2011
This damaged banner displays the Society's motto, *Nemo me impune lacesset*, meaning "no one will touch me with impunity." Some believe this motto refers to the thistle, Scotland's floral emblem, which prickled invaders landing on the Scottish coast.

The Imperial Order of the Daughters of the Empire (IODE) also contributed to the war effort from the building, staying there long after the war. Founded in 1900, this patriotic organization was divided into subgroups specializing in different areas of charity work. Some IODE chapters met in Morrin College as early as 1917. In 1940 the College board supplied the IODE with quarters "complete with sewing machines, supply cupboards, counters and other equipment, as well as a kitchen, where tea can be prepared for the workers." Members raised money and prepared packages of books or clothing for soldiers or needy families. When IODE members were informed that soldiers needed more mitts and gloves on the front, many gathered to knit and sew furiously. Children helped their mothers by knitting balaclavas or serving tea at meetings. During peacetime, members worked in many fields. Some welcomed immigrants at the port, others raised funds for educational work, and the General Turner V.C. chapter sponsored a basal metabolism machine for Jeffery Hale's Hospital.

Nature lovers and animal activists also used the building. For over half a century, the Ladies Branch of the SPCA held meetings in Morrin College. They contributed to the war effort in their own way by holding a Valentine's Day sale for the wounded horses of France and Flanders in 1918. One wonders if they got along with members of the Sportsmen's Fish and Game Protective Association, whose 1922 annual meeting in the building called for an open season on murres, guillemots, and auks.

Artists of all stripes congregated in the building during the twentieth century. Starting in 1905, Miss Boulton was given a room to teach painting. Photographers used the darkroom in the former chemistry and physics lab. By the 1950s, smaller rooms on the third floor were rented out to artists. British painter Lionel Fielding Downes rented one of these from 1956 to 1959, paying the janitor's son fifty cents an hour to pose. Artist Kathleen Shackleton, sister of the polar explorer Ernest Shackleton, also rented one of these rooms. In the 1950s and 1980s, theatre groups used College Hall for practices, set painting, and storage.

It took a long time for the College to use the building for its heritage potential. The board was nervous about allowing guided tours, as the building was exempt from taxes as long as it was used for non-commercial purposes. "Tours of the dungeons" were eventually tried out in 1971, the board agreeing to hire "a Protestant student" for the summer months. Eventually, two students were hired, showing the cells to nine hundred visitors. This has been a recurring feature ever since.

Last but not least, teaching continued in the building after the College's closure. In 1907, Professor Gunn was given a free room to continue his courses in modern languages provided he mentioned "that they are not under the patronage of the College." The McGill link was even revived, with the board allowing College Hall to be used for "McGill extension courses" on winter Tuesdays in 1926. In recent years, Professors Mary-Ellen and Thomas Reisner of Université Laval continued this tradition of offering classes on poetry and social history in the building.

IODE Room in College Hall, 1970s
Quebec City once had thirteen chapters of the Imperial Order of the Daughters of the Empire. The last one shut down in 1990. With the decline in imperial fervour, the order shortened its name to the acronym IODE in the 1970s. Nevertheless, Queen Elizabeth's portrait and the Union Jack still had pride of place in the Quebec City meeting room.

GROWING UP IN MORRIN COLLEGE

The southern half of the building's ground floor was home to a live-in custodian until 1989. The longest-serving caretaker was J.W. Strachan, who kept things in order from 1890 to 1939. The last live-in caretaker was Ernest Muise, an amateur wood carver whose set of miniature horse-drawn carriages can be seen in the library.

Hubert Bauch, a retired journalist at *The Gazette*, remembers growing up in the building. His father Gerhard Bauch was caretaker between 1956 and 1964. Hubert Bauch lived with his three siblings and two parents in the tiny ground floor apartment, with all four children sleeping in one room. They were recent immigrants from Germany. Bauch said the Jewish kids teased him for being German, the "waspy kids" were exclusive and crusty, so he ended up falling in with the Irish kids, who were "more blue collar and closer to my family's economic circumstances." His own mother's family was Catholic and his father was agnostic, but he became "a Presbyterian of convenience, on account of my father's job."

He was poor, but says growing up in Morrin College and having free run over the building was a rich experience. He credits his career in journalism to his unrestricted access to the library: "There was a box where people would deposit used magazines that I would raid on a regular basis." He also remembers playing prisoner with his friends in the jail cells. They "would burn inscriptions with candles into the ceilings." He did his homework in College Hall. When he was in trouble, his father made him sweep the stairs from the fourth floor to the bottom.

Hubert Bauch, 2007
Retired political journalist for *The Gazette*, Hubert Bauch lived with his family in the Morrin College building between 1956 and 1964. He calls himself "the last graduate of Morrin College."

The Fate of the Aylwin Library

In addition to the Society's library, the College also had its own "Aylwin Library." It contained 10,000 books stored on the top floor. Willed to the College by Judge Thomas Cushing Aylwin after his death in 1871, this collection included some two hundred rare books dating from the sixteenth to the nineteenth centuries. After the College closed, the Literary and Historical Society was paid to catalogue and revive this collection. This was done over an eight-year period between 1908 and 1916, after which the collection became accessible to Society members for a short time. Being full of old books, the Aylwin Library was probably not frequently consulted and was eventually shipped over to new shelves in the chemistry lab, where the unread books mouldered away until the 1940s.

In 1946, the College decided to dispose of the books. The collectors' editions were sold to professional buyers, bringing in $571, a little over $6,000 in today's terms. Bishop's University made a selection from the rest, leaving many of the out-dated law books. College minutes suggest that these were probably donated "to the Salvation Army for scrap."

Real Estate and Related Concerns

In addition to distributing funds, the College's major preoccupation in the twentieth century was managing real estate. The main College building eventually came to be seen as a liability.

On September 16, 1952, board members put the main College building up for sale. Calculations for the previous five years showed that they had incurred a loss of $11,017 on the main building whereas revenue from houses in the court was $3,058, leading to a "continual drain of resources on the Corporation." They tried to interest the Literary and Historical Society in purchasing it, but it could not afford such a liability.

The board invested little energy in the sale at first. It took nearly twenty years before they actually put up a "FOR SALE" sign on the building. A real estate agent was only hired in 1974. Part of this had to do with their sense of a "long-standing moral obligation toward the Literary and Historical Society." They were picky about buyers, concerned about changes to the building, and wanted to ensure that the Society would also benefit. They turned down many initial offers, while the high sale price kept potential investors away.

From 1965 onward, board member Wilfred Rourke took the lead on the sale. Born in Petite-Rivière-Saint-François, Rourke was a classic self-made man. He came from a modest background, did not complete high school, but founded seven businesses in the fields of construction and building management. He was known as a persuasive talker and a flamboyant dresser, capable of combining alligator shoes with a fur coat.

Morrin College Building, 1970s
By the 1970s, the old College building had seen better days.
The plastering on the outside walls was chipping and fading
away. At one point, a chunk of wall even fell on a car
parked behind the building.

Rourke presented many proposals for the site's re-use. The GIFRIC, a non-profit interdisciplinary Freudian research group, hoped to set up an experimental arts centre in the building. Architectural historian Luc Noppen tried to interest the library in his co-operative "Morrin Museum" scheme, which involved transforming the rest of the building into a museum on the "art, history and architecture of Quebec." He recruited over forty people, but his project was dismissed as "vast enthusiasm, much talk, many ideas, and no money."

The only early offer that pleased the board came from the provincial government in 1976. This involved turning the building into a *Maison du patrimoine*. The 1808 Duberger scale model of Quebec City would have been displayed in College Hall, among other things. The preservation of the Society's library was also guaranteed under this arrangement. A deed of sale was drawn up but never signed, as the government backed out without explanation in 1977.

Architectural drawing of a library in the prison cells, 1982
This architectural drawing was appended to GIFRIC's proposal to turn the building into an experimental arts centre. The cellblocks have been linked up and turned into an Arts library. A library clerk sits in one of the former cells. The Society's library, located above this room, would have been transformed into rooms for experimentation in dance, art, cinema, and music.

The English-speaking community also mobilized to save the building. In the 1970s, a new consciousness was developing in response to the decline of religious practice, the cultural assertiveness of the French-speaking majority, and mass migrations of English-speakers out of the province. Older ethno-religious identities (Irish-Catholic, Protestant) were supplanted by a newly constructed sense of a shared Anglophone culture. New interest groups such as the province-wide AQEM (Anglo Quebec en Mutation) were formed. As of 1978, AQEM hoped to turn the building into a focus for English-speaking Quebec outside Montreal. AQEM member Eric Waddell wrote:

> The rupture from one generation of English Quebecers to the next is almost total. . . . As the francophones have realized, a people without a past cannot hope to have a future, or values, of its own. . . . We propose taking an important step in resurrecting the Anglophone collectivity's history, giving it a *point de repère*, a living temple within the walls of Old Quebec, a pride, and some guidelines for the future.

Their project involved expanding the Society's library into a research facility on English Quebec; restoring the prison cells for tours; creating a museum on the city's history in College Hall; landscaping an enclosed court yard; and transforming the College Court homes into a mixed-use residential/commercial development. There was even talk of setting up a British consulate in part of the building. This offer interested the College board, but they came to the conclusion that the group lacked funds and was unlikely to raise the money.

The impending sale spurred the government into action to preserve the building. The building was added to Quebec's register of cultural properties on January 23, 1981. Soon after, it was designated a National Historic Site by the federal government on November 13, 1981. Although this protected the significant architectural elements of the building, it did not ensure its continued use as a library.

In 1981, Rourke said "that none of the offers so far could be accepted, and he wished to make an offer himself." He asked the board if any members were interested in joining in, stating that if they participated "at a lower sale price, they would share in the profits." In the end, he procured an option to buy the city block for $350,000 in 1981. Although this price may seem low, it matched the higher purchase offers and was much higher than the municipal evaluation. Rourke eventually exercised his right to buy a few years later. The building, courtyard, and five apartments were sold to Les Immeubles RBS Inc., a company registered to Rourke's children, on October 30, 1987. Two years later, they sold the Morrin College building alone to the City for $500,000. In other words, Rourke's family made a $150,000 profit by flipping the main property, not to mention additional profits later made from selling the courtyard and condominiums. Although the Society lost its parking spots in the process, it was satisfied with the favourable rent-free and utilities-free lease negotiated for them by Wilfred Rourke with the City.

Not everyone was pleased with this process. The sale drew criticism at a 1989 parliamentary commission to modify Morrin College's bylaws. Gary Caldwell, one of the artisans of the rejected AQEM proposal, was a vehement critic. He argued that "*le présent conseil d'administration a fait fi de l'une des traditions les plus importantes de notre culture britannique, c'est-à-dire un service public désintéressé… et il y a ici une apparence de conflit d'intérêts*" ("the current board ignored one of the most important traditions of our British culture: disinterested public service… and there appears to be a conflict of interest"). Heritage advocate Luc Noppen felt that splitting the main building off from the rest of the property had destroyed the historical integrity of the site.

The 1987 sale put an end to the Morrin College board's official connection to the site. The sale strengthened its financial position, with annual income from investments doubling in the years following the sale. This allowed more students and organizations to benefit from grants and donations.

BACK TO THE FUTURE

Many sectarian charitable organizations have become secular since the 1960s. In Quebec City, charities such as the Church of England Female Orphan Asylum and the Irish Protestant Benevolent Society banded together to form the non-sectarian Citadel Charity Foundation in the 1970s. The Ladies' Protestant Home started accepting French-speaking Catholic men around this time, and the Irish Catholic Saint Brigid's Home set up an ecumenical chapel. The same is true of schools—even ultra-Catholic Université Laval became a secular university in 1971, and English-language school boards are no longer divided on denominational lines.

Morrin College was a rare exception to this rule. If anything, the contrary happened. Joseph Morrin's Deed of Trust does not mention that his endowment should be restricted solely to members of certain religious groups, yet this is essentially what happened. Bursaries were tentatively opened up to other Protestants for a few years in the mid-twentieth-century. But since the 1960s, Morrin College has embarked upon the Quiet Revolution in reverse. All student applicants outside the Presbyterian and United Churches were excluded after 1962. Moreover, the churches themselves have now become the largest beneficiaries of institutional grants. Despite the secularization of society, Morrin College has become more about religion and less about education.

Nevertheless, this discreet organization has had a remarkable impact over its 150 years. Many of its professors and graduates achieved renown in places as diverse as the battlefields of France, the colleges of Oxford University, the Klondike goldfields, and the deserts of Arizona. Even since closing, the organization has helped hundreds of students through university. Important charitable, religious and cultural institutions were preserved thanks to the continued support of Morrin College, including the Literary and Historical Society of Quebec. The College maintained its historic building throughout the twentieth century and insisted on selling it to a buyer that would respect both its character and the Society's library. Without Morrin College to look after it, the charming neoclassical building would probably not have survived and grown into today's Morrin Centre.

TIMELINE

1794	Joseph Morrin is born in Dumfriesshire, Scotland
1861	Joseph Morrin dies in Quebec City; Morrin College is incorporated
1862	Inauguration of Morrin College in Masonic Hall
1864	Morrin College affiliates in Arts and Law with McGill
1868	Morrin College moves to former common gaol after renovations by architect Joseph-Ferdinand Peachy
1885	Morrin College opens its Bachelor of Arts program to women
1892	Death of Reverend John Cook, principal of Morrin College for 30 of its 40 years
1894	Morrin College inherits $120,000 from the estate of James Gibb Ross, three times the amount of Dr. Joseph Morrin's initial bequest
1896	Reverend Donald Macrae takes over as principal
1900	Morrin College's affiliation with McGill ends; the full-time Arts course is discontinued
1902	Regular classes at Morrin College end. Morrin College changes from an educational institution to a charitable foundation
1952	Morrin College building is put up for sale.
1981	Morrin College building is classified by the provincial government and designated a National Historic Site by the federal government
1987	Morrin College building, and the apartments in College Court, are sold to Les Immeubles RBS, Inc. for $350,000
1989	Morrin College building is sold to City of Quebec for $500,000

A NOTE ON SOURCES

Primary Sources

The archives of Morrin College are housed at the Quebec City centre of Bibliothèque et Archives nationales du Québec (BAnQ), in fonds P949. This fonds includes early founding documents; the minutes of board meetings from 1879 onward; correspondence; documents about the building's sale; and more boxes of financial documents than you could ever possibly be interested in. The High School of Quebec Fonds (P956) and the Literary and Historical Society Fonds (P948), also housed at BAnQ, are useful to understand relations with these organizations. BAnQ also holds the unpublished manuscript of Olivier Robitaille's memoirs from 1882, which challenge the established biography of Joseph Morrin.

Published course calendars were a valuable source of information, listing program and course descriptions, staff and students, and information about the way the college operated. Unfortunately, only nine of these calendars survive for the four decades of the institution. There is a more complete collection of McGill course calendars to complement the gaps; these contain annual lists of students and professors for Morrin College and provide a perspective on the evolution of the relationship between the two institutions.

Many other documents about the college can also be found at McGill University. The McGill University archives house correspondence between the two institutions. They are also home to the fascinating correspondence of former Morrin College professor George Mercer Dawson, which provides a snapshot of the life of the institution. In 1930, former student Ethel Gale wrote a short article published in the *McGill News* that looks back on her years at the College. The library of the Presbyterian College, affiliated with McGill, contains all the annual reports of the General Assembly of the Presbyterian Church in Canada, and Morrin College continues to file a report at this assembly to this day.

Keyword searches in online newspapers and old city directories were a useful complement. They brought up articles about the college and its buildings, and provided information on many of its former students and professors.

This study also drew on many documents produced by or for the Quebec provincial government. Reports of the Superintendent of education and documents issued by the Protestant Committee of the Council of Public Instruction made it possible to analyze the Morrin College School saga and changes in funding over the years. The 1860 Deed of Trust, the 1861 Act of Incorporation and discussions of subsequent modifications of the latter in the Journals of the Legislative Assembly, and the proceedings of the 1989 parliamentary committee to modify the Act (that derailed into a debate on the building's sale) were also useful.

Finally, nineteenth-century census data was also used. Reports of the decennial censuses made it possible to compare changes in Quebec City's English-speaking population to the Anglophone populations around Sherbrooke and Montreal, changes that had a direct impact on the College's fortunes. Moreover, databases covering 100% of the census data collected in Quebec City between 1851 and 1911 by the "Population et histoire sociale de la ville de Québec" project made it possible to look up individual students and professors, and to draw broader conclusions about age, religious affiliation, and professional trajectories.

Detailed references for the text are available at www.morrin.org/morrinbook.

Secondary Sources

There is only one existing history of Morrin College aside from my own previous work on the topic as part of my Masters program. This is Laura Bancroft's B.A. thesis from 1950, which uses a chronological approach and mostly draws on information in the Morrin College minute books.

Existing studies of the history of higher education in Canada made it possible to understand the broader context in which Morrin College operated, while individual historical studies of Laval, McGill, Bishop's, and Queen's provided perspectives for comparison.

The Dictionary of Canadian Biography was useful for biographical information on students and teachers.

These are the most important secondary sources used for this study:

Bancroft, Laura Isobel. "Morrin College: An Historical and Sociological Study." B.A. thesis, Université Laval, 1950.

Donovan, Patrick. "Morrin College: 1862-1902." Supervised research project for M.Sc.A., Université de Montréal, 2002.

Frost, Stanley Brice. *McGill University: For the Advancement of Learning.* Volume 1: *1801-1895.* Montreal: McGill-Queen's University Press, 1980.

Gillett, Margaret. *We Walked Very Warily: A History of Women at McGill.* Montreal: Eden Press Women's Publications, 1981.

Hamelin, Jean. *Histoire de l'Université Laval : les péripéties d'une idée.* Sainte-Foy: Presses de l'Université Laval, 1995.

Harris, Robin S. *A History of Higher Education in Canada, 1663-1960.* Toronto: University of Toronto Press, 1976.

Magnuson, Roger. *The Two Worlds of Quebec Education During the Traditional Era, 1760-1940.* London: Althouse Press, 2005.

Masters, Donald C. *Protestant Church Colleges in Canada: A History.* Toronto: University of Toronto Press, 1966.

Neatby, Hilda. *Queen's University.* Volume 1: *1841-1917: To Strive, to Seek, to Find, and Not to Yield.* Montreal: McGill-Queen's University Press, 1978.

Nicholl, Christopher. *Bishop's University, 1843-1970.* Montreal: McGill-Queen's University Press, 1994.

MOOSE IN FLAMES
THE STORY OF THE LITERARY AND HISTORICAL SOCIETY OF QUEBEC

Louisa Blair

PROLOGUE

In 1823, George Ramsay, the 9th Earl of Dalhousie, Captain General and Governor in Chief of Upper and Lower Canada, Nova Scotia, New Brunswick, and Prince Edward Island, summoned a small group of people to the Château Saint-Louis at Quebec to discuss the founding of a learned society. There was no such thing in Canada, but several in Scotland, where he came from, and he had a friend in New York who belonged to one. From such groups, he believed, "every object of national improvement may originate, and hereafter our meetings may embrace Literature, Science, Education, and all other sources from whence spring the happiness of Society."

An exploratory meeting to discuss the establishment of the Society did not go well. The brains he had chosen to educate for leadership immediately began to fight about whether the title of the new society should include the word Canada (thereby also including Montreal), or Quebec. It was the kind of petty jealousy which, Dalhousie confided to his journal, he found "truly discouraging & mortifying."

The Literary and Historical Society of Quebec (LHSQ) was officially founded in 1824, and Dalhousie gave it a kick-start of £100 per year. Once he left, the government carried on funding it and, within ten years, the LHSQ had its own charter and had become a cultural institution of seminal importance to Canadian history. It occupied the most prestigious rooms in the central government buildings of British North America, rent-free. It acted as a substitute academic institution, granting a form of accreditation before the capital city had its own university and receiving public funds to buy history and science books and scientific apparatus. It operated one of Canada's earliest publicly funded cultural institutions: a natural history museum and an art gallery that displayed works by important European and Quebec artists. It supported and published some of Canada's first comprehensive geological surveys. It collected manuscripts in England and France relating to Canada's history and published them.

This said, the Society never quite lived up to its promise. It was chronically underfunded and endured many near-fatal setbacks. It withstood several fires and numerous evictions. It survived the removal (twice) of the Canadian capital from Quebec, which deprived it of some of its most influential and educated members. It survived the departure of British officers, another enthusiastic clientele, and then an exodus of anglophone Quebecers in the latter part of the nineteenth century. Its saviours were an intermittent series of passionate presidents and librarians, a succession of solitary overworked secretaries, private benefactors, and the founders of Morrin College, where it has lodged peacefully for nearly 150 years. In the twenty-first century, having auctioned off most of its collections to stay afloat, the Society had another boost in its fortunes with new governance, public grants, and a new crop of donors.

Despite its unpromising beginnings, Dalhousie's dream proved to have remarkable staying power. The Quebec Gaol moved in and out, Morrin College came and went, but since that first squabble in 1823, the Literary and Historical Society has endured through it all, the beating heart of the Morrin Centre building to this day. Most historians who have paid it any attention have quickly dismissed it as a group of elite British colonizers feebly trying to broadcast their version of events from the wrong side of history, and a few bibliophile Quebecers know it as the only English library in town. To most Quebecers and Canadians, the Society is still largely unknown.

Quebec from the Twenty-One Gun Battery, **by Fanny Amelia Bayfield, ca. 1827-1841**
In his journal Dalhousie wrote of the "filthy state" of the Chateau Saint-Louis, his new home, complaining that the furniture was tattered, plaster was flaking off the ceilings, and rain dripped on to the dancers at Lady Dalhousie's balls. He tried to lift the tone by hanging up a portrait of the King.

Silhouette portrait of Sir George R. Dalhousie, by Jarvis Frary Hankes, ca. 1828.
Dalhousie gained his overseas appointments by raising a regiment to fight in the Peninsular War, during which he carried with him a portable library of English and French classics. A keen scientist, he collected specimens as he moved from battlefield to battlefield and sent them back to a museum in Edinburgh.

HOW TO MAKE AN ARISTOCRACY

ORIGINS OF THE LITERARY AND HISTORICAL SOCIETY

THE SOCIETY'S FOUNDER

Lord Dalhousie was appointed Governor in Chief in 1820. He had enjoyed himself as Lieutenant-Governor of Nova Scotia, where he had been able to devote himself to edifying educational pursuits such as starting up an agricultural society, a library, and a college, all of which had taken root and were flourishing.

When he was appointed Governor in Chief, he moved to the Château Saint-Louis in the capital of Lower Canada, Quebec City. His wife, Christian (Broun) Ramsay, was a keen botanist and he was a collector and patron of the arts. Both were voracious readers and brought with them to Quebec a library of some 400 books. He immediately began to patronize the Quebec Library, founded by Governor Frederick Haldimand in 1779. In 1826, this library had 4,658 books, about a third of which were French and two-thirds English. Dalhousie was a fiction enthusiast, borrowing Jane Austen novels from the Quebec Library only a few years after she published them—perhaps to read aloud to his wife, as they habitually read to each other in the evenings. Christian Ramsay had superior aristocratic credentials, but a shared love of reading had helped Dalhousie win her heart.

In Quebec things were much more complicated than in Nova Scotia, however, and there wasn't as much time for reading as Dalhousie would have liked. He was charged with overseeing four colonies (New Brunswick, Upper Canada, Lower Canada, and Nova Scotia and Prince Edward Island) containing more than half a million people. He

My Lady's Reading Habits

Lord and Lady Dalhousie read books to each other in the evenings, and sermons on a Sunday. Christian Ramsay's diary shows that her reading was astonishingly wide, in both English and French, ranging from literature to history to philosophy, from early feminist works to scientific treatises on entomology, chemistry, geology and agriculture. She often had several books going at once, polishing off Scott's *Waverley* in just one day while working through others, such as Gibbon's six-volume *Decline and Fall of the Roman Empire* (1776), over several months.

She read Shakespeare, Byron, and Scott (repeatedly), eighteenth-century women novelists such as Jane Austen and Anna Radcliffe, and travel literature such as Humboldt, Charlevoix, and Mungo Park. She read David Hume's six-volume *History of England* three times in five years, and she and her husband read it together just after he was promoted to the job in Quebec in 1820. Perhaps in preparation for her North American sojourn she read James Adair's *History of the American Indians*. In French she read Abbé de Vertot's *Histoire des revolutions de Suède (1695)* and Jean-Charles-Dominique de Lacretelle's *Histoire de la France pendant le XVIIIᵉ siècle*. She read Scottish Enlightenment works on philosophy and aesthetics, especially Lord Kames and Hugh Blair, but also William Hazlitt, Joshua Reynolds, and Edmund Burke. Among the great philosophers she read David Hume and John Locke, but preferred the Christian philosophers such as Thomas Reid and James Beattie. She also read widely on women's improvement, works such as *Letters to Mrs Montagu* (1817) and Anna Seward's posthumous *Letters* (1811), and patronized the first Canadian-born novelist, Julia Beckwith, who dedicated her first novel, the ominously titled *St. Ursula's Convent, or the Nun of Canada* to Christian Ramsay. Finally, her scientific reading included William Kirby's *Introduction to Entomology* (1815–26), Sir Humphry Davy's *Agricultural Chemistry* (1813), and Robert Bakewell's *Introduction to Geology*.

Reading played an important part in her social relations too. A favourite reading companion was a "Miss Cochrane" in Halifax. Historians have remarked that this "sociable reading" was an important stimulant to intellectual life in British North America in the 1810s and 1820s. Christian Ramsay may have communicated some of her ideas and suggested her favourite writers to readers in Quebec, and perhaps had a say in the first purchases of the LHSQ library.

had high hopes that he would get on with the elected Assembly in Lower Canada by not siding with the English or the French. But the divide between the Assembly and the executive, appointed by the Crown, was deep and bitter.

Education was sorely lacking in the new colony, and Dalhousie decided to start at the top. He saw Canada as "a country in its infancy, shewing in every corner the promise of becoming one day a valuable and powerful state." For that day to arrive, it would need a ruling class, and although it didn't have the kind of aristocracy one might hope for, as a self-respecting Scot Dalhousie believed that a decent education would go a long way to remedying a shortage of blue blood. He also worried that this fledgling state had little to show for itself in terms of a written history. Something had to be done. A learned society like those flourishing in his native Scotland might do the trick.

The Brains of the Outfit

Dalhousie picked the Society's co-founders for the credibility each man would bring to the project. Yet his diary describes some of them in scathing terms, and others would go on to let him down.

As the French-English divide had stymied other such initiatives, Dalhousie began by writing a note to Joseph-Rémi Vallières de Saint-Réal, asking him to take the lead in this initiative to preserve early documents relating to the "Aborigenes" and collect archives, scattered in private or public hands, that were "neglected and wasting." Vallières had also been involved earlier in the short-lived Société Littéraire (1808–9) along with Philippe Aubert de Gaspé and Louis Plamondon. His relationship with Dalhousie soured when Vallières joined the reformist Parti Canadien, and Dalhousie later removed his militia commission as punishment.

Dalhousie also invited William Smith, who had published a history of Canada in 1815. Smith had run up against a pitiful lack of data and so shared Dalhousie's interest in the preservation of documents. Nonetheless, Dalhousie believed that Smith was a toady who "would do or say anything to please the reigning power," a weakness reflected in his *History*. Smith, he wrote, "is the meanest most avaricious & self-interested man connected with H. M. Govt. If he can't get a dollar, he will accept a sixpence."

Jonathan Sewell, Chief Justice of Lower Canada and member of the Executive Council, was certainly a good catch for the job. But Dalhousie complained that he "jumps at every vacancy as does a trout at a fly, and within the last year has importuned me for half a dozen places for [his son] … I feel it indelicate and unworthy of his station."

As for Sir Francis Burton, the lieutenant governor, he would betray Dalhousie in less than a year. While Dalhousie was in London, Burton, who was acting governor in his absence, made concessions to the Assembly that relieved an almost permanent state of stand-off and made Dalhousie look bad. But Burton was untouchable: he was the brother-in-law of the king's mistress.

Portrait of Jonathan Sewell, artist unknown, LHSQ collections
Chief Justice Jonathan Sewell, Dalhousie's chief advisor, was the son of Loyalist parents who fled the American Revolution. He was a man of large interests, many children and little money, but with important connections and influence. He had been in Quebec since 1789, and was one of the most powerful men in the colony.

THE NEILSON-FISHER AFFAIR

John Neilson's family had been printing the *Quebec Gazette/Gazette de Québec* for nearly sixty years. But at his election to the Assembly, he joined the Parti Canadien, and when he joined Papineau in London to complain against the Union of Upper and Lower Canada, Dalhousie punished him by hiring John Fisher to publish a new official *Quebec Gazette*. Neilson sued Fisher, furious at the loss of this lucrative contract as well as of his paper's title and thereby his prestige and reputation. He was unsuccessful, but in revenge, Neilson's paper did not mention a word about the LHSQ until Dalhousie was a distant spot on the horizon, and encouraged people to form the Mechanics' Institute instead. He seemed to have quickly got over the blow, however, for in 1834 he printed a book by Fisher, and in 1838 began printing the Society's publications. He and his son appear in membership rolls on and off from 1836 to 1869. John Wilson Cook described him in a lecture to the Society in 1866 as "one of the most able and honorable of the men who have taken part in the political contentions of Canada."

Dalhousie's best appointments, ironically, had no aristocratic credentials or wealth, but their hard work and enormous intellects set the Society on a solid footing. William Green, first recording secretary, was a protégé of Sewell's, a lawyer, joint Clerk of the Peace, and the translator at the House of Assembly. He was also a passionate botanist and artist. He had already published one of the first guides to Canadian plants—probably of great interest to Christian Ramsay—and, at the Society's first meeting, he audaciously maintained "against opinions pronounced in London" that a weed used for red dye in Canada was not the same as the madder used in England, and moreover was greatly superior. Green spoke with such authority that Dalhousie later submitted his paper and some samples to the Society for the Encouragement of Arts, Manufactures, and Commerce in London, which awarded Green the Gold Isis Medal.

Another key founding member was an impecunious Presbyterian minister named Daniel Wilkie, who was not in the same social class as Dalhousie but shared his Scottish background and some of his liberal ideas. Both were deeply influenced by Scotland's recent meteoric progress in education, science, and the arts.

Scotland was having its own Enlightenment, and was teeming with liberal ideas in every sphere. Political and economic theory were revolutionized by David Hume's *Treatise*, Adam Ferguson's *Civil Society*, and Adam Smith's *Wealth of Nations*. Because there was intense traffic of people and books between Scotland and Quebec, these ideas were to change the fate of Canada and other British colonies for all time.

Scientists and philosophers were studying geology and geography and coming up with new theories about the origins of the world, attacking superstition, and keeping God at the edge of their thoughts. Some, under the influence of Diderot, Montaigne, and Voltaire, believed that experiment alone, and not inherited truth, should define the business of living. Many others studied the new sciences alongside theology, and developed a new vision that blended them. They had egalitarian, even democratic ideas.

Scots were also reading the novels of Dalhousie's old school friend Walter Scott, whose romantic view of the old Scotland, especially the Highland clans, was opening a whole new perspective on traditional societies. This was to have a deep impact on the Literary and Historical Society's views of First Nations and French-Canadian cultures, too. Most of these ideas were debated and developed in the context of the learned scientific societies that met in the salons and libraries of Edinburgh. These included the Philosophical Society, the Select Society, hosted by David Hume, and its subsidiary the Edinburgh Society for Encouraging Arts, Sciences, Manufactures, and Agriculture in Scotland which awarded prizes for Scottish enterprise. Literary societies of the antiquarian or bibliophile variety were also popular in late-eighteenth-century Scotland, while public-lecture lyceums flourished in the United States. The Literary and Historical Society of Quebec would manage to combine all these models into one.

Wilkie ran a school that educated most of the city's elites, both French- and English-speaking. Their school fees provided his income, but in the evenings he gave courses for young working adults. With Joseph-François Perrault, his fellow Clerk of the Peace, he had been appointed in 1823 to a House of Assembly Committee to study education, and one of their conclusions was that the country badly needed a university. The LHSQ—significantly aided by Wilkie's longstanding involvement (1830 to 1851)—would go some way to making up this deficit.

After its incorporation, the Society moved out of the Château to an equally prestigious but less leaky location—the Union Building (now the Tourist Office), owned by Sewell and leased to the government. Dalhousie wrote to ask for the King's patronage, and gave the Society a substantial grant. Since none of the minutes from the Society's first meetings survive, exactly how those early times unfolded will remain forever a mystery.

With its roster of political heavyweights, the Society was immediately attacked by opposition newspaper *Le Canadien*, in which a young Étienne Parent wrote, "nothing will be good or true that comes out of this Society." A rival society, made up of people who wanted to establish an intellectual milieu that distinguished itself from the Governor's clique, soon sprang up to challenge the LHSQ. With much lower entrance

LHSQ Coat of Arms and Seal. In 1834 the Society ordered the design of a seal to be engraved on the diplomas and medals it awarded. It depicted "a shield charged with a view of the new country, partly under wood and undergoing improvement, with the sun just rising." (See page 179.) The inscriptions were in French and Latin.

fees, it struggled for survival, and Sewell suggested a merger—many members of the Society for the Encouragement of the Arts and Sciences in Canada (SEASC) were LHSQ members as well anyway, and many who weren't signed up too, including Étienne Parent. The battle for a new name was won by the LHSQ, which got to keep its name. Sewell renewed the Society's commitment to objectivity and inclusivity:

> We were originally two societies, we are now one, we are all fellow labourers in the field of science, and cherish … a common desire to render our labours beneficial to the land we inhabit, either as the place of our birth, or as the country which we have maturely chosen and adopted.

The Society soon had a growing library—and a museum, which was set firmly on its feet by Christian Ramsay's donation of a Canadian herbarium of 382 pressed plants that she had collected at Sorel, Bytown, and Quebec. The Society was poised to play a major role in the intellectual life of Quebec, and of Canada as a whole.

Only four years after its founding, Lord Dalhousie left Canada, a disappointed man. In this period of conflict between the Parti Canadien and the British Party, he had consistently refused to stand down and concede a single traditional prerogative of the Crown to the Assembly, an obstinacy that indirectly led to the Rebellions of 1837–38. Shortly after petitions with 87,000 signatures arrived in London supporting his recall, he was appointed to India.

He left behind him several enduring monuments, however, including Dalhousie University in Halifax, the Wolfe-Montcalm monument at Quebec, which commemorates the death of the two generals on opposite sides of the battle of 1759, and Dalhousie Gate at the entrance to the Citadel, built mostly under his rule. He also left behind the Literary and Historical Society of Quebec, of which he was proudest of all. "There is no act in the whole period of my administration of the Government in this Province," he said in his farewell speech, "which has afforded me so much satisfaction as that of having accomplished the formation of the Literary and Historical Society of Quebec."

A RAVENOUS AND UNSELECTIVE APPETITE

Intellectual Enthusiasms

In the late eighteenth century, educated amateurs were discovering that noting similar characteristics among the things in the New World was fun—a kind of crowdsourcing of scientific research—and were feverishly organizing everything into taxonomies. While Darwin was busy on the *Beagle* trying to work out how the Galapagos animals fit into Linnaeus' system of orders, subgenera, and classes, LHSQ members were busy identifying and classifying the virgin territory of North America. The world was an open book, or a giant specimen cabinet just waiting to be organized. The Society's attitude in the early nineteenth century seems, to the modern mind with its interests and academies now so successfully divided into watertight compartments, a ravenous and unselective greed for knowledge of every kind.

When it petitioned the government for a grant in 1830, the Society received a handsome grant of £250 for the purchase of "mathematical instruments and other objects to enable it to promote science in this province." In this early period of enthusiasm for a higher education in science, the Legislature had given the Society a mandate to be a public museum and a kind of national science research council.

The Society sent a shopping list of instruments with Lord Aylmer to London with requests for two globes, an electrical cannon, a solar microscope, various telescopes, barometers, thermometers, and hygrometers, and cases of various kinds of acids and glass apparatus. In addition to being used for scientific experiments and demonstrations to illustrate public lectures, these "mathematical instruments" could be borrowed by researchers "to carry out investigations connected with the objects of the Institution."

By 1831 the Society was running a fully fledged, publicly funded library, art gallery, natural history museum, and publication program. The scientific apparatus, books, museum exhibits, and other collections had been deposited in the Society's rooms, the early officers wrote proudly to Lord Aylmer that year, "and are now open to the public." It began to purchase sculptures that were shipped from London, including the capital of a pillar from the ruins of Carthage which must have added a British-Museum-style ambiance of classical antiquity.

Daniel Wilkie believed that patronage of the arts was an important function of the Society and that artists should be decently paid for their work. "Painting appears to have struck its roots among us," he said in 1827. "Already several artists have, notwithstanding extraordinary disadvantages, and amidst the almost total want of encouragement, made distinguished progress in this elegant department." Wilkie was a great supporter of the painter Joseph Légaré, who found support at the LHSQ that was not available anywhere else in town.

The Society particularly encouraged artistic creation directly related to Canadian history and scenery. Wilkie was thrilled when Légaré branched out from his religious themes into Canadian landscapes. "He has emerged from the dusty and prozing society of vigil-worn saints, and other goodly canonized nobles," Wilkie wrote in the *Quebec Gazette*. The Society offered medals and prizes for:

- the best poem on any subject relative to British North America;
- the best historical oil-painting; the subject relating to Canada;
- the best landscape of Canadian scenery, in oil or in water colours;
- the best piece of sculpture model, on plaster cast.

The Society was also running a public lecture program. Sewell, who bemoaned the lack of a "scientific" law school in Quebec, declared at the LHSQ's very first lecture that:

> the elements of science are best inculcated by public lectures—rightly conducted they awaken the attention of the student, abridge his labour, enable him to save time, guide his enquiries, relieve the tediousness of private research, and impress the principles of his pursuit more effectually upon his memory.

Someone sent a printing press from the United States for the Society to "advance its views." One fledgling literary review even proposed that the Society become a kind of Ministry of Education and take charge of all educational institutions in the province, Protestant and Catholic—a suggestion that was roundly denounced by a rival review whose editor asked "How would it be possible to reconcile the different religious opinions of parents?"

The Society concentrated instead on science education, and ordered the latest scientific tomes, including Michael Faraday's *Chemical Manipulation* (1827); *Reliquiae Diluvianae* by Buckland, who was the first man to identify a dinosaur; and a book on North American zoology by John Richardson.

Books, scientific instruments, historical manuscripts, and specimens began to pile up, and soon the Society was cramped for space. Its application to the House of Assembly for £1,500 to create a "suitable edifice for the convenience and free use of the public" suggests the scale of its ambitions: the new premises would include a library, a museum of natural history ("a repository of arts and sciences, models and inventions"), a lecture and music hall, an observatory, and a "gallery of painting and sculpture." This was the first of many applications for its own building over the next 150 years, none of which came to fruition.

Soldier-Scientists and Economic Independence

Seeking to advance the state of science was not only an open-ended search for knowledge; above all, it was practical and economical. In the early nineteenth century, thousands of immigrants were arriving, evicted by the industrial revolution in Britain, and needed land upon which to settle—most of which had not yet been surveyed. The government also needed people to build roads and canals and chart the rivers. It hastened to send out engineers, hydrographers, and surveyors across the country.

The incentives driving this thrust for scientific inquiry were multiple, and coalesced like the horizontal and vertical planes of a surveyor's theodolite. "We are all interested in obtaining information relative to … the more useful rocks and minerals," said Dr. Skey, which would "extend rapidly the productive powers of the country" and make it "independent of a foreign supply." The Lower Canadian merchants were hoping for miniature Birminghams, Manchesters, and Boltons to spring up in North America and compete with their British namesakes.

Because of the military importance of rivers, roads, and canals, many of Canada's pioneering scientists such as Frederick Baddeley (geology), Edward Ashe (astronomy), and Henry Bayfield (hygrography) were military men, trained in Britain. As members of the LHSQ, when they came back from their expeditions they could flesh out their measurements and statistics with tales of their adventures, complete with romantic encounters with Indians, in lectures at the Society—which would then publish their findings in its 400-page periodical, the *Transactions of the Literary and Historical Society of Quebec*. These scientist-explorers also filled up the Society's geology and mineral display cases with donations.

Soldier-geologist Lieutenant Frederick Henry Baddeley, considered the best geologist in Canada, had been commissioned in 1827 by the Legislature to explore the Saguenay with Andrew Stuart for settlement purposes and mineral identification. In their company were several voyageurs including Guillaume Gill (most likely a Métis), a number of unidentified Aboriginal guides, and the surveyor Joseph Hamel, who helped with measurements and made drawings of what he saw. They also took a theodolite for surveying, and a barrel of

"Bark of thuya gigantea & cordage made from its fibre – in common use by the inhabitants of Vancouver Island," a specimen from the Canadian Wood Collection at the LHSQ. The canal engineers and surveyors who explored, dug up and measured the country brought back information about sources of gold, petroleum, building materials, medicinal plants, and fibre for clothing and rope.

rum. Every night, while the voyageurs were making supper, Hamel and Baddeley collected minerals, rocks, soil samples, and plants, measured the magnetism in the rocks, and used the theolodite to take survey measurements. On his return, Baddeley gave the samples to the LHSQ natural history museum and read a paper before the Society describing his expedition in more detail. He went on to explore the geology of the Labrador coast, Charlevoix, the Eastern Townships, and the Magdalen Islands.

The surveying of the country as a whole was uncoordinated and imprecise, however. In 1841 the LHSQ and the Natural History Society of Montreal petitioned the Legislature to undertake a systematic geological survey of Canada. That year the sum of £1,500 was voted for the purpose, and the Geological Survey of Canada was born. This was the first but not the last time that the Society lobbied for a national body to push forward one of its many vocations.

ACCREDITED INTELLECTUALS

To encourage research, the LHSQ conferred honours on people who distinguished themselves in some area of knowledge. In 1831 it awarded thirty-two prizes for essays on a variety of subjects. Its leading lights established "Classes" or departments in Useful Arts, Science, Literature (led by *Gazette* publisher John Fisher), and Natural History (led by surgeon Dr. William Kelly). In 1834 a Fine Arts class was added, given by Abbé John Holmes, Catholic priest, theologian, and teacher at the Petit Séminaire. Dr. Joseph Morrin took charge of the library.

Dr. James Skey, Deputy Inspector of Hospitals, sent out a letter throughout the province encouraging "the rising youth of the country" to submit papers on Natural History, a subject "admirably calculated to occupy their leisure hours agreeably and usefully." The Editing Committee prepared the best submissions for publication. The reward for all this activity was the promise of a Diploma of Fellowship, or a Corresponding Membership of the Society, especially for those "who furnish it with well authenticated facts, and also enrich its cabinet by their contributions."

The Society in the nineteenth century was dominated by a small number of families of colonial officials, doctors, lawyers, judges, and churchmen. Members were distinguished by a high level of education, whether in medicine, divinity, law, engineering, or all four. And most had secondary scholarly interests that that they pursued at least as passionately as their official duties. Both James Douglas and Daniel Wilkie had degrees in divinity but were chemists and mathematicians too. James MacPherson LeMoine was trained in law but published forty books and some 400 articles, in French and English, on history, botany, and ornithology.

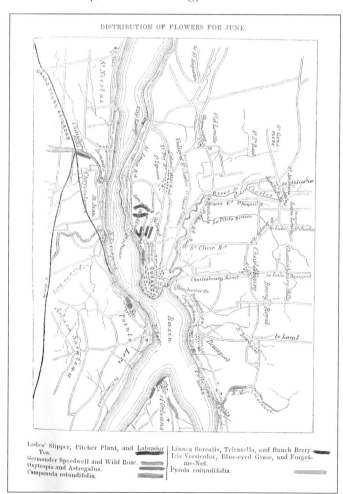

DISTRIBUTION OF FLOWERS FOR JUNE.

Ladies' Slipper, Pitcher Plant, and Labrador Tea.
Germander Speedwell and Wild Rose.
Oxytropis and Astregalus.
Campanula rotundifolia.

Linnea Borealis, Trientella, and Bunch Berry.
Iris Versicolor, Blue-eyed Grass, and Forget-me-Not.
Pyrola rotundifolia.

Wildflower map of Quebec, by Samuel Sturton, published in the LHSQ *Transactions* in 1864-5. Quebec pharmacist Samuel Sturton had an apothecary at 1½ St. John St., but spent his summers rambling around the Quebec city region, mapping and collecting wildflowers. "I delight in flowers, especially in those which are natives of the locality where I dwell," he explained in a Society lecture in 1860.

Phrenology pen holder, from the mid-nineteenth century, in the LHSQ collections. The Society dabbled for many years in phrenology. A book on the subject in the Society library explained that "in proof of the prodigious difference of size in cerebral parts, we may contrast the small head of an idiot with the large head of Franklin."

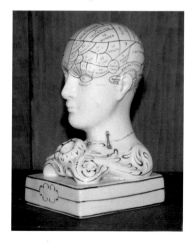

Scientific inquiry was a perfect way to meet like-minded and suitably classed people. It was a good excuse for a trip out to the Montmorency Falls in a cariole, for example, or an expedition up the Chaudière River. If one brought home contributions to the museum's geological cabinet or herbarium, these pleasant rambles in the countryside could be renamed scientific expeditions. A hunting trip, or even a walk around the city, could double as a scientific expedition. In 1863 James Douglas and William Anderson made an expedition to the local hatter's shop, for example, and found it provided a perfect laboratory for their investigations in the field of phrenology, a popular pseudo-scientific racial theory by which the mental strengths, abilities, and personality traits of persons—and races—could be determined from the shape of the skull. Douglas and Anderson reported their observations at an LHSQ lecture, which appeared in the newspaper the next day. Barely a thought that occurred to any of them went unpublished.

As a kind of protean university, the LHSQ became a different faculty at every monthly "standing meeting," as its evenings of public lectures were called. Hungry for information, members listened to a vast spectrum of what other members knew about. LHSQ members seem to have been interested in absolutely everything, whether it was agriculture, wildflowers, shells, biblical studies, geology, history, mapping, poetry, Aboriginal languages, or mathematics. The approach was a kind of intellectual melting pot, but an intentional one. Wilkie hoped that if many fact-collectors threw all their observations together, something interesting would emerge. "Insulated and apparently unimportant facts," he wrote eagerly, "become valuable when collected and grouped in a common centre, by which their relations to each other can be established and their anomalies explained."

Eligible lecturers did not need academic qualifications—they had simply applied themselves in some field of research. Chief Justice Sewell lectured on Russian stoves, while John Hale, the Receiver General, gave a lecture on crickets. One of the first lectures was by Harriet Campbell, who had become an expert in invertebrates. Using the system of classification proposed by the pre-Darwinian evolutionary theorist Jean-Baptiste Lamarck in his *Système des animaux sans vertèbres*, she classified the shells she found in the environs of Quebec, noting that several of them "do not accord with any

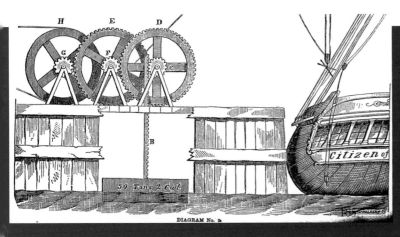

DIAGRAM No. 2

Edward David Ashe's wave power machine, published with his article "Water Power of Quebec" in the LHSQ Transactions, 1855. Lieutenant Ashe, a naval officer and Fellow of the Royal Astronomical Society, is known for having been one of the first to experiment with astronomical photography. He was appointed to direct the Quebec Observatory in 1851 and was a popular lecturer at the LHSQ.

mentioned in the books we have." Like her close friend Lady Dalhousie, she was not going to restrict her interests to entertaining the guests of her husband, the shipbuilder and lumber merchant William Sheppard (one of the founders of the LHSQ), on their 100-acre estate in Sillery.

Hunting the Orchids of Sillery: Women Scientists in Nineteenth-Century Quebec

Some of the most remarkable scientists in nineteenth-century Quebec were wives of LHSQ members. While their names are not on the membership rolls, they were involved in the Society nevertheless. Harriet Sheppard (née Campbell) was the first to publish a book on the birds of Quebec City. She gave a lecture on the subject at the LHSQ in 1833, in which she roundly opposed French naturalist Georges Buffon's extraordinary claim that North American birds do not sing (in winter, she conceded, they are perhaps frozen into silence). She and her husband had an aviary at Woodfield, their property overlooking the Saint Lawrence, in addition to their gardens, greenhouses, a 3,000-volume library, an art gallery, and a natural history museum. Her lecture on shells in the region, published in the *Transactions* with descriptive notes, is considered the first publication on Quebec shells. She was clearly aware of the Linnaean taxonomy, read French well, knew much of the current literature on shells, and used the evolutionary theorist Jean-Baptiste Lamarck's classification system thirty years before Darwin's *Origin of Species*—remarking carefully, however, that his taxonomy did not describe many of the species she had found.

She and her friends Christian Ramsay (Lady Dalhousie) and Anne Perceval (the châtelaine of Spencer Wood, now the Bois de Coulonge) regularly went on botanizing expeditions throughout the large Sillery estates to collect specimens to send to British botanist William Hooker, the director of the Royal Botanic Gardens at Kew.

Another of their haunts was Sorel, the governor general's summer residence. Lady Dalhousie, who had set the LHSQ on its scientific feet with her gift of 1824, compiled a catalogue of about four hundred Canadian plants, which was published five years later in the first volume of the *Transactions*. William Hooker included some of her discoveries in his massive *Flora Boreali-Americana* (1840). Most of her herbarium has been repatriated to the Royal Botanical Gardens in Hamilton, Ontario. Christian continued botanizing after the Dalhousies were posted to India, and her name is commemorated in a genus of perennial climbing shrubs, *Dalhousiea*.

Anne Perceval (née Flower, appropriately enough), the third of the botanizing trio of the 1820s, was also a contributor to Hooker's tome as well as to Torrey and Gray's *Flora of North America* (1838–43). Daughter of the Lord Mayor of London, she assumed the role of Lord Mayoress at the age of nineteen after the death of her mother, and later married Michael Perceval, Collector of Customs for Quebec and a member of both the Executive and Legislative Councils of Lower Canada. She had ten children and in her spare time roamed the woods of Sillery with Christian and Harriet collecting plants, including two species of rare orchids. She made several albums of herbarium specimens, one of which is now in the possession of Agriculture Canada and is thought to be the oldest series of plant specimens in Canada (1820).

Other women did not achieve public recognition but made quieter, private contributions to science. Fanny Amelia Bayfield, the wife of another prominent LHSQ member, Admiral Henry Bayfield, was a keen watercolourist. She did not even sign her paintings, but bequeathed an album of beautifully observed botanical illustrations, entitled *Canadian Wildflowers*, to her son on her death.

A herbarium sheet of *Carex laxiflora* sent by Harriet Sheppard (née Campbell) to Kew Gardens.

Despite this early, promising start, however, the Society quickly flagged. Would it fulfil Dalhousie's botanical prophecy that "it may droop and die as almost all foreign or European plants do in this Province"?

Even the awards and medals offered for the best essays did not seem to flush out latent scientists in the wings, according to a depressed annual address by Daniel Wilkie. The same old people were repeatedly coming forward to deliver lectures. Ruminating on why people were failing to respond to this intellectual call to arms, he wondered if it was because they lacked "confidence in the judgment of the Society and its Officers." Or could it be "the fear of failure, and the mortification that would thence ensue"?

In 1844, just before the Society was expertly steered into good fortune again by Georges-Barthélemi Faribault, only seven papers were read in the Society rooms. Four of them were by Wilkie.

International Specimen Cabinets

From its earliest days the Society collected international contacts as voraciously as it collected insects, dead mice, and intestinal worms (see page 192). The LHSQ quickly set about establishing its international credentials.

As soon as it published its first set of *Transactions* in 1829, the LHSQ sent them off to other learned societies around the world in exchange for their own publications. Thus fifty-nine of the volumes on the library shelves in 1830 were periodicals and transactions published by its sister societies.

With its connections in France as well as across the British Empire, the Society was able to cast its net wide. In its international exchanges it offered the world what it was learning about Canada, and gave its members a way to learn about the world beyond. Members who were sent on missions to colonial posts overseas or made trips to Britain

Literary and Historical Society Periodicals Register
At the turn of the century, librarians were kept busy by a tsunami of journals arriving in the mail from all around the world. Fifty-one periodicals arrived weekly from Canada, the US, the UK and France. All these periodicals had to be sewn together and bound.

and France returned with books, maps, and other artefacts. The Society also engaged in exchanges of specimens and even animal skins with museums elsewhere. By 1836 it had sixty-one international honorary members in Europe and the United States, and ninety-six corresponding members worldwide.

This exchange of intellectual riches among sister societies became almost as busy as the internet in our own time, with literally dozens of publications arriving by post every day. By 1864 the library catalogue listed publications (in order of importance) from Scotland, Germany, Holland, Russia, Italy, Belgium, India, Portugal, Switzerland, Ireland, Australia, Denmark, Spain, Greece, and Poland.

Meanwhile, however, Canada's local inhabitants remained something of a mystery.

On his travels across Canada, Dalhousie had developed a romantic admiration for his Aboriginal guides and boatmen. In his diaries he describes a guide called Toma in glowing terms:

> He … views the scene and decides the course of the stream he shall take. After that there is no changing or wavering, no possibility to alter his line; he turns to his helmsman a look as if to desire him to be attentive but says not a word. His eyes as keen as a hawk, not a muscle of his countenance alters. With his broad paddle he brings himself right into the stream, and then poising his pole horizontally, he guides or fends off as necessary. I could not have imagined so much coolness, so much collected intrepidity and intelligence and decision in these wretched Indians, and it strongly convinces me of the impolitic manner in which we treat them.

Many early presidents rued the fact that science had taken the upper hand at the Society, instead of inquiry into Aboriginal history, as Dalhousie had intended.

There was an initial flurry of activity around this mandate in the early days of the LHSQ. In its first two volumes of the *Transactions*, the Society published five papers on First Nations, including a Huron grammar found among the papers of the Lorette mission, translated from the Latin by John Wilkie (probably Daniel Wilkie's son). Partly through the good offices of Abbé John Holmes, the library acquired various histories and accounts of New France containing descriptions of the First Nations, such as those written by Charlevoix, Bacqueville de La Potherie, Lahontan, the Jesuits, Colden, and de Pauw (who'd never actually been there).

One of the first members of the Society, Joseph-Marie Bellenger, a Roman Catholic missionary and a fluent speaker of Micmac and Abenaki, donated an Aboriginal arrowhead found in a field. Others found calumets, pottery, and stone hatchets, which were displayed in the Society museum. Artists also chose First Nations as romantic themes for their paintings.

The artist Major Alexander Mercer drew up a "Catalogue of Remarkable Coincidences" to support the theory that the First Nations originally migrated from Asia. One conclusive piece of evidence, according to Mercer, was the existence among

Self portrait by Zacharie Vincent, n.d. Zacharie Vincent, the Huron-Wendat leader, was inspired to start painting when Antoine Plamondon painted a portrait of him in 1838 and won an LHSQ prize. Vincent sold several of his own paintings to the Society in 1850, and it acquired two more later.

First Nations of catamites, or "boys kept for infamous purposes," who wore girls' clothing and performed traditionally feminine tasks. "That this abomination exists in China is pretty fully established," declared Mercer triumphantly.

These initial attempts to record First Nations history quickly withered. However, the Society executive still experienced the odd frisson of guilt for its infidelity to Dalhousie's mandate. By 1866, James Douglas felt it was already too late. The assimilation of the First Nations had destroyed their customs and removed their interesting otherness, and was a regrettable loss to science:

> Every year the Indian tribes are perceptibly fading away before the influence of European civilization, either dying out under its uncongenial system, or losing their identity in the unequal amalgamation … much of the natural character of the aborigines in our neighbourhood has been lost … many an interesting point, which could still be decided, will be left without the possibility of solution.

A MUSEUM OF NATURE AND ART
A BASKET OF INSECTS

In its first twenty years, science was the Society's chief vocation. It was more exciting than dusty old manuscripts, and far more likely to draw a crowd. Like the travelling zoos and freak shows that were popular in Quebec at the time, science qualified as a novelty. The solar microscope, "the most agreeable and entertaining microscope yet known," was popular in Europe, and the LHSQ's purchase of one from J. Newman in London in 1830 would have been a star attraction. People were prepared to stand in line to look at objects magnified thousands of times. The Society regretted, however, that "the interest of the microscopic objects in the Society's possession is much impaired by the want of a proper list and description of them."

The government grant of 1830 for the purchase of mathematical instruments and other scientific objects included a condition: that its museum be open to the public. By 1831 the Society had a Royal Charter signed by King William IV and elegant lodgings in the Union Building. The Society occupied pride of place in the building—rooms on the second floor overlooking the square, including the President's Hall, the largest room in the building. Originally a ballroom, the President's Hall must have housed the large natural history and curiosities collection, including the collection of minerals (1,310 specimens) and Lady Dalhousie's herbarium.

The rooms contained pieces of sculpture imported from Britain, including a bust of Wolfe, and a large exhibition of fifty-three works, many of which were owned or painted by local artists such as Joseph Légaré. This mutual arrangement provided Légaré with an insured space in which to show his collection, and gave the LHSQ added attraction for visitors. On display was a collection of copies of Rubens, David, Raphael, and Van Dyke, depicting classical and biblical themes, which Légaré was intending to sell to the many parishes and religious communities that were his clients. Original paintings bought by him from European collectors were also on display. A collection of paintings that had been confiscated from the Church by the French state during the Revolution, and sold to Légaré by Abbé Desjardins, caused a particular sensation—Quebecers had seen little art produced in Europe, and were delighted with the Italianate landscapes filled with romantic Renaissance ruins, blasted pines, and shepherdesses.

An increasing part of the premises, however, was taken up by the natural history museum, which frequently threatened to get out of hand. Like the lectures on offer, donations made to the museum and library show a voracious and somewhat scattershot approach to acquisitions. "No object in Natural History," urged the museum curator, "… is in reality insignificant or useless. All have their uses in Art as in Nature. Any and every donation will prove of use, and all will be thankfully received."

Members took this open invitation seriously. Among the donations received in the first six years of the Society's existence were the following:

> Dr. Carter. — An Anatomical variety from a Cows throat.
>
> Hon. Mr. Justice Taschereau. — A Manuscript vol. containing an authentic statement of the officers, non-commissioned officers and privates of the Militia of Quebec, during the siege of that city in 1775–76.
>
> Sir John Caldwell. — A basket of Insects.
>
> Chief Justice Sewell. — The original Diploma of Bachelor of Arts conferred upon an Indian, D. Ludovicus Vincent, by the College Dartmouth, in 1781.
>
> Mr. C. J. R. Ardouin. — A specimen of Intestinal Worm.
>
> Chief Justice Sewell. — The Manifesto published by General Wolfe on his arrival in the St. Lawrence, and his General Orders issued on board the Sutherland Ship of War off St. Nicholas the night before the battle of the 13th September, 1759, on the Plains of Abraham.
>
> Dr. Wm. Fraser, Murray Bay. — A white Mouse.
>
> Mme Augustin Germain. — A vol. Engravings, "Recueil de cent Estampes representant differentes Nations du Levant gravées sur les tableaux peints d'apres nature en 1707 et 1708, par les soins de M. Le Hay, à Paris, 1714."
>
> Town Major Frost. — A singular specimen of the potato.
>
> Felix de Brunner, Ecr. Lt. Col. — Mémoire sur l'emploi des vases clos portatifs pour la fabrication du charbon végétal, minéral et animal — *par Brevet d'Invention*, par Felix de Brunner, membre correspondant de la Société d'Encouragement pour l'Industrie Nationale de France.
>
> Revd. Dr. Harkness. — Five old Coins.

The curator of the museum not only had the thankless task of arranging the most recent donations for display at each meeting ("placing them on the table"), but also had to organize them intelligibly in the museum's cabinets.

Several specimen cases were necessary, one each for birds, eggs, rocks, minerals, insects, shells, coins, medals, plants, and wood specimen collections. Carpenters and glaziers had been hired to build shelves and cases. A final specimen case was reserved for curiosities that baffled even the most cunning taxonomists.

The curator also offered helpful suggestions as to preserving animal skins before donating them. Put a little cotton wool in the mouth of the beast, he advised, skin it, and then anoint the skin with "arsenical soap" (recipe provided—with the proviso that it should be "kept very close" as it is "deadly poison.") Once skins were received, the assistant curator sent them off to the taxidermist to be stuffed. Some of the Society's curators earned extra cash by doing it themselves.

Fisher and Hawkins's *Picture of Quebec*, published in 1834, describes the Society's museum specimens as "admirably arranged and scientifically classed." A British visitor, writing in his diary a year earlier, was less impressed:

> There were the usual objects of a museum here … common things putting on the wonderful by dint of hard name and particular date, albeit with the name of the donor more conspicuous than the gift, showing a love of ostentation rather than of science. Monstrosities made more monstrous and inexplicable by the distorting powers of the glass bottles, others rendered indiscernible and unnatural by the thickness of the spirits, etc. However, the museum, considering its age, is a promising youth.

After it moved into Parliament House in 1841, the Society acquired another natural history collection formerly belonging to Pierre Chasseur, who had opened a museum in 1826 in response to the new public enthusiasm about science. The public's enthusiasm, however, had not been sufficient to maintain his museum, and in 1836 the government bought it and moved it into Parliament House. The Chasseur collection included 500 specimens of birds, nearly 100 specimens of mammals, and about forty reptiles and fish. It also contained some Aboriginal artefacts, a Chinese umbrella, an axe once wielded by a famous murderer, and a bronze cannon supposedly lost in the Saint Lawrence by Jacques Cartier.

In spite of twice being cleaned out by fires (see page 197), the museum soon outstripped its allotted space, as well as its caretakers' ability to classify the specimens being bought or donated. In 1862 President James Douglas had to appoint separate subcurators for the archaeology, botany, zoology, mineralogy, geology, and ornithology collections, including James MacPherson LeMoine's renowned collection of 177 Canadian birds. In 1873, the museum also contained 225 bird's egg specimens, thirty-two stuffed animals, sixty-four medals, about forty rock, fossil, and mineral specimens, two cases of "foreign" butterflies and insects, sixty Canadian wood samples, and 101 wood samples from Australia, Mexico, California, and the Caribbean.

The following year, D. R. MacLeod suggested remedying the shortage of space by "causing the birds to roost more closely together." He also proposed the addition of a beluga whale stuffed with straw and hung from the roof of the museum, since the whale fishery in the Lower St. Lawrence would soon render them extinct. With the

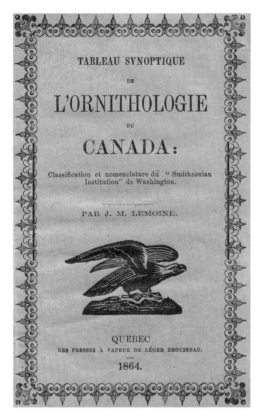

Title page of Tableau synoptique de l'ornithologie du Canada, by James MacPherson LeMoine, 1864.
LeMoine was a pillar of the Society—and of many other societies too. By the time he died in 1912, he had acquired memberships in 31 clubs and learned societies across North America, France and Great Britain. These enabled him to promote his own publications and exchange with like-minded people around the world.

Eider duck, LHSQ collections.
LeMoine, who lived at Spencer Grange (now Villa Bagatelle), left his vast collection of stuffed birds to the Society. He had a rich ornithological library, and his own *Ornithologie du Canada* (1861) was the first book on Canadian birds to appear in French. This duck is now the only bird left in the LHSQ collections.

same withering logic, he also suggested that the Society should have wax models of Aboriginals, Madame Tussaud–style, "squatting on the floor of the library waiting to get into the museum." These could also illustrate the evolution of their clothing from Jacques Cartier's day down to "the latest Lorette fashions, and the Historical Document Fund could be drawn upon to pay at least the tailor's bill." The obsolescence of the science apparatus also fell victim to his satirical glee. "The present curator of apparatus has nothing to do but navigate the solitary globe the whole year round," he wrote. "For that reason a nautical gentleman is usually put in charge."

THE ESCAPE OF PARASITES

William Couper, the entomologist who served as the Society's caretaker in the 1860s, was not only interested in insects themselves; he also collected insect nests, cocoons, and other structures that bore witness to their architectural genius. In 1863 he announced that he had assembled more than 6,000 specimens, mostly vegetable matter, which illustrated activity by larva or adult insects. Perhaps this heap of dried vegetation, perforated by millions of insect holes, is what doomed the handsome bank building on St. John Street that lodged the Society from 1859 until it too burned down in 1862.

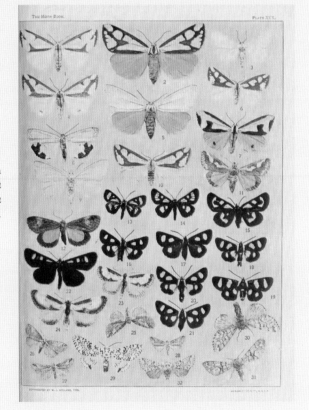

"Langton Forester Moth," illustration in *The Moth Book: A Popular Guide to a Knowledge of the Moths of North America* by W.J. Holland, 1903.

As soon as he had settled his wife and family after their traumatic eviction, he offered to begin the Society's insect collections again and build new cabinets to house them. He was proud of his custom-designed insect cabinets which, he boasted, had hinged doors "to prevent the escape of the small parasitic Hymenoptera etc., which from day to day may appear."

In 1864 Couper and the Sorbonne-trained Quebec botanist Abbé Louis-Ovide Brunet started up a Quebec branch of the Entomological Society of Canada. In March they asked if their Quebec meetings could be held in the Society's rooms. In return, the minutes recorded, the Society would be provided with a cabinet stocked with "insects from all parts of Canada, properly named and classified." Within two years the Society complained that, although it had been provided with more than 700 specimens, this consisted of cases and cases of unidentified bugs.

Whether it was because a number of the small parasitic *hymenoptera* did in fact escape through Couper's clever cabinet lids, or whether the Society was sinking under a deluge of other unidentified and perhaps not-quite-dead creepy crawlies, Couper was dismissed in 1865, upon which, according to legend, he refused to give back the minute books and threatened the assembled council with a poker.

But Couper believed that a well-placed *coleoptera* could heal all wrongs, and that year, perhaps as a way of apologizing, he dedicated a moth he had discovered to the LHSQ president, John Langton—the Langton Forester, or *Alypia langtoni*. He then consoled himself by setting off to survey the insects of Anticosti and the coast of Labrador, but his knack for making himself unpopular never left him. While he was there, he criticized local First Nations' salmon fishing techniques and, in revenge, they destroyed his collections.

LeMoine, with his magpie-like enthusiasm, had aimed that the LHSQ acquire a specimen of every single animal in Canada, the United States, and Europe, but he eventually abandoned that goal and the museum began to decline. In 1885 the Society's annual $750 government grants ended, and in 1889 Morrin College reclaimed the Society's museum and newspaper room. At the annual general meeting, it was suggested that "a taxidermist [be] employed to look over the contents, especially with a view to protecting them against the ravages of moths." The following year the High School of Quebec bought a selection of specimens and cases from the collection for $250, and the rest was advertised for sale in the newspapers.

MOOSE IN FLAMES
FIRES, EVICTIONS, AND POLITICS

In 1841 the Society suffered the first of its many evictions. It not only had to move its valuable book collection but also the contents of the museum, including a stuffed bear, a lynx (bought at the market for £1-5s), a deer, a moose, a fox, a seal, and thousands of birds and other specimens in glass-fronted cabinets, as well its growing collection of paintings and sculptures.

All of its possessions were moved into a group of rooms situated directly under the cupola in the centre of Parliament House, which had been vacant since the government's removal to Kingston in 1839. Situated on what today is known as Montmorency Park, the Society's new home had been built as the Bishop's Palace between 1693 and 1695. The colonial government began renting the building in the 1760s, and bought it in 1830.

The removal of the government freed up some space for the Society's stuffed animals but deprived it of many active and influential members. Much of the remaining intelligentsia was devoting its energies to politics, and membership was dropping like a stone. The Society's initial generous government grants had dried up after a committee declared in 1835 that "the support of such societies should depend upon private contributions, and, consequently that they should not look to legislative aid." In 1849 the Society had to change its by-laws to reduce quorum, and by 1850 only fourteen members had paid up, down from its 124 charter members twenty years earlier. When Parliament returned to Quebec in 1852, the Society regained a few members but was squashed into an even smaller space.

Parliament buildings in Quebec, artist unknown, ca. 1850.
The Society's home from 1841 to 1854 was a building that, according to one Gazette journalist, looked just like a Lancashire cotton factory. "The style of architecture was neither Grecian, Roman, nor Gothic, but Canadian," he wrote. "—a poker and tongs style of architecture."

The great fire of June 28 1845, by J. Murray and G.T. Stanford, 1845.
Fires regularly devastated Quebec. After the Society's second fire in 1862, LHSQ secretary Henry Thielcke published a notice begging people to bring back "any of the books, papers, minerals, animals or birds, as well as any of the apparatus" they may have removed "by the care to save them from the fire."

On February 1, 1854, disaster struck. In the coldest part of the winter, when the water cisterns had not yet been refilled after a fire two weeks earlier, the Parliament buildings caught fire. At first the police and soldiers tried to put out the fire with heaps of snow, but soon flames tore through the attics, the roof of the museum fell in, and the whole building was in flames. Summoned by a peal of bells from Notre Dame de Québec, people arrived with sleighs to save what they could. While soldiers kept the exits open, LHSQ members, including Daniel Wilkie's nephew Daniel and Mayor Narcisse Belleau,

> ran back and forth, while sundry stuffed animals ... caught fire and from time to time interrupted the removal of books, records etc. By those means the entire collection of books, manuscripts etc. some of which are originals of great value, and dated several hundred years since, were removed carefully to the vestibule of the French Cathedral.

The loss of the "sundry stuffed animals" was keenly felt. D. R. MacLeod reported twenty years later that entering the premises one was "immediately struck by the absence of the gigantic moose, the fleet caribou and the affectionate bear." However, the fire may have been just what the Society needed to kick-start it into action again. George Henderson (none other than the former disgraced gaoler!) rented it rooms above his grocery store on the corner of Sainte-Ursule and Saint-Louis streets, the Legislature gave it $250, membership increased, classes were formed again in Literature, Useful Arts, Fine Arts, and Natural History, and the British Museum sent some specimens to get the museum going again. Soon more specimens were flooding in, eleven lectures were given that year (as opposed to three the year before), and two issues of the Society's *Transactions* were published.

Henderson's rooms were expensive, though, and the Society soon moved into two floors of a new building on St. John Street considered to be "one of the handsomest in the city," but had to share it with two banks and a music store. William Couper, the Society's caretaker and in-house entomologist, moved in to the space—bringing with him his wife, children, and large insect collections—and work began again on restocking the museum and library.

In 1862, however, fire struck again. This time, in spite of George Thomas Cary's attempts to save some of the books (those he had printed himself, perhaps) by throwing them "ruthlessly" out of the windows onto the heads of the people in the street, the Society lost 1,680 of the 2,350 volumes in its library, most of its precious specimen collections, and its apparatus, including a Dolland telescope (worth £75) given by Lord Durham, an orrery, and its electrical and transit machines. "After the fire," said James Douglas four years later, "we sold all that remained of our apparatus for old brass." From its original purchases in London in 1831, one solitary globe remained.

The Society was adequately insured this time, however. Daniel Wilkie, with $3,000 in hand, scoured the auctions for books. Edward Meredith went to Boston and bought

Burnt copy of *New Voyages to North America*, Vol. II, by Baron Lahontan, 1703.
The fire had the effect, wrote James Douglas, of "awakening our fellow townsmen to a recollection of our existence." In the eight years before the fire in 1862 an average of 65 books per year were borrowed from the library. The year afterwards, members signed out 900 books.

$776 worth of books from Little, Brown and Company. LHSQ also acquired the Quebec Library Association's collection, adding another 4,000 or so books to the "700 sodden and coverless books" left over from the fire. Donations of specimens also came thick and fast: birds were sent from India and Australia, and "a young bald eagle" from Ringfield, in Limoilou.

Couper dispatched his children to hunt for birds' eggs—night herons, yellow warblers, thrushes, and flycatchers—and gave them to the Society. The Free Public Museum of Liverpool sent casts of dodo bones, while the Smithsonian Institution sent an opossum. Colonel William Rhodes, known for bringing sleighloads of caribou home from his hunting trips, sold the Society a fisher, or Canadian weasel, for five dollars.

While it restocked its library and museum, the Society also gamely started up its seasonal lecture programs again, and put its publishing program back on schedule. "The fire . . . created such sympathy in our favour," said Douglas, "that an increase of members rapidly followed."

After the 1862 fire, the newly minted Morrin College came to the Society's rescue. Dr. Joseph Morrin, a member of the Society, had given money to establish a private Protestant college affiliated with McGill, and appointed Dr. John Cook as its principal (see Morrin College section). The College had rented rooms in the Masonic Temple on Desjardins Street while waiting for convicts in the old gaol on Saint-Stanislas Street to be moved to a new prison on the Plains of Abraham, at which point it began fitting the building out for students instead.

Cook suggested a deal that was the beginning of an extraordinary 150-year relationship that explains the Society's existence today. Morrin College would join with the Society in rebuilding a museum and library that would service both the Society and the College: on June 25, 1868, the Society paid four men 4s-6d per day for four days, and a carter with a horse and wagon 10s a day, to move the LHSQ from the Masonic Hall to Morrin College, which was now housed in the old gaol. The Society has been there ever since.

The Questions that Shouldn't Be Raised

Many of the members of the LHSQ were related by blood as well as mutual interests. The Society was a good match-making sieve: new members were introduced by other members and voted in by ballot. People of the wrong class were neatly filtered out, and daughters of members married sons of other members.

But while the Society's members may have shared a high level of education, they did not necessarily speak the same mother tongue, attend the same churches, enjoy similar income levels, or share political opinions. They could only enjoy the common pursuit of intellectual goals if they could steer the conversations at the Society away from politics.

The Society's intention was to be bilingual, as Dalhousie had made clear in his appointment of Vallières de Saint-Réal. The Society's name, which appeared in French, and not English, on the common seal, was another sign of this intention. The 1831 charter reflected a careful commitment to neutrality: "Questions relating to party politics or religious controversy, shall on no account be admissible in the debates or discussions."

Quebec art historian John Porter suggests that the Society managed to dissociate politics from culture, and to foster the setting aside of personal opinion for the sake of the advance of knowledge:

> How else can one explain the exchanges that went on at the LHSQ between a Catholic and an Anglican bishop, between Abbé Demers and Reverend Wilkie, between Caron and Stuart, and even between Légaré [a *Patriote*] and Symes?

Francophone membership dropped off following the Rebellions. Some left, as James Douglas said, because the Rebellions "diverted the public mind from any quieter pursuits than politics"—the country's constitutional difficulties seemed more urgent than measuring skulls or classifying moths. Society member Robert-Shore-Milnes Bouchette was imprisoned in Montreal, then exiled to Bermuda. After 1837, the name of the artist and *Patriote* Joseph Légaré no longer appears in the Society records; in 1838, another member of the Society, magistrate Robert Symes, after conducting a secret inquiry, threw him into the Quebec gaol for sedition. It is hard to imagine how they could have sat peaceably at a meeting together after that. However, in 1840, there were still enough francophones involved at the Council level to form an active French editorial committee, which published early issues of the Society's *Historical Documents* series.

By 1851, perhaps because of the founding of the Institut Canadien three years earlier, only fourteen out of the eighty-four members of the LHSQ were francophone. As the century progressed, francophones may have been put off by the effect on public opinion of the Ultramontane wing of the Roman Catholic clergy and publisher Jules-Paul Tardivel. Bishop Ignace Bourget of Montreal disapproved of literary societies altogether because they could expose people to the possibility of reading material unapproved by the Church. He wrote in 1854:

> When it is an established practice that a literary institute has books harmful to faith or morals, that readings are given there which are anti-religious, that immoral and irreligious newspapers are read there, one cannot admit the sacraments to those who are members of it.

While the repression of liberal thought was less evident in Quebec City than in Montreal, Tardivel and his supporters dissuaded Université Laval from granting the American historian Francis Parkman an honorary degree because, they said, he was "*hostile à la religion*" and "*très injuste contre les missionnaires.*" The LHSQ, of which Parkman had long been an honorary member, kept officially silent but pointedly invited him to speak in the Society rooms. They were rewarded by being given his complete *Historical Works* in eight volumes.

Membership generally and finances were at a low ebb in the 1840s and 1850s; but, by 1866, one-third of the membership was again francophone, and Society librarian John Wilson Cook, eldest son of Morrin College Principal John Cook, gave a lecture that was openly sympathetic to the *Patriotes*. In discussing the role of the press leading up to the Rebellion, he said:

> *The Mercury* supported out and out the Legislative Council: the *Gazette*, edited by Mr. John Neilson—one of the most able and honorable of the men who have taken part in the political contentions of Canada—leaned, though with wisdom and moderation, to the popular side. But *Le Canadien*, the French newspaper, was needed to maintain the rights of the French population, and to instruct them in parliamentary warfare.

Portrait of Philippe Baby Casgrain, by Charles Huot, ca. 1886-1903, LHSQ collections.
Longtime Liberal MP, the bicultural Casgrain was twice president of the LHSQ at the turn of the century and found congenial company at the LHSQ. James MacPherson LeMoine, another bicultural Quebecer, published a list of 135 "unfrench alliances" (francophone-anglophone) among "our best-known families," including "no less than eleven sages of our Bench."

Detecting how many members and/or presidents were francophone, which has been a preoccupation of most critical studies of the LHSQ, is a misleading exercise, however. Anglophone and francophone historians have both claimed James MacPherson LeMoine as one of their own, and many of the "francophones" were members of Quebec's closely interlinked bicultural families such as the Baby, Garneau, Bouchette, and LeMoine clans, who happily moved back and forth between French and English among their kinship networks and other overlapping intellectual and religious circuits.

LeMoine might be lecturing in English one night at the LHSQ and in French the next at the Institut Canadien, and he wrote voluminously for newspapers in both languages. Bicultural Quebecers were able to use their multiple memberships in Quebec's many societies to escape the prejudices of one community or another. When he was tired of the sedentary masculine formalities of what became known as the Lit and His, LeMoine could skip across to the Club du Quadrille Canadien-Français, which he had founded precisely to let off steam. When he was tired of that, he could take his seat at the Royal Society of Canada, of which he was a founding member. Pierre-Joseph-Olivier Chauveau, another longstanding member of the LHSQ (he was Council Secretary in 1845), also co-founded the Société Saint-Jean-Baptiste of Quebec City. He was elected as the first premier of the province of Quebec in 1867 and president of the LHSQ the following year.

LeMoine wanted to keep the LHSQ as bicultural as possible. As soon as he became Society librarian in 1865, he set about increasing the francophone membership (about 33 percent at the time) by planning several lectures in French for the upcoming year and placing advertisements in the French press, which, he claimed, received "a responsive echo." In 1898, the resignation of three prominent francophone members, J. E. Livernois, Théophile Ledroit, and Edmond Joly de Lotbinière, prompted the president to bewail the fact that "when the Society was incorporated in 1831, it was composed of gentlemen belonging to every nationality and creed in Quebec. The French-speaking part of the population had a fair and proportionate number in the ranks of the Society. We regret to observe that the same zeal has not been shown during the last decade." It maintained its attempts to attract francophone membership, however, once again establishing editing committees in both French and English.

Trying to figure out who was Catholic and who was Protestant in the LHSQ membership is an equally misleading exercise. Many bicultural Quebecers in that era had allegiances in both camps, especially those with social class and education in common. Language was even less of a division, and for some, religion was not an immovable part of one's identity either. The Presbyterian John Neilson, for example, was married to Marie-Ursule Hubert, niece of the Roman Catholic bishop. They educated their girls as Catholics and their boys as Protestants. James MacPherson LeMoine was married in a Presbyterian church, his funeral was in a Catholic church, and he was buried in Mount Hermon Protestant graveyard.

In 1875, a third of the council were francophones, and most of their ancestors had made "nonfrench alliances," as James LeMoine put it, and had thus taken part in *both* sides of the great battles. Until the late nineteenth century the LHSQ was to some extent a refuge for Quebecers who had both francophone and anglophone ancestors.

The late nineteenth century was the heyday of imperial fervour in Quebec. Many of the Society's bicultural families were monarchists, and saw the kinship ties among the French and English monarchy as indicative of the state of things in their own milieux. Royalty was a more promising symbol of the future than the tensions between French and English, which, in their eyes, were fleeting diversions led by political or religious demagogues. Empire, too, gave them an international identity that relieved them of having to be British.

While the Society almost never refused offers of friendship, it did draw the line, in 1901, when the American Humane Society asked it to sign a petition to stop horses and mules being shipped from the United States to South Africa, probably for the purposes of the Second Boer War. The Society suspected the underlying reason for the petition was U.S. antipathy to Empire. "Why not stop the cattle trade with Europe altogether?" it wrote back sarcastically. "But that would not suit your people's sentiments, or pockets."

In happier times the Society had counted such francophone notables as Charles Panet, Étienne Parent, Georges-Barthélemi Faribault, Charles Drolet, the Roman Catholic Bishop of Quebec Joseph Signay, George-Paschal Debarats, Jacques Crémazie, Thomas Amiot, Dr. Charles-Jacques Frémont, Pierre-Joseph-Olivier Chauveau, Charles Baillairgé, and F. X. Garneau among its officers and members. But by the 1940s the Society had become markedly less bilingual, and membership dropped to an all-time low. At one general meeting, at which the members decided once again not to merge with the Institut Canadien, the members were reminded that theirs was a private, not a public library, and that new members should not only be able to pay the fee but, more importantly, be "congenial to the mood of the library & to other members." In 1943, the Society abolished the membership committee and decided to stop admitting any new members at all, as it considered the membership sufficient and wished to limit it to "individuals congenial to each other on personal grounds."

William Wood, ca. 1929.
Colonel Wood was president of the Society three times between 1900 and 1941. He was rumoured to be an illegitimate great-grandson of the Duke of Kent, Queen Victoria's father. A keen historian, naturalist and prolific writer, he lobbied to preserve many of Quebec's historic sites and buildings.

Pileated woodpecker, from John James Audubon's *The Birds of America*, 1827–1839. Audubon visited Quebec in 1842 to promote his book, and LeMoine showed him around the Sillery estates. A government grant in 1837 had enabled the Society to purchase only the text. In 1871, Marion Torrance (Gibb) gave the Society twelve Audubon engravings and "thirty odd specimens of French and Italian birds."

Regularizing the Ladies

Lady Dalhousie had launched the museum with her botanical collection, and women had always been allowed into the library, because subscriptions were (and still are) by family, but individual women could not become voting members. In spite of this exclusion women made generous donations to the museum—unless they were just doing a bit of spring cleaning. In 1872, for example, Mrs. Dixon contributed twenty stuffed birds, while Mrs. Gibb gave a collection of European birds, some missing Audubon engravings, as well as "medals, coins, casts, and natural curiosities," and Mrs. Algernon Sewell gave a knife from India.

In 1859 the daily paper reported that, "the admission of ladies, and the introduction of Coffee after the reading of the papers, have imported a novel and agreeable feature to the stated periodical meetings." But if women wanted to borrow books, they had to do so through their male relatives.

In 1879, a Mr. H. S. Scott noticed that, "there were several ladies who would be willing to join the Society for the privilege of taking out books, and suggested the expediency of examining the Bylaws as regards the Admission of Ladies." Scott was a former president of the Quebec Library Association (QLA). The Quebec Library, which the QLA had absorbed, had been admitting women since at least 1822. Three years later the suggestion had still not been taken up, and the Council declared it was "not aware that the ladies of any member's family have ever been refused admission to the Rooms of the Society."

In the end, the impetus to admit women as individual members probably had little to do with a sudden opening of the imperial mind. Almost the day after the government grants dried up in 1886, women were admitted as members for four dollars per year, while "lady teachers" were admitted for only two dollars. In 1923, women's memberships were "regularized" in that they were to pay the full five dollars, but they still had no right to vote.

The following year a group of women members under the supervision of a "Ladies' Convener" were permitted to elect two representatives to sit on the Book Committee, the group that chose which books the Society should buy—but in a purely advisory capacity. The Council hoped that, this way, the women would come to understand the difficulties of choosing books on a limited budget, especially those women who were "disposed to be censorious at the doings or misdoings of the Book Committee."

In 1939, a woman was finally proposed as a Council member. Although William Petry observed drily that, "the Society had been in existence for 115 years and had got along well without a lady member of Council," women provided not only a decent supply of contemporary novels, at last, but money, literary connections and longevity. By 1940 there were three women on Council, including Mrs. Frank Carrel, whose husband published the *Quebec Daily Telegraph* and was a generous benefactor of the Society. Adèle Stuart, who remained a Society member for seventy-two years, also restored the Society's bicultural pedigree: she was a great-granddaughter of one of Quebec's first and finest novelists, Philippe Aubert de Gaspé.

Adèle Maud Stuart, ca. 1920.
Adèle Maud Stuart (1889–1987), longtime member of the Society, was the daughter of Mary O'Meara and James de Gaspé Stuart. She lived in the "Maison Henry-Stuart" on Grande Allée from 1918 until her death at the age of 98, and spent every morning gardening until the day she died.

A LITERARY LIMPET
THE LHSQ LIBRARY AND ITS LIBRARIANS

The most important physical remnant of the Literary and Historical Society today is its library, which has remained in exactly the same spot for nearly 150 years. Over that time it has been repainted, reappointed, repolished, recarpeted, restocked, and finally lovingly restored, but it still feels like a forgotten corner of a remote British colony, perhaps Mombasa or Mandalay. The walls are lined with dark wooden bookshelves and a narrow wooden spiral staircase leads to a graceful gallery circling the large, high-ceilinged room.

A dwarfish statue of General Wolfe stands in one corner pointing at the Travels in the Antipodes shelves. A model of the *Cosmo*, built in Quebec in 1877 by an LHSQ Council member, the shipbuilder Henry Fry, perches aloft on a bookcase. Some comfortable old chairs, a leather-upholstered sofa, and a desk that once belonged to the Father of Confederation Sir George-Étienne Cartier have all been there for as long as anyone can remember. None of the concessions to modern norms—a ban on smoking, modern lighting, and a computerized catalogue—have been achieved without years of testy discussion. But the book committee still meets and argues over what books are appropriate purchases, the honorary librarian still reports to the annual general meeting, and the magazines are still auctioned off once a year to pay for subscriptions—a practice that has gone on for over a hundred years.

The library has withstood the years of itinerancy, the two major fires, several devastating auctions and sales when funds or space were lacking, and, when liberal feeling was lacking, a period of Victorian piano-leg-style censorship. Society membership dropped in 1856 to fourteen paying members, and its operating funds to £39. It has stooped to hiring thuggish collectors to collect its debts, bribed its librarians with commissions to chase members in arrears up and down the country, and even threatened lawsuits to collect their dues. It has instituted library fines, and taken them away again.

But after each setback it started again, and someone or something stepped in to save it. After the first fire in 1854, the government stepped in. After the second fire in 1862, Rev. John Cook and Morrin College were its saviours. When it had no more money left and had sold most of its valuables, James Douglas, a mining magnate and former Society president, stepped in and gave it an endowment with which the Society is still purchasing books to this day. Its limpetlike tenacity was also due to its members, whose dedication

Statue of James Wolfe, 1779, LHSQ collections.
This wooden statue was commissioned by a butcher who had fought alongside Wolfe. It stood in a niche at the corner of Rue Saint-Jean and Côte du Palais, where a statue of a saint had once stood. In 1838 it was kidnapped and taken to England by Navy officer cadets. Some time later it arrived back in a wooden crate addressed to the mayor.

to the Society has bordered on the pathological—William Couper risked his life to save specimens during the fire of 1854, while Daniel Wilkie nearly died to save books.

The Society lost its art gallery, sold its museum, and had most of its historic documents requisitioned by the government—losing its chartered vocations one by one. But the library kept going, because until now, some people still like to read. At the time of writing, the Society has recovered some of its cultural vocation, but the jury is still out as to whether people will still be reading books by the time the library celebrates its 200th anniversary in 2024.

Hunger for Reading Matter

As soon as James Kempt replaced Dalhousie as Governor in Chief, the Society wrote asking him to support its petition for a legislative grant to buy books as well as science apparatus:

> Your petitioners have begun to form a … library of historical and scientific books, and that they purpose to increase both at their own expense for the benefit of all, who in the execution of any literary work, or in the course of their studies, may wish to avail themselves of either.

By 1830 the library held 152 books, which according to Joseph Bouchette were "valuable standard scientific and literary works" that were both "new and important." Fifty-one were science-related, and they included books on medicine, botany, ornithology, paleontology, astronomy, geology, mineralogy, and phrenology.

In spite of government grants, the Society relied heavily on book donations. Some of the merchant members, such as William Sheppard, were well enough heeled to give the library their leftovers. When Sheppard brought back books from England to stock his large private library at Woodfield, his villa in Quebec, he also brought back books for the Society. While its noble patron in 1838, Lord Durham, may not have given the Society the new building it requested complete with laboratories and an observatory, he did give it over a hundred volumes of the latest translations of the Greek and Latin classics, some of which are on the shelves to this day. As for one Captain Wright, he thoughtfully donated a work entitled *Parliamentary Reports on the Bogs in Ireland*, in five folio volumes.

The prime movers of the Society, however, were a handful of well-educated and literate professionals living in Quebec. They were starved for reading matter in English and, in the boom-and-bust economy of the colonial capital, were often strapped for cash. Access to a library was worth more to these men than modern Google-book surfers can possibly imagine. Other than almanacs, textbooks, and prayer books, few books were published in Quebec, and buying books and periodicals from Europe and Britain and shipping them was prohibitive for most individuals. Forty-two per cent of the books on the shelves of the Library in the 1860s were published in Great Britain, nineteen percent in the United States, nine percent in France, and fewer than five percent in Canada. A decent reference book might cost twice the monthly wages of the Society's single employee, whereas the Society now spends on books three percent of what it spends on wages.

Gradually the Society's predominantly scientific interests ceded to its avocation for history. In the library catalogue drawn up by Fred C. Wurtele in 1864, modern history is the largest category. But not everyone wanted to read geological surveys, historical documents, or the musings of imperial war strategists. And not all those who wanted to were allowed to. A battle ensued around this time in the library that has lasted ever since.

A Bookless Continent

Society members have been bewailing the fact that people are too busy to read ever since its founding. Today they blame modern technology, but in the early nineteenth century they blamed the fact that people were too busy making their fortunes. Society president William Sheppard explained in 1834 that in these "ungenial and hyperborean regions" the active members of society were "devoted of necessity to business one half the year, and during the other half more generally seeking recreation from toil in ordinary amusements" rather than in literature or science.

Early-nineteenth-century France already had half a million books in its largest library, and the Bodleian at Oxford had 150,000. North America lagged behind. Harvard had 12,000 books in 1800, and the Library of Congress had only 3,000 before it was torched by the British in 1814.

There were few libraries in Quebec when the LHSQ was founded. The Quebec Library, a proprietary subscription library with shareholder-members (its collection was later subsumed into the LHSQ library), had been founded by Governor Haldimand in 1779. The parliamentary library was only open to MPs, and others, such as the Advocate's Library founded by Elzéar Bédard and the small collection belonging to the Legislative Council, were for specialized professionals only.

Most of the general libraries of the nineteenth century were attached to learned societies. Subscription libraries were common in Scotland in Dalhousie's day, many with their very own aristocratic patrons. The LHSQ took pains to make sure it maintained its royal credentials, reminding every single governor of the colony (and the turnover was rapid) that he was its patron in no uncertain terms. The Society has "a strong presumptive claim to your Lordship's favour and support," wrote the president to the Earl of Gosford in 1835. Although the patron rarely featured in the day-to-day running of the library, he supported it with his prestige, his authority over the colonial government, his transatlantic connections, and his precious book donations.

THE DESTRUCTION OF FAMILY LIFE

The library kept a recommendations book in which the readers began to make repeated demands for novels, but the powers that were kept a lid on it, harking back to charter phrases such as the "prosecution of historical and scientific research" and "from which public benefit may be expected"; or later, using the conditions of the Douglas bequest or simply the phrase "the dignity of the Society."

PRACTICAL HINTS.

Published Mar.1.1820. by Taylor & Hefsey Fleet Street

Frontispiece from *Practical Hints for Young Females on the Duties of a Wife, a Mother, and a Mistress of a Family,* by Mrs. Taylor of Ongar, 1815. The arrival of novels undermined the good influence of books such as this one for young women "in the middle ranks" whose education made them feel "degraded by domestic occupation." Marital happiness, says Taylor wisely, is made up largely of "trivial attentions, nameless kindnesses, and habitual tenderness."

PRACTICAL HINTS

In a lecture in French in 1866, the writer Narcisse-Henri-Édouard Faucher de Saint-Maurice pronounced upon the evil effects of "bad" literature, which, he declared, destroyed family life. After reading novels, he declared,

> a good and affectionate husband becomes morose and anxious … cunning and affected; home life now disgusts him, because he read this morning that "family" is nothing more than a word. His domestic happiness now pales…. He reckons his fate is unbearable, and plunges into an idealized, impossible world existing only in foul ideas … that wither his heart and keep his brain in turmoil. The woman, meanwhile … shuts herself in her dressing room, far from her children … and to console herself, weeps over imaginary tragedies.

The Society must have approved of his attitude: he was voted librarian in 1869, and was able to maintain a stern vigilance over the Society's acquisitions. He believed circulation could still be increased: "Did the young French-Canadians of our city know of the treasures of literature, philosophy and history that are to be found in our Library?" These treasures included "the best and oldest editions of the French classics" and "the best work of the most esteemed modern authors."

211

Cover of *Charles Guérin*, by Pierre-Joseph-Olivier Chauveau, 1853.
In a lecture in 1874 on "The Present State of Literature in Canada", librarian James Douglas noted that French-Canadian novelists were producing better work than English Canadians. He praised Chauveau's novel *Charles Guérin* and Napoléon Bourassa's historical novel about the Acadian deportations, *Jacques et Marie*, among others.

Not enough young men were coming to the library, said president James Douglas, but he was determined not to succumb to the temptation of heart-withering novels to attract them. "We have to work upon those who are disinclined to literary occupation.... That can be done without filling our shelves with novels," he said.

The lack of public libraries, he added, was "a crying disgrace to Canada."

If readers wanted something racy and knew their stuff, of course, they could always sit down in the back room with Laurence Sterne's or Rabelais's collected works. Otherwise they could sit at the table and read the periodicals, which ran fiction in serial form, and to which the librarian apparently turned a blind eye. At the magazine auction each January, a member could buy a whole year's worth of periodicals and, at last, take them home to read in bed.

The stage was set for change with the purchase of the Quebec Library Association later in 1866, when the LHSQ acquired over a thousand English and French novels, a specialty of the Quebec Library, for $500. Haldimand had established the Quebec Library in 1779 in the hope that it could bring together the French and British peoples of the colony, not by force, but through the expression of ideas. The Quebec Library Association (founded in 1845) had merged with the bankrupt Quebec Library and now it, too, had run out of money. This purchase increased the library's "modern literature" collection by two-thirds, and set the Society on its feet again. Thus by 1873 there were nearly 9,000 volumes on the shelves, making it an important draw to the *literati* of Quebec.

Dead Authors Alone

With its new vocation as a major collection of literature as well as of science and history, James MacPherson LeMoine resolved that the Society should promote Canadian literature and "acquire the leading Canadian works written recently in the English and French language relating to History, Literature and Poetry." Most of the additions were in French, because James Douglas, for one, believed that "French Canadian littérateurs … produce upon the whole better romances and novelettes than the English."

The *Morning Chronicle* reported breathlessly that the shelves now contained

> the essence almost of all that human intelligence, human thought, human wit, man's invention and ingenuity has as yet brought to light…. The student and littérateur, the bibliophile and dilletante novel reader [are] the most frequent visitors here.

In 1879 there were 12,000 volumes in the library, "few which are not either of high standard character, or which, if of indifferent intrinsic merit, do not bear upon the history or literature of this country." But some members were still not happy. Mr. Russell wrote that year to say he had been paying his dues for forty years, and finally showed up to borrow a book for the first time—*The Last of the Mohicans*, by James Fenimore Cooper—only to find it missing. "My surprise was extreme when I was told that the works of this eminent American author are excluded because they are 'Novels'!"

This contempt for historical fiction was part of a campaign led by Society historians to dissuade readers from accepting as factual the multiplying romantic versions of Canadian history to be found in fiction. Readers were advised instead to return to sources—the kind of sources the Society's had been publishing in its *Historical Documents* series since 1838 (see page 219). Historian Dr. William Anderson pursued this campaign in a lecture on the difference between Longfellow's *Evangeline* and the real story of the Acadian deportations, which could be found in archival documents from Nova Scotia published by the Society.

But the "dilettante novel readers" continued to request lighter reading—requests which must have been met, as James MacPherson LeMoine wrote a formal protest in 1892 against "the admission on our tables, in the library, [of] additional light current literature, such as the popular novels of the day."

James Douglas, by then a mining tycoon established in New York, recalled later that, "we had a terrible fight about the admission of novels, and a compromise was reached by which the works of dead authors alone were admitted as classics." Douglas still feared an impending avalanche of frivolity, however, and when he made his second book bequests in 1919 he insisted on a novel quota of no more than one-third.

At around the same time, the Society was given access to the far-from-frivolous 10,000-book collection of legal, philosophical, and historical books, some of them dating from the sixteenth century, that had been bequeathed to Morrin College by Judge Thomas Cushing Aylwin, one of Daniel Wilkie's most brilliant and able alumni and a founding member of the Society (see page 163). But this collection, with its ancient Latin law books, passed almost unnoticed in the heat of the debate over purchases of contemporary fiction.

Questions of the proportion of non-fiction to fiction, and literary to popular fiction, are still debated fiercely at the LHSQ. "I always felt I had a duty," said Irene Calfat, who worked in the library in 1999, "because we have no money, to keep a balance between a permanent collection of books of value, and popular novels—Judith Kranz by the yard."

International Fish and Fowl

At the turn of the century librarians were kept busy with a deluge of journals arriving in the mail from all around the world. A library bulletin in 1904 lists its exchanges with 150 institutions. It received all official reports of both the federal and provincial governments, as well as reports from agricultural, antiquarian, and historical societies, libraries, and military and cultural institutes and academies in the United States, India, Australia, New Zealand, Brazil, Scotland, England, Ireland, Germany, and Spain. In addition, it subscribed to fifty-one weekly periodicals from Canada, the United States, Britain, and France.

A fierce loyalty to the British Empire continued to affect book orders and subscriptions for many years to come. During the Great War in 1916, the Society returned to the post office a journal edited "with great cunning" by the pacifist Norman Angell whose purpose, the minutes record, was to "give German views, to give publicity to anti-war speeches, and to the [pacifist] Quakers." They had quickly forgotten Prime Minister Robert Borden's 1914 pronouncement against militarism, indeed as had Borden himself:

> War is an economic crime. It is pitiful to think of the suffering and starvation that prevail throughout the earth, while nations are spending untold millions in preparation for subjugating each other, or in contending for the mastery of the world.

After the war ended, in 1919, the New York journal *The Nation* was also discontinued, as the Council considered it "very anti-British & pro-German during the War, and still antagonistic to everything connected with the British Empire." The LHSQ wasn't the only one to suspect the *Nation*—U.S. security agencies have monitored the magazine into our own time.

FEEDING THEM PEPPERMINTS: THE ASSISTANT LIBRARIANS

The Society's first librarian on record was a Scottish surgeon who taught at Wilkie's school, Dr. John Whitelaw. The librarian's duties included the "care and custody of the Books, Manuscripts, Maps, Charts, Plans, Diagrams, Prints, Engravings, Paintings and other objects deposited in the Library." But there's more: "And [he] shall class them and arrange them in scientific or methodological order."

With a job description of such magnitude, the council librarian needed an assistant. The men who filled the position in the early 1830s were various sons of the president Chief Justice Sewell who continued to jump, trout-like, at positions for his numerous children.

A succession of staff followed the Sewells down the centuries. Some were scientists, artists, and publishers; others were barely literate. Some were clergymen; others were inveterate alcoholics—and sometimes both at once. It was only in the late 1990s that the Society began to employ more than one person on a consistent basis. Most of its achievements until then depended almost entirely on the volunteer activities of its Council and membership.

The Society sometimes hired its own officers who were out of pocket or out of a home—the job provided a place to live and a small wage.

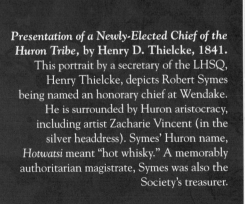

Presentation of a Newly-Elected Chief of the Huron Tribe, **by Henry D. Thielcke, 1841.** This portrait by a secretary of the LHSQ, Henry Thielcke, depicts Robert Symes being named an honorary chief at Wendake. He is surrounded by Huron aristocracy, including artist Zacharie Vincent (in the silver headdress). Symes' Huron name, *Hotwatsi* meant "hot whisky." A memorably authoritarian magistrate, Symes was also the Society's treasurer.

Impecunious artists sometimes filled the position, including Henry Thielcke, a portrait artist from England. Thielcke's father had been George III's groom of the royal bedchamber, and his mother, as the Queen's wardrobe woman, had assisted Queen Charlotte with her underwear and corsets. Henry had thus grown up in Buckingham Palace and, perhaps owing to his privileged acquaintance with royal anatomy, became a royal portraitist.

Thielcke moved to Quebec in about 1832 and soon tapped into the market for religious art among Quebec's religious communities. He exhibited his works in a studio provided for him in the Chambre de L'Assemblée, right next door to that of Antoine Plamondon, whose bread and butter was the same clientele. Plamondon wrote a lengthy attack on Thielcke's work in the papers: in his opinion, there was *rien de plus monstre et de plus ridicule* than Thielcke's depiction of John the Baptist, for example. Thielcke turned to the Anglo-Protestant clientele, and in 1839 submitted to the Society's Class of Fine Arts a work entitled *The Landing of General Wolfe*, which earned him a silver medal. Medals didn't buy him bread and lodging, however, and Daniel Wilkie, indefatigable patron of the arts, hired him to teach art, German, and French at his High School. No doubt it was Wilkie who suggested that the LHSQ hire him, too.

By 1850, Thielcke was not only a lowly assistant secretary but President of the Class of Fine Arts, responsible for organizing art competitions, judging them, and handing out the medals. The Society was tickled pink to have the aristocratic and talented Thielcke with his royal manners and accent welcome them to the rooms, and lamented that the finances of the Society did not allow them to "remunerate him as adequately as his talents demand." But inadequate also was Thielcke's devotion to his duties, and he was fired in 1854. Shortly afterwards the key to the strongbox was replaced. The hiring in 1860 of another artist and member of the Society, William Bingham, also ended badly. This time the Council librarian and Bingham resigned together; the Society refused to accept their resignations and resolved never again to "pay any member of the Council for any services whatever."

The library staff were often the guardians of the premises as well, having an apartment onsite where they could make sure no one broke into the mineralogical cabinets or made off with a valuable manuscript. Sometimes they were also the assistant secretary and the "sub-curator" too. This meant they did everything the council, the curators, and the librarian told them to, as well as making sure the coal scuttles were full, carting the rubbish, cleaning snow off the roof, washing the windows, escorting visitors who wished to "inspect the museum," and sending the latest batch of *Transactions* off to Poland or India.

The salary was meagre, but they could supplement it by chasing down members in arrears, for which they received a commission that sometimes amounted to nearly 10 percent. This gave them both the incentive to hound the members and the privilege of receiving their wrath in return. At other times the Society hired a separate collector, a thuggish character whose job was to go from house to house collecting the dues and noting down the reasons for their refusal in a register. The officers of the Council finally concluded that "a large amount of subscriptions remain uncollected ... because of the ill repute of the collector," and let him go.

No less pugnacious was William Judd, an auctioneer and boxing aficionado who was hired on and off for several years. He did everything from buying candles and chalk to sewing periodicals together, and the Society paid him two dollars extra to keep the library open in the evenings. Bored to tears, he began to turn one of the vast old Quebec Library borrowing registers into a scrapbook, pasting into it newspaper clippings about all the boxing matches he was missing.

Finally there were the assistant librarians who are almost within living memory. Mr. Hardy was remembered by one member as keeping children quiet in the library by feeding them peppermints, while J. W. Strachan, his successor, terrified them into good behaviour by banging his cane on the floor. In 1916 Strachan joined a labour union, and four years later his salary had doubled to $800 a year.

In 1929 the Society sent Strachan's daughter, who assisted him in the library, to attend summer school at McGill's Redpath College for a course in library science. When her father died, Evelyn Strachan thus became the first professional librarian in the history of the Society. With her new training in the Dewey system and the help of three paid assistants, she spent two years reorganizing the library completely, resulting in the addition of ninety-seven new members in one year alone. Strachan's delicate, bird-like appearance belied her tyrannical disposition. "Does your mother know you're reading that?" she would ask young people who were reading in the library unchaperoned. She ran her own private censorship scheme, keeping an index of books that she only allowed certain people to borrow. Mary McGreevy, the treasurer's wife, recalled that

> she was ... a terrible snob, wore tweed suits and Henry Heath hats, dowdy but very well tailored, that lasted a lifetime. If she liked you she'd do anything for you. Oh yes, you got all sorts of privileges if you were a friend of Miss Strachan's. But she didn't like people coming in and trying to *run* her. To get past her wasn't simple.... But she knew nothing about books, except for the pennyfeather novels.

The advent in 1964 of an Englishman, Mr. Parkes, changed the atmosphere. His literary preferences reflected his passion for model trains—the library mysteriously acquired shelves and shelves of books about them—but there was no more talk of letting the wrong sort of people in. "You no longer had to be part of the elite to belong," said John McGreevy. "If you had the money and you didn't have a jail sentence, you could be a member."

Unsuitable and Objectionable Books

When women were finally allowed to sit on the Book Committee in 1924, their presence had an effect that was quite the opposite of what the Council had desired, and apparently led to the purchase of some racy "sex stories." Two years later "Maj. W.H. Petry … made enquiry as to what methods were used to in any way check the flow of unsuitable and in many ways very objectionable books finding their way into the library and thence into the homes of the subscribers."

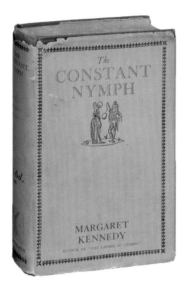

The Constant Nymph, by Margaret Kennedy, 1924.
A library bulletin in 1906 reminded members that the Book Committee would not buy "will-o'-the wisp" novels, but promised to provide a corner for "frivolous books which contain the most representative absurdities of the day—even though the fashionable tinsel of one season is always found in the scrapheap of the next."

As a result of this concern, the Library formed its first and only Censorship Committee "with the authority to order the immediate destruction, at their discretion, of any books of an undesirable nature." Before it was disbanded, the Committee managed to destroy sixteen "books of an immoral nature" such as Margaret Kennedy's *The Constant Nymph*, which described shocking scenes of adolescent sexuality in the Austrian Tyrol. The Committee also questioned books of a politically objectionable nature, such as those by Poultney Bigelow, an American journalist who was a close friend of Kaiser Wilhelm II.

In 1926, fifty-five enraged women members signed a petition for the disbandment of the censorship committee. The Lit and His, they said, was "not a school library for the immature" but a "library for the thoughtful and educated." It took another year of conflict before the Censorship Committee gave up the struggle, but not without arguing that they had simply been trying "to rid the library of books … disguised as modern fiction [and which] rely solely on their so-called 'frankness' in dealing with sex questions." Meanwhile, Major Petry was bringing the banned books home, where his teenaged daughter devoured them before he had time to throw them on the fire.

DAMP CELLARS
EARLY CANADIAN ARCHIVES

Dalhousie had noticed as he made his rounds of the government and military offices, scattered around the city, that public records were lying in piles in the corners, gathering dust, or being sold as waste paper. As for records of the French regime, many of the official records of New France were in archives in France, and especially in Paris. In 1823 Dalhousie wrote in his diary that "to have these collected or copied would be in itself a work of use, and to bring the attention of the Literary men of our day to the subject of these scientific & Antiquarian inquiries will be a public service which future ages only can appreciate."

After the Society received its Royal Charter in 1831, its by-laws legislated a seven-member Historical Committee to collect "original documents and authentic materials" to be "preserved for the public benefit among the archives of the Society." The Legislature accordingly granted the Society £300 for the "procuring, copying & publishing historical documents relating to the early times of this province."

Its approach to what constituted a historical document was broad, and included "unrecorded traditional accounts of early events" and information on a variety of aspects of life in Canada, gathered "from able persons on this continent." This definition set the scene for Canada's particular vision of public archives as not just official administrative records, as in most of Europe and the United States, but also private material and other "old and curious papers," as Andrew Cochran called them, bearing on the cultural and political history of its communities.

In 1835, the Governor in Chief gave the LHSQ responsibility for the safekeeping of the Records Commission, confiding copies of the official colonial records from London to the LHSQ "until the libraries of the Legislative Council and Assembly [may be] united." The Society promptly gave itself the mandate to "render these records accessible to all the public authorities in the country, as well as to the community generally." The most obvious way to render them public was to publish them.

Portrait of Georges-Barthélemi Faribault,
Archives du Séminaire de Québec
Author of the first published bibliography of Canadian history (1837), Faribault's goal was to provide resources for writers of Canadian history. Under his presidency, the LHSQ commissioned copies of French and British colonial records and published them, playing a key part in early Canadian historiography.

In 1836, Georges-Barthélemi Faribault, who had been a Society member for at least four years, was voted Honorary Librarian of the LHSQ. Faribault was a passionate bibliophile and archivist, parliamentary translator, assistant clerk of the House, and advisor to the Assembly librarian, Étienne Parent. When Faribault published his *Catalogue d'ouvrages sur l'histoire de l'Amérique, et en particulier sur celle du Canada*, the first Canadian historical bibliography, the Society noted the importance of this work and voted him Vice President of the Society and member of the Historical Documents Committee.

Over the next twenty-two years, under the auspices of the Society, Faribault was responsible for energetically tracking down, repatriating or copying, cataloguing, and publishing thousands of documents that were seminal for piecing together Canadian history. One of his staunchest supporters in this venture was Lord Durham, who appeared to be trying to remedy the "people with no history, and no literature" situation by giving the Society manuscripts from Versailles, copied at his own expense, in 1838. That very year the Society published the first of its *Historical Documents* series, and began to send these documents around the world. The first four issues in this series were all in French. With an annual publishing grant from the government, it continued to collect and publish an impressive number of historical documents until 1915, providing access to anyone who requested it.

In the period between 1835 and 1840, when the political situation in Quebec was explosive, Faribault's major partners in this enterprise presented an unlikely quartet: Andrew Cochran, firm believer in the royal prerogative; Lord Durham, the arch-assimilator; Patriote leader Louis-Joseph Papineau; and John Holmes, a Catholic priest. Between them they copied or had copied thousands of manuscripts relating to the early history of New France and the British colony of Canada from England, France, and the United States.

A number of them were memoirs, such as that written by Governor La Jonquière's secretary who arrived in New France in 1749. Some of his comments on the administration of the time were "invective, a great deal of it flagrantly unfair." But it was through these memoirs that historians first learned of Intendant Bigot's corruption and pillage of the colony.

Many Quebec historians have seen the LHSQ's primary goal in publishing such memoirs as a promotion of a pro-Anglo-Protestant historiography. But Faribault's main goal was to provide resource material for contemporary historians such as William Smith, Robert Christie, and Michel Bibaud, whose work, in Faribault's estimation, was inferior and "*ne rendaient point justice aux Canadiens.*" These early published memoirs may have inspired French Canadians from old families, such as Éliza-Anne Baby, Jacques Viger, Henry-Raymond Casgrain, James MacPherson LeMoine, and others to publish their own memoirs. Many of these memorialists came from families whose oral memories dated back to the Conquest and before. Their memories were anecdotal, but at the same time they were aware of the history the LHSQ was publishing. So although their memoirs have a conversational tone, as among convivial raconteurs around a fire, they produced knowledgeable, if not always factual, records of key moments in Quebec history.

Writers such as Philippe Baby Casgrain (president of the LHSQ in 1898–99 and 1906-7) and James MacPherson LeMoine (president in 1871, 1879–82, and 1902–3) also wanted to bring out the links between the two communities and educate their fellow Anglo-Canadians about French Canada. Louis-Philippe Turcotte wrote in his history of the LHSQ, published in the *Transactions* of 1879, "*si je ne craignais de blesser sa modestie je vous dirais combien M. Le Moine a travaillé à mettre plus d'union entre les deux populations, combien il a réussi à faire connaître notre histoire à la race anglaise.*"

Miraculously, the Society's historical documents survived its numerous evictions and both fires. Once it was firmly ensconced in Morrin College, the Society converted one of the cells beneath the library into "a fire-proof vault" for the storage of its historical documents and fitted it with a brand new iron door. It became a game of one-upmanship among the members to see who could root out the most interesting historical artefacts or documents at the lowest price, such as James Murray's *Journal of the Siege of Quebec*, a trophy that William Anderson had acquired "from the Record-office at London, without any cost to the Society." An honorary member who lived in Saint-Malo, France, Desmazières de Sechelles, sent the Society a detailed genealogy of Jacques Cartier and other manuscripts relating to his fellow Malouin. He even tried to acquire for the Society some relics prised from the walls of Jacques Cartier's seigneury in Limoilou, France; but, he wrote, "the landlord is inflexible in spite of the gold I offer him."

The situation of public records was, in LeMoine's words, one of "chaos and neglect." Henry Hopper Miles spoke to the Society in 1870 about the lamentable state of the public archives. He had visited the basement of Government House in Montreal and found it stuffed with bundles of unsorted documents and loose papers:

The vaults were usually musty and damp, and scarcely safe for the purposes of search without the use of a stove. I gathered, in fact … that at least two persons had accelerated their premature decease by too assiduously prosecuting there the work of searching for documents and sorting old papers.

Miles, who was acting secretary of the Council of Public Instruction of the new province of Quebec, was trying to write school history textbooks and having trouble establishing the facts. "So much of our knowledge of the past is allowed to be based upon tradition or mere *hearsay*, yet … we all know how often unreliable, indefinite, and even contradictory, is this sort of record." His concern for historical accuracy led him to accuse William Anderson in 1872 of misrepresenting fact in relation to a manuscript of James Thompson's Journal that the Society was about to publish, and the Council became so hilarious that the President, Captain Ashe, had to intervene three times. Miles was not amused, published a pamphlet in 1872 refuting the Society's claims, and wrote to Ashe that he could not "be expected to submit myself, personally, a third time, to the interruptions and even rudeness" of Council.

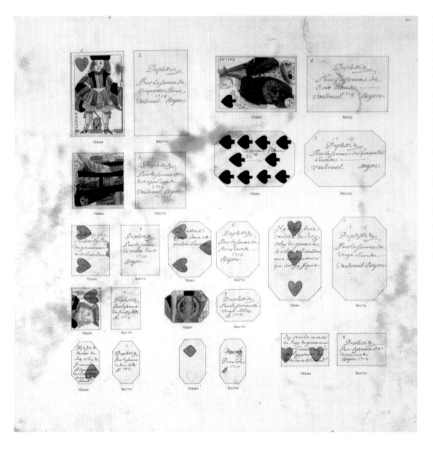

Early twentieth-century illustration of the playing card money used in New France, by Henri Beau. To overcome a currency shortage in New France, card money was introduced which was to be redeemed in cash when the king's ship arrived. It was a topic dear to the heart of LHSQ president and banker James Stevenson, who wrote an eighty-page essay on the topic for the Transactions in 1875.

By this time, the LHSQ had abandoned the idea that it alone should be the government record-keeper, but it was deeply concerned about the issue of public records. It lobbied both the Governor General and the House of Commons, and on 24 March 1871 presented a petition—signed by leading authors, clergy, and educators in Montreal and Quebec—to the House of Commons, for the establishment of a Canadian public archives. Its concern was that, with the "the diverse origins, nationalities, religious creeds, and classes of persons represented in Canadian society," history was being written according to "the political and religious bias or the special motives which may happen to animate the narrator of alleged facts."

Silver commemorative tray, 1997, LHSQ collections.
Presented to the LHSQ on the 125th anniversary of the National Archives of Canada, this gift was "in commemoration of the instrumental role played by that organization in the establishment of the National Archives of Canada in 1872."

The petition resulted in the establishment of a preliminary records commission. A sum of $4,000 was allocated for the purpose, and the following year Douglas Brymner was appointed Dominion archivist. He was given three empty rooms in the offices of the Department of Agriculture in Ottawa and told to get going. Brymner started off energetically, but in a few years his reports had dwindled to a few paragraphs, and the government records remained scattered in four different government buildings in Ottawa. The Society was not content. It presented another petition to both federal and provincial governments in 1877, and again in 1879. Finally the government devoted the necessary funds, and a proper archival program was underway.

In 1884, the Quebec government cut its grant of $750 and demanded that the LHSQ hand over the London and Paris archives, claiming that they were government property. The Society appointed a committee to study the question in 1888, and then referred the question to arbitration. Council members finally "satisfied themselves that the claim of the Government was legal, and that the Society was the custodian and not the owner of the papers in question." It handed over ten volumes, but when it inquired as to why it had not received its grant that year, discovered that the government wanted seventeen more. This unleashed a fierce debate over the Society's role and what constituted "public" archives, and it fought bitterly to reclaim some of the documents. It won the battle, but at the cost of its annual government grant.

The relationship with government improved later in the century with the close friendship that developed between William Wood, historian and pillar of the Society for fifty years, and Pierre-Georges Roy, provincial archivist. Between 1926 and 1938, largely thanks to their collaboration, the Society turned over its remaining collection of historical documents to the Province on condition that they would be kept in "an entirely separate compartment" and that the LHSQ members and their successors would be the "only custodians." In 1942, when the LHSQ was under the presidency of Judge G. F. Gibsone, the government handed over $10,000 in payment for the documents, and the matter was closed.

An attempt was made in 1986 by the Voice of English Quebec, headed by historian Marianna O'Gallagher, to revive the role of the LHSQ as an anglophone cultural centre and repository of anglophone archives. Anthony Price, descendant of Quebec City lumber merchant William Price, became involved and solicited large grants from the Webster Foundation and other donors, enabling the Society to hire a professional archivist and assistants. The Society had become the repository of the archives of defunct anglophone organizations such as the St. Andrew's Society, the Ladies City Mission, the Quebec Playground Association, and the Lake Edward Sanatorium Association. These archives needed organizing and cataloguing. The call went out to all Quebec City anglophones to deposit their family archives with the Society, but tracing these families was a challenge, as Price noted, because most had died out, or else the few survivors had left Quebec and deposited their family archives elsewhere in Canada.

Providing the proper climate for archives other than damp prison cells or dusty old classrooms was going to cost $90,000. The province offered encouragement and professional advice, but was not prepared to offer enough money to pay for a full-time archivist or bring the facilities up to standard. When the archivist left in 2001, a part-time archivist was hired for two months a year, but in 2009 the Society's archives were donated to the Quebec National Archives (BAnQ), which has since catalogued them and made them accessible to the public.

Royal Arms of France, by Noël Levasseur, 1727.
Commissioned by Gaspard-Joseph Chaussegros de Léry, this coat of arms hung prominently in Quebec until James Murray brought it back to Britain as a trophy. LHSQ president William Wood repatriated it to Quebec in 1925 through his connection with Sir John Jellicoe, First Sea Lord of the British Admiralty.

Model of the Royal William, ca. 1930, LHSQ collections. Built by 21-year old James Goudie at Quebec in 1830 in George Black's shipyard, the Royal William was the largest passenger ship in the world and the first seagoing steamship built in Canada. The LHSQ once owned a "crow's nest" builder's model of this ship, made to show shareholders what the ship would look like, and lent it to the Royal Naval Exhibition in London in 1891. Historian Eileen Reid Marcil discovered this model languishing in the office of a car dealership.

DRUM AND TRUMPET
COMMEMORATION AND CONSERVATION

> For now they met, not as they met before—
> Not as they used to meet in days of yore…
> But met as bitter foes, in deadly strife,
> Each wildly panting for the other's life.
>
> Helen Johnson,
> *The Surrender of Quebec*,
> LHSQ medal-winner, 1853

On 14 December 1834, a small group of Quebecers, led by John Fisher and Georges-Barthélemi Faribault of the Literary and Historical Society of Quebec, gathered on the banks of the St. Charles River to commemorate the three-hundredth anniversary of the arrival of Jacques Cartier. They planted a wooden cross with an inscription in front of the new Marine Hospital, and declared that a more permanent monument should be raised. Over half the committee appointed to carry out the plan, including Mayor René-Édouard Caron, consisted of members of the Society.

226

Although the plan never came to fruition, the Society's vocation as keeper of the public memory included building monuments as well as publishing historical documents. Inspired by Dalhousie's obelisk commemorating Montcalm and Wolfe, the Society continued raising wooden crosses, pinning historic plaques to rocks, or lobbying to save Martello towers from destruction well into the next century. It also worked with an almost religious fervour to protect historic sites from development. It campaigned to save the Plains of Abraham—not because a big park seemed like a good idea, but because such an important battlefield was sacred space.

SHOULDER TO SHOULDER

In its zealous historical flag-waving, the Society was loyal to Empire but strictly non-partisan when it came to the heroes of Canadian history. Lecturers rarely spoke of the Battle of the Plains of Abraham, won by the English, without also speaking of the Battle of Sainte-Foy, won by the French.

But it was the Siege of Quebec in 1775–76 that the LHSQ loved to remember most. The Americans had hoped to convince the *Canadiens* to join the Revolution, and had already taken Montreal and the rest of the colony. Only Quebec held out. At Quebec they were roundly defeated by a defence force that included some *Canadiens*. In the LHSQ version of history, this was the moment when French Canadians, less than twenty years after the Conquest, proved themselves as loyal to the British Empire as their British-origin compatriots in repelling the invading Americans.

The Society's celebration of the centenary of the battle included a full brass band belting out classical overtures, French-Canadian quadrilles, Irish jigs, Scottish folksongs, and "The British Grenadiers," and finishing up with "Vive la Canadienne" and "God Save the Queen." Readings of eye-witness accounts of the battle (brought up from the vaults) were rounded off with a stirring call to communal loyalty: "The immortal Wolfe and Montcalm had scarcely returned to their kindred dust," James MacPherson LeMoine reminded the crowd, "'ere the Briton and the Gaul were shoulder to shoulder repelling the invader of our sacred soil."

The Society's interest in this battle continued into the next century. In 1904, it installed two bronze tablets in the shape of shields, one weighing a thousand pounds and embedded in the cliff-face, the other bolted to the Molson Bank. The inscriptions were written by William Wood, an avid fan of the predestined-fusion-of-the-races historiography. He glorified the "old and new defenders" who protected Quebec from the Americans: "And on this sacred spot each and all of these widely different ancestors of the present 'Canadians' took their dangerous share of empire-building."

Wanton Desecration: The Plains of Abraham

Well before the bronze tablets, however, Quebec City's historic sites and buildings, including the city fortifications, were being threatened by modernity. Quebec had long been a popular tourist site. In the summer of 1870, seven hundred international visitors per day visited the city. Visitors included European royalty and British and American literary figures, among them Charles Dickens (1842), the Prince of Wales (1860), Prince Napoleon (1861), Henry James (1871), and Rudyard Kipling (1907). According to the London *Telegraph*, the beauty and historic significance of the Plains of Abraham, their chief destination, attracted more visitors than the battlefields of Waterloo. LeMoine and Wood were well aware of history's role in Quebec's popularity. Both passionate amateur historians and deeply acquainted with the LHSQ's collection of primary sources, they were in a perfect position to exploit that history. The Literary and Historical Society was often called upon to give distinguished visitors a tour of the city.

Their role as tour guides drove home to these two men the dilapidation or disappearance of sites and buildings that they liked to point out to visitors. Ruins of old civilizations may have been romantic, but ruins eventually disappear; and there were plenty of local forces, or "vandals" as LeMoine called them, ready to hurry the process along.

In particular, hundreds of acres of "the Heights and Plains of Abraham" were gradually being eaten away by development. "The three most conspicuous objects on the most famous site in the whole New World are a gloomy gaol, a hideous factory, and a wantonly desecrated tower," wrote William Wood and Arthur Doughty, the Dominion Archivist.

But when the Ursulines put their Marchmont estate on the Plains, divided into 800 lots and nineteen streets, on the market in 1899, the Society was roused to vigorous action. Philippe Baby Casgrain lectured in French at the Society on the importance of the Plains, James Douglas paid for an alarmist brochure, and on February 28, 1901, the Society held a public meeting to which it invited a large group of influential citizens, including the mayor. The outcome was a delegation to Ottawa suggesting that the government purchase the Ursuline property and others on the Plains so that they could be preserved as "historic grounds."

Prime Minister Wilfrid Laurier was game, the Ursulines were game, but the other owners were less compliant. After three years of quick property turnovers (the mayor was rumoured to be involved), acrimonious negotiation, and accusations of scandalous overpayment, Laurier raised money throughout the Empire to buy the site for $80,000.

Still the Society was not satisfied. It petitioned the government to buy the Cove Fields segment of the Plains, owned by National Defence, as well. The historic grounds should be landscaped according to "a design or plan," and a prize offered, "as the beauty of such parks in afteryears will depend mainly in the manner in which it was originally laid out."

MONUMENT WOLFE
PLAINES D'ABRAHAM

SOUVENIR OFFICIEL DES FÊTES
DU IIIe CENTENAIRE DE QUÉBEC
1608 – 1908

Souvenir postcard of the Wolfe Monument, 1904.
The Wolfe monument was a favourite point of interest for visiting British dignitaries – and a favourite target of French-Canadian nationalists. First erected in 1832 by Lord Aylmer, it has been replaced five times, the first time due to the predations of souvenir hunters and the last time after it was knocked down and destroyed by the Front de libération du Québec (FLQ) in 1963.

When Governor General Lord Minto's term ended in 1904, he urged the preservation of the Plains on Lord Grey, his successor, and when Lord Grey came to inspect his new charge, Wood was delegated to take him on the rounds. He pointedly took Lord Grey to Wolfe's monument. Grey could not fail to notice the desecrations, and reacted exactly as hoped, declaring that he would "never rest until such sacred ground became the heirloom of all Canada and the Empire."

STAMPED TO DEATH

Human beings also sometimes qualified as historic relics, and were more interesting preserved in their natural state. This applied especially to First Nations and French Canadians.

In a lecture in 1860, LHSQ Council member Noël Hill Bowen extolled the historic and cultural virtues of the Île d'Orléans, whose inhabitants had "preserved the manners and customs more closely than probably [in] any other part of Lower Canada, and been up to the present uncontaminated by the fashions and follies of 'the town.'" Modernity, in the form of the new steam ferry to the Island, was clearly not to his liking although he himself had built the wharf that made it possible. The inhabitants themselves, however, were relieved to be able to bring their goods to market in vessels other than canoes, and Bowen himself admitted that he enjoyed being able to gallop along the Route des Prêtres on his horse. He later built some summer houses for anglophones at Sainte-Pétronille.

Quebec rural scene by Horatio Walker, ca. 1880.
American painter Horatio Walker (1858-1938) began to frequent the Ile d'Orléans in the 1870s. His paintings depict traditional rural life in Quebec as romantic and mythical, and his paintings of Quebec brought the highest prices ever obtained by a living painter in North America.

Animals and birds were also worth preserving in their natural state, in the opinion of William Wood, the first Canadian to propose bird sanctuaries. Wood was deeply distressed about the disappearance of "our kindred of the wild," and worried that they were being killed more quickly than they could breed back. He had met fishermen who recalled shooting great auks, and was disgusted by some of his friends in Quebec, one of whom, a "gentleman of large means and good education," once shot six caribou in the hills near Quebec just to see how well a particular sight was working on his new rifle. People were hunting wildlife into extinction, he wrote in 1911, for the sheer fun of it.

> "C'est un plaisir superbe" was the description given by some voyageurs … who had spent the afternoon chasing young birds about the rocks and stamping them to death. Deer were literally hacked to pieces by construction gangs on new lines last summer. Dynamiting a stream is quite a common trick wherever it is safe to play it. Harbour seals are wantonly shot in deep fresh water where they cannot be recovered, much as seagulls are shot by blackguards from an ocean liner.

230

PERIL AND SHAME: HISTORIC SITES

The Society's experience with the Plains of Abraham demonstrated the power of collaboration. In 1905 the Society began to correspond with other historical societies with the idea of forming a national body or "Canadian Landmarks Commission" to protect and identify other such sites.

The idea was taken up with alacrity by the Royal Society of Canada (founded 1882), which had already successfully lobbied to preserve the Château Ramezay in Montreal. In 1907 the inaugural meeting of the Historic Landmarks Association (HLA) took place at the annual meeting of the Royal Society, with William Wood as its founding president. Its definition of "landmark" was fashioned by his vision of history:

> It may be a monument set up by pious hands; a building, a ruin, or a site; a battlefield or fort; a rostrum or poet's walk; any natural object; any handwork of man; or even the mere local habitation of a legend or a name … Its spirit makes every true landmark a talismanic heirloom, only to be lost to our peril and shame.

In Quebec City, several additional sites related to the history of Canada should be purchased for the purposes of commemoration, Wood wrote, including the house where Wolfe made his headquarters and a corner of ground at Pointe-aux-Trembles, "where Vauquelin fired his last shot from the gallant *Atalante*."

Kiosks on Dufferin Terrace, ca. 1885.
When Dufferin Terrace was extended in 1879, the LHSQ successfully petitioned City Council to name one of the new kiosks after Frontenac, the "illustrious and warlike Governor of Quebec" and suggested erecting a statue of Champlain "facing the site where the good old Governor lived and died."

Women in the Quebec tercentenary pageant, 1908.
The climax of the tercentenary celebrations was a vast historical pageant intended to heal divisions between First Nations, French Canadians and English Canadians. William Wood and William Price became a kind of theatrical press gang, recruiting 3150 local volunteers to act out the roles played by their forebears.

As 1908 approached, the Saint-Jean-Baptiste Society suggested that the city celebrate the tercentenary of its foundation. The idea was greeted with enthusiasm, and as historian H.V. Nelles has shown, eventually appropriated by numerous religious and ethnic groups for their own purposes. The LHSQ began to join deputations to Ottawa to further its own vision of a celebration that would, as William Wood characteristically explained, "show the French and British régimes as two halves of the one connected whole." The Society proposed that the city should reconstruct Champlain's habitation and they advised that the guides be dressed up in period costumes—a suggestion Quebec historic sites have followed assiduously to this day.

As for the Historic Landmarks Association, its job of cataloguing and researching historic sites was taken over in 1919 by a government agency, the Historic Sites and Monuments Board of Canada which, in a postmodernist twist of the history of history, was later to designate the foundation of the LHSQ itself as a historic event.

In 1922 the Historic Landmarks Association changed its name (with LHSQ approval) to the Canadian Historical Association and established links with public archives and the newly established history departments in Canadian universities. The LHSQ continued its activism at a local level, lobbying to preserve Martello Tower Number 4 (in Saint-Jean-Baptiste) in 1906, and to prevent the demolition of several New France–era houses in the old city, including Kent House (1650) and the Vallée (1650), Montcalm (1677), and McKenna (1720) houses. In 1930, the Council reported that the Society's "strong representations … stopped the work of demolishment." That same year it suggested that *all* the buildings within the walls be conserved.

William Wood died in 1947. A few years later, in another ironic twist, his own house, 59 Grande Allée, was torn down to make way for the premier's offices, a brutalist building known today as "the bunker."

DIVEST, DISARM, INVEST
THE LATER YEARS

The era of William Wood, with his detailed knowledge of history, his aristocratic background, his passionate belief in the British Empire as something all nations could identify with, his love of the French language and of French Canada, and his contempt for modern architecture, came to an end with his death in 1947. He was mourned by his many friends and colleagues at the LHSQ and the Royal Society of Canada, but has remained strangely ignored as a colourful and mysterious character, an interesting historian, and one of the most active and prescient conservationists of his era.

In 1943, the LHSQ by-laws had been formally changed to reflect the Society's demise as a learned society. Among other changes, the Society eliminated the requirement for an apparatus committee and an archives committee "by reason of there being no apparatus conserved by the Society" as Colonel William Petry pointed out, and because most of the archives were now in government vaults. The committees were replaced by a membership committee and a finance committee, and indeed, it was a period when the minutes mention almost nothing but declining membership and money.

The Society consisted of little more than a group of elderly men who sat around deciding how to invest the interest that still trickled in from the Douglas, Carrel, Turnbull, and Richardson endowments—or at least those are the conversations they recorded in the minutes. Once in a while, there would be a flurry of letters—say, to suggest a new Canadian flag (a maple leaf with a union jack in the background), or to petition for a streetcar stop closer to the Society rooms. But these men had less energy and perhaps less time for the campaigns and petitions than had the younger LeMoine, Douglas, and Wood of earlier years. In 1944, even the task of finding new members began to seem onerous—the Society was quite content to totter along without the irritant of new people who might not laugh at the same jokes. That year George Love suggested a freeze in membership recruitment, "as the membership is now quite sufficient."

According to one member, even the smell of the library was off-putting. "It smelled like cabbages and pigs' ears," recalled Rita Laframboise, who had moved around the world all her life in the company of her husband, Canadian ambassador and Quebec diplomat Jean Chapdelaine. "It felt like those little British outposts in Egypt or Brazil, but it smelled just like Dublin."

Dufferin Terrace, n.d.
The Society once supported artists such as Joseph Légaré and Henry Thielcke, and in later years artists Kathleen Shackleton (1884–1961) and Lionel Fielding Downes (1900–1972) were fellow lodgers at Morrin College. Fielding Downes had painted alongside Arthur Lismer and the Group of Seven before settling in Quebec.

Mary McGreevy (née Gavan Gray), whose husband John McGreevy was treasurer of the LHSQ for forty-eight years, declared in 1999 that the Society in that era "was like the most exclusive private club… Going there was like going back to Victorian times. It was really a men's organization. The ones who weren't there were at the Garrison Club, it was as simple as that."

She also noted that subscriptions were almost exclusively to English newspapers and magazines: "There was the *Tatler*, the *Spectator*, the *Illustrated London News*, *Country Life*, the London *Times* (although quite a few days old). None of them were Canadian that I remember. And if you had a British accent, that got you a long way." But for all her husband's financial husbandry, the place was still falling down: "Last time I went, the bannister gave way as I was climbing the staircase, and I fell flat on my face. I haven't been since," she said.

Gradually the exclusive grip of masculinity lost its hold on the Society. More and more it was women who chose the books for the library, who used it, and who raised money for it. Richard Parkes died in 1974, generously leaving his entire collection of train-related books to the library, including his own *Railway Snowfighting Equipment Methods* (1961). A special section of the library was dedicated to his memory.

Quebec Passports

Three years later, his assistant Cynthia Cook-Dooley took over as librarian. She was the great-granddaughter of Dr. John Cook who had given the Society its first taste of security over a hundred years earlier when he took it under the wing of the new Morrin College. "I grew into the job," she said. "We lived in Morrin College, and our family has been a member forever. I was here all the time."

Mary Hilda Freeland Stephens and her "Quebec Collection," ca. 1991. Hilda Stephens (1911-1999) was an artist and collector of antique china and toys. In 1991 she donated her entire collection of treasures belonging to the "old families of Quebec" to the Society, including dolls' clothes, toy furniture and miniature china dating back 200 years.

Bilingual and with truly eclectic interests in the best of the Society's tradition, Dooley also played her part in its survival by organizing endless bake sales, Christmas sales, raffles, luncheons, flea markets, auctions, and wine and cheese parties. The Society also owed its survival to a steady stream of quiet donations by members such as the McGreevys, Rosemary Power-Cannon, Hilda Stephens, Hazel Breakey, and Donald Ross, all from old Quebec anglophone families for whom the Lit and His was home.

The LHSQ suffered its third fire in 1966, and this time it was arson. A young Argentinian named Alberto Oscar Pipino, a fierce opponent of the British claim to the Falkland Islands, decided to vent his spleen on the statue of Wolfe standing in the library, a symbol of what he considered Britain's similar relationship with Quebec. He brought in two Molotov cocktails, placed them on the shelves behind the librarian's desk, and left. Just as a hundred years earlier, firefighters saved books by throwing them out of the windows—but put out the fire quickly. Damages were around $2,650, and Pipino was sentenced to two years in prison and then deported. Judge Achille Pettigrew pronounced that "Canadians know what they want and don't need foreign agents to tell them how to … protect their independence."

Librarian Cynthia Dooley was nevertheless sanguine about the politics of the day. In 1976, just before the Parti Québécois came to power, PQ heavyweight Claude Morin came to the library to talk about sovereignty. "The little old ladies drank it up," she said, "asking questions like 'will we need passports?' Then they fed him cake, and he ate piece after piece, and the women were all thrilled with him… Those old ladies probably all joined the PQ." She also recalled with pleasure the occasion when the entire Parti Québécois cabinet showed up to launch Graham Fraser's book on René Lévesque. "There was no security," recalled Irene Calfat, who also worked in the library. "They were all amazed; none of them knew the place existed… There was René Lévesque, Parizeau—the lot—plus the press gallery, so the wine really flowed, and they all sat about and wandered around until late in the evening."

Book launch at the LHSQ of Graham Fraser's *René Lévesque and the Parti Québécois in Power*, 1984.
Journalist Graham Fraser, later Canada's Commissioner of Official Languages, launched his book in the Library on the eighth anniversary of René Lévesque's election. At the time, tensions were brewing in the PQ cabinet, and within a few days of the launch half of his cabinet quit over the question of independence.

236

Rosemary "Posy" Cannon, Cameron MacMillan, Ross Cowan and John McGreevy, LHSQ Collection, c 1980. Charles Power was an avid reader, and his daughter read every book he brought home. As first woman president of the LHSQ, Rosemary Cannon had to confront an old-boys club culture that was centuries old. At her inauguration in 1978, she expressed the hope that the founders of the Society "do not agree with Kipling, who said that 'a woman is only a woman, but a good cigar is a smoke.'"

The LHSQ was still a well-kept secret, and not only from the Parti Québécois. The Public Archives of Canada telephoned in alarm that year, having heard from McGill University that the Society had closed its doors. In the charged political atmosphere of the late 1970s, the Society was keeping such a low profile that it was in danger of disappearing from sight altogether.

With the election of Rosemary Power-Cannon in 1977, the Society was finally under the official direction of a woman for the first time. "I was the last choice," she said diffidently. "They couldn't find anyone else to do it." But the choice was a formidable one. Theatre director and TV host, Cannon was the daughter of Chubby Power, a prominent cabinet minister in Mackenzie King's government, and had married into another powerful political family. She had been coming to the library since 1947.

Cannon plunged fearlessly into the political labyrinth of one of the last anglophone institutions in town. The first thing she did was crack open the incestuous method the Society used for nominating Council members so that control of the Society did not constantly rotate through the same old suspects. She opened up the Society's reading matter, too. When there was a furor over the purchase of Pierre Vallières's book *White Niggers of America: The Precocious Autobiography of a Quebec "Terrorist"* (1971), Cannon stood up for the book's remaining on the shelves: "You can't worry about how controversial a book is; people should be able to read what they want to. It's only fair to have both sides of a current debate." It was also during her presidency that the approval of a new member by two-thirds of the other members was dropped. Henceforth, anyone could join the Society if they paid their $60 membership fee.

It was a period when unilingual anglophones did not feel welcome in Quebec. The vicissitudes of the LHSQ's signs have always literally been a sign of the times, and in this period even a French sign that the LHSQ had put up was pulled down. After much fretful discussion, the Society had tried a bilingual sign in 1970, but it was vandalized. Almost the day after it was replaced, a law was passed forbidding any signs in English at all. "If we get in trouble with the Government, I guess we'll take it down," Cannon said to a visiting reporter from the *Globe and Mail*, but she "doubted the Government would pick on a struggling library serving an ever-shrinking English-speaking population." For several decades there was no sign to indicate the library's presence at all other than a piece of paper stuck in the window. A permanent bilingual sign was finally affixed to the building in 2012.

In 1981, a Morrin College governor and vice-president of the Society, Wilfred Rourke, made an offer to buy the city block that included Morrin College, offering to sell the building to the Society at a reduced price if he could convert the other buildings on the lot into condos (see page 163). The City of Quebec under Mayor Jean-Paul L'Allier bought the Morrin College building from Rourke in 1989.

Getting Rid of Books — by the Ton

The same year, the Society sold a large chunk of its own assets—books and manuscripts that it had been collecting since 1824.

The story of how the LHSQ dispossessed itself of its collection of historical documents and ancient books is the story of a half-century conflict over visions of its two remaining vocations—that of book museum and lending library—and how to best use its few resources. The Society's active vocation as the national collector and publisher of historical documents had ended long ago, and it was crowded for space and short of money. The items in its collection that made their way into the public archives, such as the large collection of documents deposited there in 1888, are now clearly where they belong. Some of its books, manuscripts, maps, and works of art, sold at auction or privately, ended up at Canadian universities. Others were lost to Quebecers and to all Canadians.

William Wood cared enough about the Society's historical documents that he personally catalogued the entire collection at his own expense, and he was only too aware of the Society's limitations in maintaining and storing it. In 1934 he expressed what he saw as a realistic redefinition of the Society's role when he wrote to the president suggesting that the Society might sell "works which might have a high value in the market, but which are not Canadiana, not works which our members might read, and not even works which scholars engaged in research would think of seeking on our shelves."

Wood and the librarian made a list of some 400 volumes that fell into this category, including the original copies of the *Moniteur universel*, the newspaper of the French Revolution dating from 1791 to 1803, nine volumes of the House of Commons Journals (England) covering the period of the Civil War, and a number of books printed in the seventeenth century. Approaches to Maggs & Quaritch auction houses in London, however, produced disappointing results. In 1939 Wood tried again, writing to his friend, the Montreal bookseller Louis Melzack, with a list. Melzack wrote back to offer $173 for forty-seven of the books, adding, "I do hope your Irish housekeeper is well again and that she stays in your employ for another thirty years."

In 1947, the year Wood died, numerous volumes from the Society's collection were given to McGill University by the Society president, McGill alumnus E. C. Woodley. Among them were unique sixteenth- and seventeenth-century legal, historical, and philosophical treatises from the Quebec Library and the Aylwin Library, in the keeping of the Society. The books were then purchased by a McGill historian of philosophy and book collector, Raymond Klibansky, who eventually gave them back to McGill.

In 1965, Society librarian Richard Parkes quoted Wood's letter in an attempt to persuade president John McGreevy that it was time to consider another sale of books. "The books represent tied-up capital on which no interest is earned," he wrote. "Converted into cash and invested in suitable stocks, the interest would help pay for library operating expenses (for which we are hopelessly short of funds) and for much needed improvements, e.g. lighting in the Reading Room." McGreevy, Parkes noted, "agreed with my views."

The following year, Society president J. H. Bieler, hoping McGill or the Parliamentary Library at Quebec would be interested, invited McGill librarian John Archer and archivist Alan Ridge to Quebec to evaluate the LHSQ's holdings and make suggestions. Archer brought a friend with him, the antiquarian bookseller Bernard Amtmann.

Archer subsequently wrote a long and thoughtful letter to the Society listing its possible courses of action. One option, he wrote, was that the Society seek public, provincial, and municipal funding to develop the library as a public lending library along with the Institut Canadien. In that case, it would be wise to get rid of pre-1900 books and periodicals from the United States and Britain as well as almost one hundred years' worth of transactions received by way of exchange from other learned societies around the world.

"The library wants to keep Canadiana," he wrote, but incomplete runs of periodicals "could fill out broken runs in university and research libraries." The main function of the Society's library, he argued, was to function "as a library and not a museum," and any "surplus material" relating to Quebec or Canada should go to the provincial archives and the National Gallery. The Society's own archives should go to the Quebec archives on loan, with ownership to remain with the Society in perpetuity. He was concerned that anything sold should reach Canadian and American libraries ("since library service is international"), and suggested that the "fairest and most financially rewarding" method would be to sell the collection at public auction. The best place for this, he added, would be Montreal, and the best man for the job, Bernard Amtmann.

As soon as the Society agreed to this plan, Amtmann formed Montreal Book Auctions, Ltd., Canada's first book auction house. The value and importance of the LHSQ's collection made this a historic moment for the world of antique books in Canada, and a career-making moment for Amtmann.

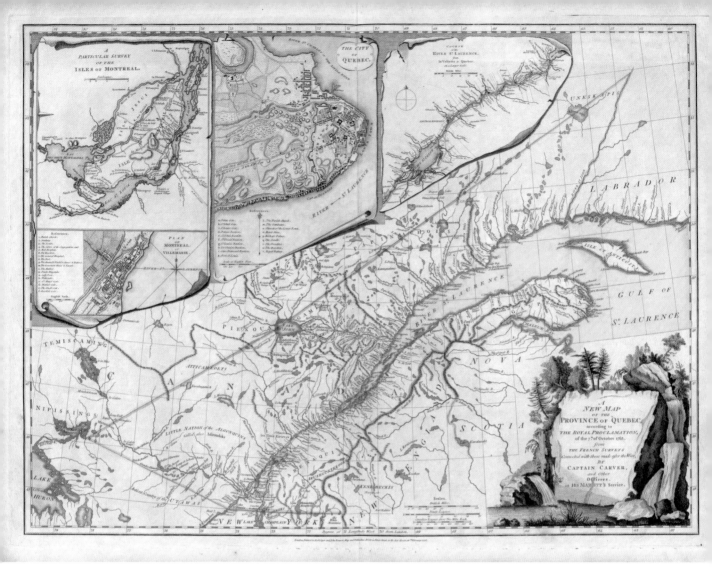

Map of the Province of Quebec from *Ameri[c]an Atlas*, by William Faden, Geographer to the King, ca.1777.
One of the most valuable items on the auction block in 1967 was this unique bound collection of "33 maps and battle plans of the Revolutionary War in North America." These hand-coloured maps were intended for a British public eager to see the latest developments in the Revolutionary War. A Montreal collector bought it for $6500.

The LHSQ shipped nine tons of books to Montreal, where they were auctioned over the next two years in the plush rooms of the Ritz-Carlton hotel. As each successive auction approached, the Society was persuaded to part with more and more Canadiana to sweeten the offer, including *Grammatica huronica*, 1822, a book that had been presented to the LHSQ by Andrew Stuart in 1833, and *Champlain's Voyages*, printed in Paris in 1632, which was bought by a Toronto collector for $4,000. Ironically, one of the last historical treasures the Society shipped off for auction was a portrait by Théophile Hamel of the Society's greatest collector of valuable historical documents, Georges-Barthélemi Faribault, donated by the artist in 1877. The books went to universities in Canada and the United States, as well as to British and American book dealers.

Altogether, the LHSQ items fetched $43,139 on the auction block. The Society ended up with $29,411—plenty of money to pay for new lighting in the reading room.

Parkes was perhaps the only one who enjoyed the whole process immensely. "We have had a lot of fun getting books auctioned," he wrote to Archer, who was by now librarian at Queen's University.

Frozen pigs, St. Anne's Market, Montreal. Alexander Henderson, ca. 1870.
Alex Henderson was a Scottish immigrant who learned photography in Montreal, and travelled widely in Quebec and Ontario. *His Canadian Views and Studies by an Amateur* (1865) was donated by to the LHSQ in J. T. Ross in 1923 and sold at auction for $7,200. It is now at Library and Archives Canada in Ottawa.

"Dilapidation Pure et Simple"

There was no love lost between the Society and the province in this era. While William Wood had had many close francophone friends with shared cultural interests, in the 1970s many anglophones did not trust the Quebec government to protect the Society's cultural interests—or its possessions. The Society continued to survive on donations, endowments, and subscriptions, as well as the sale of IODE calendars, poppies, and Grenfell Mission cards. The government grant of $500 from, oddly, the Ministère du Loisir, Chasse et Pêche, secured through William Wood long ago, continued to arrive, but was not enough to pay more than a month's salary for the librarian. The Society even stooped to accepting money from the DuMaurier Tobacco Co. In 1981, John Mappin evaluated the remaining Canadiana belonging to the Society at $80,000. At an impromptu meeting two years later, four members of Council decided to sell a collection of Canadian photographs, known as the Henderson Album, to the National Archives for $7,200. At the Annual General Meeting, McGreevy explained that the sale "fitted in with the Society's policy of adding to the endowment funds which subsidize the current lending library function of the Society."

The selling off of the family silver continued in 1988 when Rourke, the new owner of Morrin College, claimed an upstairs room full of books for the use of his company. The Society secretary wrote that "naturally no directories or Canadiana or books of particular interest to us are involved and we will be extremely careful in choosing the discards."

Rosemary Cannon and John McGreevy picked out about 4,000 books "of no disputed historical or sentimental value," and sold them to Quebec City bookseller Maurice Villeneuve for $12,000. The deacquisitions, as the Council called them, included Canadian journals, maps, and Bibles published from 1858 to1861 in thirty-three languages. The Society also sold books to dealers in Ontario and maps to Université Laval.

In an interview with CBC, Canadian historian Graeme Decarie called the sale of the building "tragic," as was the sale of part of the Society's "magnificent collection." Quebec historian Claude Galarneau, interviewed by *Le Soleil* on April 23, 1988, called the sale "*dilapidation pure et simple du patrimoine québécois*," and the National Archives complained that it had not even been told about the sale.

Luddites vs. Tour Guides

This was a period of grave uncertainty as to where the Society was to live, calling up memories of its wanderings in the nineteenth century, but the uncertainty ended with the purchase of Morrin College by the city in 1989. With no more rent, heat, or lighting bills to pay, the Society was on a more secure footing again. Meanwhile, the library was going through a parallel, non-material identity crisis. There was skepticism over the first purchase of a computer (1987) and, more controversial yet, the conversion of the card catalogue to a digital one. Irene Calfat, who worked at the library for years, expressed the loss most succinctly:

> I loved filing the cards, and learned so much from them. I was forever seeing something that I didn't know we had. I love looking over the list of people who've read a book. Some have died, and it's a way to fondly remember them. Then some members ask me if they've read a book before, and I can look it up and see that they read it thirty years ago. Members are always saying to each other, "I see you've read such-and-such, what did you think of it?" … I'm opposed to anything electronic, but that's just because I'm a Luddite. A couple of libraries in San Francisco are now going *back* to card filing, because they realize what they've lost.

In large part the Society's survival had always depended on low wages paid to its staff. "I adored working at the library," said Calfat. "Mary McGreevy once objected to us getting a pay raise, saying 'but they love working here'—and it was true. To tell the truth I'd have done it for nothing." It also relied on the unpaid work of volunteers who fell in love with the library the minute they walked in and were quickly dragooned into becoming members of busy committees or offering their services for free.

When books needed mending, the librarians left them on the desk for Jacques Roy, a motor vehicle inspector who repaired books in his basement as a hobby using old leather coats. He had discovered the library through an ad in the papers. "There was a beautiful collection of books there, but some of them were in rough shape," said Roy. "So I've been taking some of them home to repair ever since. I rebind one or two a week, more in the winter." The Society's only contribution was a few old coats and a life membership.

Many people who spent their days in the library wanted it to stay the same forever. In a 1998 article in the *Canadian Forum* I wrote that, "it would be nice to know that this priceless piece of Canada's history won't all moulder away in complete obscurity. On the other hand, if it was higher on the list of Quebec's heritage priorities, it would have been all tarted up and turned into another theme centre with little signposts and have-a-nice-day guides and possibly a Gifte Shoppe. Then I'll stop going."

The Literary and Historical Society Library in 1999.
Having barely changed since it moved into the building in 1868, the Library attracted the attention of crime writer Louise Penny, who used it as the setting for a murder in her novel *Bury Your Dead*. With its publication in 2010 the Society finally gained true literary notoriety, and fans of her novels came from far and wide to visit.

For the following fifteen years, however, this was exactly the direction the Society, under the new umbrella of the "Morrin Centre," was headed. More and more tourists were recognizing the library for its beauty and hidden-treasure quality. A new dynamic staff set out to bring in more revenue and rectify the perennial shortage of funds, while trying not to undermine the spirit of the place or drive its older members away. The year 2004 marked the passing of the old to the new: the staff grew and professionals were hired to oversee restoration work; that same year, accountant John McGreevy, who began his service as president in 1961 and retired as treasurer in 1997, and TV host Rosemary Cannon, first woman president of the LHSQ, both died.

Attempts to solve the library's problems by linking up with the public library network failed for a variety of reasons. From the 1940s to the 1980s, the Society turned down repeated offers by the Institut Canadien, which manages Quebec City's public libraries, to merge the two systems. After that there were overtures on both sides, and the consequent questions of where to establish the edges of a distinct anglophone cultural institution. Each side was suspicious of the other, with the intensity and direction of suspicion fluctuating depending on the individuals running the respective institutions. Would the Society library continue to be the only English library in Quebec City? Would it lose its historic institutional character? Would it have to hire unionized staff? Would it continue to be able to choose its own books? Would there be, horror of horror, *fines*? In the twenty-first century, when the Society became eager to join the public system so that it could achieve core funding, the City was no longer in the mood to expand its library system.

Restoration and Revival

For over a century and a half, the Society had devoted itself to documenting, collecting, and conserving historic documents, archives, and artefacts, lobbying to preserve buildings, and putting up tablets to commemorate historic events. Finally the thought occurred that the Society itself was worth preserving.

The first mention of this in the Society's minutes was by Jean-Paul Grenier, a member, who suggested in 1964 that the building should be made known as a historic site. In 1984 the Society was designated of national historic importance by the Historic Sites and Monuments Board of Canada.

Various committees were established to decide What To Do. Gary Caldwell suggested that the building should be used as a new liberal arts school for Protestant anglophone youth. Marianna O'Gallagher proposed a trilingual Celtic studies institute. Others recommended a museum, a nursery school, an art gallery with a tearoom in the courtyard.

The LHSQ, it was suggested, could restore its archival vocation, publishing program, and lecture series. Meanwhile, however, the building urgently needed basic repairs. In 1988 Voice of English Quebec (VEQ) took up the banner and began to agitate for the building to be restored at Canada's expense. A shared-cost restoration project was finally agreed to, and John Keyes, a college history teacher, formed the "Morrin College Project" in 1992 in collaboration with VEQ. An agreement was signed with Parks Canada, the City of Quebec, and the Province of Quebec for restoration of the exterior of the building for $2.3 million, a project that was mostly completed in 1994.

In 1996 Mayor Jean-Paul L'Allier announced that he would commit one million dollars to help turn Morrin College into a cultural centre, which would include the library, and turned over the building to the freshly named "Joseph Morrin Historical Centre Foundation." A city architect recommended that it should be a *centre d'interpretation* rather than a museum, but someone was going to have to raise private matching funds.

John Keyes handed over the fundraising project to the LHSQ in 1998. It was a daunting prospect for a small group of English speakers who liked reading. David Blair, former president of VEQ, believed that the last tenant of the building, the Literary and Historical Society, could raise the money, starting by creating a children's library. He had been visiting the building since he was a *calèche* driver in the 1980s, when the caretaker would give him and his clients unofficial access to the untouched and atmospheric prison cells. Blair, who became LHSQ president in 1999, was determined to put the Society and its hidden treasures on the map again. Its annual budget at the time was $38,000.

He and a new, younger LHSQ Council and staff began energetically raising money to restore the entire building. Canadian Heritage promised half a million dollars if the city and the province would match funds. The province dragged its feet for a couple of years, finally coming up with $190,000 in 2004. Mayor L'Allier, however, boldly took the side of the "Anglos." Upping the ante, he repeated his promise of a million dollars, saying, "A city has to have a complete history and not a partial one." Meanwhile, the Society had managed to raise $160,000 in private funds.

The City of Quebec and the LHSQ signed an emphyteutic lease which, in spite of sounding like a terminal lung disease, gave the LHSQ and its subsidiary, the newly named Morrin Centre, possession of the building for ninety-nine years.

Two part-time staff were replaced by four full-time staff in 2004, and a regular program of cultural activities and guided tours began, including tours through the old gaol cells and the Morrin College chemistry laboratory. The Society also began publishing again for the first time in eighty years. Membership rose, the staff doubled again, and the library moved briefly to the church hall opposite while major renovations began on the interior of the building under the management of the new executive director, architect France Cliche and historic preservation consultant Patrick Donovan.

The Society began to effervesce in a way that hadn't been seen since the late nineteenth century. Historical and philosophical lectures were revived, and an annual literary festival brought renowned Canadian authors to a city where English-language literature is thin on the ground. It put on a Celtic festival and an opera by eighteenth-century Quebec City writer Frances Moore Brooke. The *Transactions* were fully digitized and made accessible through the new Morrin Centre website, and a witty virtual exhibition gave people around the world access to the Society's history and treasures. The library added children's books, young adult and graphic novels, and missing classics. It was fully catalogued and made available through an online database.

For several years, the minute books were mostly full of bricks and mortar, business plans, and grant applications. The LHSQ and anglophone culture were finally being recognized as important cultural assets at the federal, provincial, and municipal levels. Instead of keeping a low profile and hoping militant anglophobes would not notice its continuing existence, the Society's new survival strategy was to seek the public eye with all its might.

Altogether it raised $4.5 million, and in 2011, with much pomp and ceremony, the Society officially launched its newly restored building, including a museum exhibition on the prison.

While the new Morrin Centre attracted many new members and a higher proportion of francophones, some of the older members left, never to return. Fundraising events that had become community traditions, such as the Christmas sale, fell by the wayside—they didn't raise enough money to pay for the staff overtime needed to run them. "We were going from selling muffins to giant corporate fundraising—it was huge shift in culture," said Diane Kameen, who sat on the Council for twenty years. But without core funding, she said, "I'm afraid we've changed a small-scale need for funds into a large-scale need for funds."

It was Kameen who had the idea of turning to another anglophone institution, the Jeffery Hale Foundation, for more sustained help. The Jeffery Hale Foundation had gathered up all the assets of the defunct or depleted anglophone associations in order to redistribute them to the remaining ones.

The Jeffery Hale Foundation came up trumps, promising $100,000 per year for ten years. A 2013 donation of another $100,000 from the Quebec cooperative bank, Desjardins, suggested a broadening appreciation of the Society beyond the old Quebec Protestant alliances and government to private francophone institutions. Meanwhile, the Society keeps reaching out for a broader clientele—Irish anglophones, francophones, allophones, teenagers, and children.

Conflicting visions made public news when the library moved back into the newly restored rooms in 2008 and the spectre of the old book auctions made a new appearance.

In the move, the staff identified hundreds of books that were falling apart, duplicates of editions in better shape, or in incomplete sets. Hundreds of these books were weeded out and put up for silent auction, provoking a burst of outrage among some members. Thomas Reisner, retired literature professor and former lecturer at the LHSQ, called the auction "a pointless and barbarous purge," and a past president, Thomas Feininger, wrote a scathing letter to the papers about what he termed a "mindless sale."

The Society rejoiced in more press attention than it had enjoyed in years but shut down the silent auction, asked members to send recommendations of books they would like to keep, and in the meantime left the books in a room to wait for a reincarnation of Jacques Roy to come and repair them.

Fourteen voyageurs and four gentlemen in Dalhousie's Vice Regal canoe, by John Elliott Woolford, 1821.
Walter Scott said of his friend Dalhousie, founder of the Literary and Historical Society, that he had "excellent sense ... the most perfect equality of temper, and unshaken steadiness." History has remembered his regal recalcitrance, but his favourite project, the Lit and His, survives at the heart of the Morrin Centre today.

SOLDIERING ON

In the background, certain things never changed. The Book Committee soldiered on, meeting monthly to choose reviews from newspapers, specialized periodicals, and websites, processing requests, and still arguing over the correct balance between bestsellers, literary fiction, and non-fiction. It still pays for the books out of interest on mining magnate James Douglas's endowment, and purchases more than a decent armful every month. The magazine auction, whereby the Society pays for its magazine subscriptions by selling off back issues to the highest bidder, still takes place every year at the Annual General Meeting, as it has for over a hundred years. Lecturers still draw a small but respectable crowd, and fines have not yet been reinstituted. In spite of the guided tours that may interrupt a quiet afternoon of reading, the library no longer smells of pig's ears, and people still stop by to talk about books, and everything else, in English.

The Society has always been the sum of its parts, its parts being its members. It cannot be said to have had a single, unchanging personality over the course of its nearly 200 years of existence. At times its members defended the royal prerogative in a British colony; at other times they defended the Rebellion. At times the Society played a seminal role in scientific development and research, and in the collection and conservation of historical documents about Canada's history; at other times it played chess and auctioned off precious documents. At times it collaborated with provincial authorities; at other times it was deeply distrustful. At times the membership was made up almost exclusively of Protestant anglophones; at other times it counted Jewish businessmen, Catholic clergy, and a large percentage of francophones among its members. The Society has been continually shaped and reshaped, not so much by its by-laws, but by the interests of its most active members, each with their own specific blind spots, passions, and visions of the world.

TIMELINE

1824	Founding of Literary and Historical Society of Quebec
1825	Population of Quebec City: 20,000
1829	First volume of the 35-volume *Transactions* published (last in 1924): Of its 17 articles, 3 are historical, 14 scientific
1830	Library and museum open
1831	Royal Charter; Joseph Morrin named Honorary Librarian. Membership 23% francophone
1832	Government grants begin for procuring, copying and publishing historical documents relating to New France and British North America
1833	LHSQ moves from Chateau Saint-Louis to Union Building (government offices)
1838	First volume of 8-series *Historical Documents* published, in French (last in 1915)
1841	LHSQ moves to Parliament Building and acquires Chasseur collection
1842	Charles Dickens visits the LHSQ
1850	Only 14 people paid their dues, 12 of whom were Council members
1854	Fire in Parliament building: LHSQ museum burns, most books saved
1862	Second fire in LHSQ rooms: most books burned. LHSQ moves to Masonic Hall
1866	LHSQ acquires Quebec Library Association collection, including Quebec Library collection.
1868	LHSQ moves into former common gaol, along with Morrin College
1871	LHSQ petition to create Public Records Office
1873	Members ask for legal opinion about the playing of Chess in Society rooms
1875	Lavish commemorations of Quebec's repulse of the Americans in 1775
1886	Women officially admitted to Society rooms
1888	Government requisitions transfer of historical documents to new public archives
1890	Most of museum contents sold to High School of Quebec
1904	LHSQ installs tablets at spot where Montgomery and Arnold were repulsed in 1775
1915	James Douglas (junior) gives $15,000 for books
1916	LHSQ takes over supervision of Aylwin Library
1924	Final publication of *Transactions*
1930	LHSQ suggests saving all buildings within the walls of Quebec City
1944	Censored books are returned to the shelves
1945	First female member of Council
1946	Sale and disposal of remainder of Aylwin Library
1966	Arson attempt at LHSQ library by Alberto Pipino, Argentinian student/poet
1967-69	Major auctions of LHSQ books, maps and paintings in Montreal
1977	First female president (Rosemary Power-Cannon)
1981	Building designated as heritage site
1988	Further sale of books, many from Quebec Library
1989	Building sold to city
1992-1993	Major restoration of exterior
2001	LHSQ Council takes over project to restore and occupy the building
2002	Launch of *Society Pages*
2004	LHSQ signs 99-year emphyteutic lease for building with Ville de Québec; regular program of cultural activities and guided tours begins
2006	First phase of interior restoration completed; inauguration of restored LHSQ library and Morrin Centre
2012	Second phase of interior restoration completed
2013	Morrin Centre awarded Prix du patrimoine de la Ville de Québec for its restoration project

A NOTE ON SOURCES

Primary Sources

The main works consulted for this section of the book were the **publications of the Literary and Historical Society of Quebec**, including the 35 volumes of the *Transactions of the Literary and Historical Society of Quebec* (1829-1925), containing texts of lectures, reports of annual general meetings and solicited and unsolicited scholarly articles, catalogues, lists, letters etc.; the eight series of *Historical Documents*, the Literary and Historical Society of Quebec's publication of the historical manuscripts previously in its collection (1838-1906); and *Society Pages* (2002 to the present). I also consulted the **Archives of the Literary and Historical Society of Quebec** at Bibliothèque et Archives nationales du Québec in Quebec City. This consists of two separate fonds. The first, P948, "Fonds Literary and Historical Society of Quebec"), contains the administrative records of the Society, including the minutes and correspondence; it also contains the remaining registers of the Quebec Library. The second, P450, "Collection Literary and Historical Society of Quebec" contains the original historical documents amassed by the Society. P948 was not yet fully described or classified at the time of writing. I also consulted records located at the Society itself, including correspondence, clippings, catalogues, addresses, annual and other reports, minutes, and various notes by Lorraine O'Donnell, Patrick Donovan, Louisa Blair and Katimavik volunteers (HRS 200). I was also given access to the private papers of Diane Kameen (correspondence, clippings, reports, minutes). I searched published **government records** via the indexes of the *Journals of the House of Assembly of Lower Canada* (1820-36) and the *Journals of the Legislative Assembly of the Province of Canada* (1841-66), as well as Elizabeth Nish (ed), *Debates of the Legislative Assembly of United Canada, 1841-56*; the *Débats de l'Assemblée législative du Québec*, 1867-99; and the *Sessional Papers of the Dominion of Canada*, 1840-1890. I also consulted several archival sources located at Library and Archives Canada, notably MG24 A12, the Dalhousie papers (indexed in *Report on Canadian Archives* 1938, Appendix II), and RG4 A1, Civil Secretary's correspondence, volumes 348, 358, 446 and 539. I also found articles and notices in contemporary newspapers such as the *Quebec Gazette, Quebec Mercury, Le Canadien, Quebec Morning Chronicle, Quebec Daily Telegraph, Quebec Saturday Budget, The Head Quarters, The Star and Advertiser, Quebec Chronicle Telegraph, Le Soleil, Montreal Gazette, Ecclesiastical and Missionary Record, The Pearl, Hamilton Gazette, Financial Post, The New York Times* and *The Scotsman*. Finally, I consulted transcripts of **interviews** I have done with former members of the Society, including Cynthia Dooley, Irene Calfat, Mary and John McGreevy, Alex Addie, Rita

Chapdelaine, Hubert Bauch, Rosemary Cannon and Jacques Roy (all in 1999), Diana Petry (2008) and Diane Kameen (2012).

Detailed references for the text are available at www.morrin.org/morrinbook.

Secondary Sources

No complete books have been written about the Literary and Historical Society of Quebec since William Wood's 1924 *The Centenary Volume of the Literary and Historical Society of Quebec*. Few scholarly articles have focused on the Society other than Bernard Andrès recent piece. Two masters' theses have been written about the Society, both before 1980: Laura Bancroft's in 1950 and Ginette Bernatchez's in 1979. Below are also some of the other theses, articles and books that are useful for understanding the history of the Society. Quite a few of the Society's members, as prominent individuals in Canadian histiory, also have articles in the *Dictionary of Canadian Biography* (http://www.biographi.ca/)

Theses

Bancroft, Laura. "The Literary and Historical Society of Quebec: An Historical Outline Written from the Sociological Point of View." M.A. thesis, Université Laval, 1950.

Bernatchez, Ginette. "La Société littéraire et historique de Québec (The Literary and Historical Society of Quebec), 1824-1890." M.A. thesis, Université Laval, 1979.

Kuntz, Harry. "Science Culture in English-speaking Montreal, 1815-1842." Ph.D. thesis, Concordia University, 2010.

Porter, John. "Un peintre et collectionneur québécois engagé dans son milieu: Joseph Légaré (1795-1855)." Ph.D. thesis, Université de Montréal, 1981

Towsey, Mark R.M. "Reading the Scottish Enlightenment: Libraries, Readers and Intellectual Culture in Provincial Scotland c.1750-c.1820." Ph.D. thesis, St. Andrew's University, 2007.

Articles

Andrès, Bernard. "Des mémoires historiques aux Mémoires littéraires. L'apport de la Société littéraire et historique de Québec." *Voix et Images* 35(3)(2010): 15-32.

Bernatchez, Ginette. "La Société historique et littéraire de Québec (The Literary and Historical Society of Quebec) 1824-1890". *Revue d'histoire de l'Amérique française* 35(2)(1981): 179 192.

Donovan, Patrick. "The First and Oldest: How Does the Literary and Historical Society of Quebec Compare to Other Societies?". *Histoire Québec* 14(1)(2008): 8-10

Duschesne, Raymond and Paul Carle, "L'ordre des choses: cabinets et musées d'histoire naturelle au Québec (1824-1900)." *Revue d'histoire de l'Amérique française* 44(1)(1990): 3-30.

Gagnon, Hervé. "Pierre Chasseur et l'émergence de la muséologie scientifique au Québec (1824-1836)". *Canadian Historical Review* 75(2)(1994): 205-238.

Jarrell, R.A. "The Rise and Decline of Science at Quebec, 1824-1844." *Histoire sociale / Social history* 10(19)(1977): 77-91.

Weilbrenner, Bernard. "Les archives provinciales du Québec et leurs relations avec les archives fédérales, 1867-1920". *Archives* 15(3)(1983): 37-55.

Wilson, Ian E. "'A Noble Dream': The Origins of the Public Archives of Canada." *Archivaria* 1(15) (1982-83): 16-35.

Books

Lacasse, Danielle and Antonio Lechasseur. *The National Archives of Canada 1872-1997*. Ottawa: Canadian Historical Association, 1997.

Lemire, Maurice and Denis Saint-Jacques, eds. *La vie littéraire au Québec*. Volume 2: *1806-1839. Le projet national des Canadiens* and Volume 3: *1840-1869. «Un peuple sans histoire ni littérature»*. Sainte-Foy: Presses de l'Université Laval, 1992 and 1996.

Fleming, Patricia Lockhart, Gilles Gallichan and Yvan Lamonde, eds. *History of the Book in Canada. Volume 1: Beginnings to 1840*. Toronto: University of Toronto Press, 2004.

Chartrand, Luc, Raymond Duchesne and Yves Gingras. *Histoire des sciences au Québec: de la Nouvelle-France à nos jours*. Montréal: Boréal, 2008.

Munro-Landi, Morag J., ed. *Old World - New World: Scotland and its Doubles*. Paris: L'Harmattan, 2010.

Stanworth, Karen. *Visibly Canadian: Imaging Collective Identities in the Canadas, 1820-1910*. Montreal: McGill-Queen's University Press, 2014.

Villeneuve, René. *Lord Dalhousie: Patron and Collector*. ABC Art Books Canada Distribution, 2008.

Whitelaw, Marjory, ed. *Dalhousie Journals*. Ottawa: Oberon, 1978.

Wood, William *The Centenary Volume of the Literary and Historical Society of Quebec, 1824-1924*. Quebec: L'Evénement Press, 1924.

INDEX

A

Abenaki (language), 189
Aberdeen, University of, 133
Acadians, 212–13
Adair, James, 174
Alarie, Charles, 61-62
Alexander, Maria, 87
Allan, Christianne, 75
Allen, Edward, 99
Alleyn, Charles, 99
Alma Mater Society (Morrin College), 123, 131, 148
American Association of University Women, 146
American Humane Society, 204
American Revolution, 26, 28, 33, 63, 110, 176, 227, 240, 249
American Women's Hospital, 146
Amiot, Thomas, 204
Amtmann, Bernard, 239
Anderson, William, 185, 213, 221–22
Angell, Norman, 214
Angers, François-Réal, 55, 81
Anglicans, 37, 69, 106–7, 128, 132, 138, 153, 201
anglophones, 37, 58, 165; culture, 13, 165, 224, 246; and gaol, 58, 64–65; institutions, 12, 105, 167, 224, 237, 244, 246; Quebec City, 13, 62, 108, 120, 151, 165, 172, 178, 236–38, 241, 245–46; relations with francophones, 204, 221, 232. *See also* Anglo-Protestants and British
Anglo-Protestants, 108, 119, 143, 153, 216, 221, 244, 248; Quebec City, 12, 105, 108, 114, 151. *See also* Protestants
Anglo Quebec en Mutation (AQEM), 165–66
anthropology, 123, 136–37
Anticosti, 196
Archer, John, 239, 241
architecture, 16, 37, 118, 121, 233; of gaol, 31, 34–35, 37; of current Morrin Centre building, 16, 165–66; of Morrin College, 117–19, 167
Ardouin, C.J.R. (Mrs), 192
Argentina, 236, 249
Arizona, 126, 136, 167
Arnold, Benedict, 249
art and artists, 35, 63, 109, 177, 186–87, 189, 191, 201, 216, 230, 235, 240; LHSQ and, 13, 171, 180–82, 189–91, 197, 209, 215–16, 234, 244, 249; Morrin College and, 157, 161, 165
art gallery, of LHSQ, 171, 180, 182, 209
Artillery Barracks, 26, 28, 30, 34, 37, 39–40, 65, 68, 98
Arts (faculty and curriculum), 105, 117, 123–27, 129, 132, 138, 143, 148, 152, 167

Ashe, Edward David, 182, 185, 222
Aubert de Gaspé, Philippe, 17, 19–20, 24, 35, 60–62, 80, 99, 175, 206
auctions, 236; of LHSQ books and collections, 207, 238–41, 246–47; magazine, 212, 248
Austen, Jane, 173–74
Australia, 50, 55, 82, 189, 193, 200, 214
Austria, 158, 218
Aylmer, Baron (Matthew Whitworth-Aylmer), 180–81, 229
Aylwin, Thomas Cushing, 163, 214
Aylwin Library, 163, 239, 249

B

Baby, Éliza-Anne, 221
Baby (family), 203
Bacqueville de La Potherie, Claude-Charles, 189
Baddeley, Frederick Henry, 182–83
Baillairgé, Charles, 95, 117–19, 204
Bakewell, Robert, 174
Bancroft, Laura, 122
banishment (punishment), 23–24
Batiscan, 38
Bauch, Gerhard, 162
Bauch, Hubert, 155, 162
Bayfield, Fanny Amelia, 172, 187
Bayfield, Henry, 182, 187
Beatson, Henry, 68
Beattie, James, 174
Beauport, 38, 51, 92, 110
Beauport Asylum, 51, 110
Beccaria, Cesare, 31, 33, 61
Beckwith, Julia, 174
Bédard, Elzéar, 210
Bédard, Jean-Baptiste, 37
Bédard, Pierre-Stanislas, 37
Belgium, 189
Bell, John, 26
Belleau, Narcisse, 199
Belleau, Pierre, 56
Bellenger, Joseph-Marie, 189
Bennett, John, 127
Bermuda, 201
Bernier, Joseph-Elzéar, 158
Berthelot d'Artigny, Michel-Amable, 34
Bibaud, Michel, 221
Bible, 20, 69, 127, 135, 242
Bibliothèque et Archives nationales du Québec, 54, 224, 239
Bibliothèque Sainte-Geneviève, 117
Bieler, Jean-Henri, 239
Bigelow, Poultney, 218
Bigot, François, 221
Bingham, William, 216
Bishop's College / University, 107–8, 111, 116, 119, 125, 128, 138, 151, 163
Bishop's College School, 119

Black, George, 226
Black Hole, 42, 74, 91–92, 97
Blacks, 29, 59, 68, 158
Blackwood, John, 34, 41
Blair, David, 245
Blair, Hugh, 174
Bland, Salem, 139–40
Bloody Code, 23, 47
Bodleian Library, 210
Bodmin Gaol, 35–36
Boer War, 204
Bois de Coulonge, 186
Bon-Pasteur, Soeurs du, 70
Book Committee, of LHSQ, 206–7, 218, 248
Borden, Sir Robert Laird, 214
Boston, 57, 199
botany, 143, 173, 177, 179, 183–88, 192–93, 205, 209
Bouchette, Joseph, 40, 209
Bouchette, Robert Shore Milnes, 81, 201
Bouchette (family), 203
Boulton, Miss, 161
Bourassa, Napoléon, 212
Bourget, Ignace, 107, 202
Bowen, Neil, 229–30
Boyle, Margaret (née Stewart), 66, 99
Brazil, 214
Breakey, Hazel, 236
Britain, 26, 32, 124, 182, 188, 191, 209, 214, 225, 236, 239
British: Empire, 69, 161, 188, 204, 214, 227, 229, 233; immigrants, 12, 48; merchants, 33–34; military, 22, 26, 28, 30, 33–34, 37–38, 48–49, 54, 60, 64, 67–68, 96, 99, 109, 172, 182, 199, 208, 219 (*see also* prisoners); prisoners, 58
British Museum, 181, 199
British North America, 45, 106, 108, 171, 174, 181, 249
British Party, 179
Broadbank, Samuel, 99
Brooke, Frances (née Moore), 246
Brown, Albert J., 139
Brown, James, 54
Browning, Wesley, 99
Browning, William, 99
Bruce, Robert, 156
Brunet, Louis-Ovide, 196
Brunner, Felix de, 192
Brymner, Douglas, 223
Buckingham Palace, 216
Buckland, William, 181
Buffon, Georges, 186
burglary and robbery, 11, 23, 53, 55–56, 62, 81–82
Burke, Edmund, 174
Burton, Sir Francis Nathaniel, 175
By, John, 73

P. 4 Sophie Imbeault; Morrin Centre; LAC, RG4 A1 vol. 446, file 1835-01; p. 7 Sophie Imbeault; p. 8 Morrin Centre; p. 10 Sophie Imbeault; p. 14 Sophie Imbeault; John Howard, "A Plan for a County Gaol," *The State of the Prisons in England and Wales*, Warrington, William Eyres, 1777; François Baillairgé, "Plan d'une maison de travail de plaisir et de correction," 1807, Musée de la civilisation de Québec, Z-161, 4-7, dessus module 4, 3-4, 7, D-2, T-226A, E-14, T-13, no 14; p. 16 James Cockburn, "The Jail on St. Stanislas Street," c. 1830, LAC, C-42292; p. 18 BAnQ-Q, P560,S2,D1,P1550; p. 22 "The Cazan's or Prison in Quebec," Isabel M. Calder, ed., *Colonial Captivities Marches and Journeys*, New York, Macmillan, 1935; p. 27 LAC, RG4 A1, vol. 20, p. 6397; p. 28 Sempromius Stretton, "Artillery Barracks," 1805, LAC, C-14828; p. 30 John Marr, "Plan of the Artillery Barracks," 1771, University of Michigan, William L. Clements Library, Maps 4-C-23; p. 32 John Howard, "A Plan for a County Gaol," *The State of the Prisons in England and Wales*, Warrington, William Eyres, 1777; p. 34 François Baillairgé, "Plan d'une maison de travail de plaisir et de correction," 1807, Musée de la civilisation de Québec, Z-161, 4-7, dessus module 4, 3-4, 7, D-2, T-226A, E-14, T-13, no 14; p. 35 John Call, "Plan, Elevations, and Section of the Gaol, Bridewell and Sheriffs Ward, Lately Built on Bodmin," 1779, British Library, Maps K.Top.9.32.1; p. 38 François Baillairgé, "Plan of the Foundation Walls...," 1808, LAC, NMC 21182; p. 40 Joseph Bouchette, *Topographical Map of the Province of Lower Canada*, London, W. Faden, 1815; p. 41 Sophie Imbeault; p. 42 Morrin Centre; p. 43-44 Donald Fyson; p. 45 Sophie Imbeault; p. 46 Linda Moser, 1950, BAnQ-Q, P728,S1,D1,PWQ-97; "Plan of the Old Jail Lot and Buildings Quebec," LAC, NMC 2619; p. 49 Sophie Imbeault; p. 50 LAC, RG4 A1 vol. 486, file 1836-07; p. 51 Morrin Centre; p. 55 BAnQ-Q, P1000,S3,D1392-0042 and 43; François-Réal Angers, *Les révélations du crime ou Cambray et ses complices*, Quebec, Fréchette, 1837; p. 56 Sophie Imbeault; p. 57 John Neal, *Appeal from the American Press to the American People in Behalf of John Bratish Eliovich*, Portland, Argus Office, 1840; p. 60 Detail of Cockburn, LAC, C-42292; p. 61 BAnQ-Q, E17, 1960-01-036/1693, Fonds du ministère de la Justice, Livernois, Québec, 1864; p. 63 BAnQ-Q, P560,S2,D1,P1253; p. 66 BAnQ-Q, E17, 1960-01-036/1646 (196), fonds du ministère de la Justice, Prison de Québec, register of prisoners' activities, 1859; p. 67 Ville de Québec, Service d'urbanisme, Centre de documentation, ÉCOSS.44, Cartes et plans; p. 72 *Quebec Mercury*, 28 June 1831; p. 73 Scale Model of Quebec, Artillery Park, Fortifications of Quebec National Historic Site, Donald Fyson; p. 74 BAnQ-Q, E6,S8,P424; p. 77 BAnQ-Q, E17, 1960-01-036\1692; p. 78 LAC, RG4 A1, vol. 284, file 1829-04; p. 81 Robert Shore Milnes Bouchette, *Les Captifs*, 1838, Musée national des beaux-arts du Québec, 1956.302, photographer Patrick Altman; p. 85 "Blotter," BAnQ-Q, E17, 1960-01-036\1607 item 58a; p. 86 Sophie Imbeault; p. 88 LAC, RG4 A1, vol. 230, file 1824-09; p. 89 *Quebec Gazette*, 26 Aug. 1813, and *Quebec Mercury*, 6 October 1840; p. 90 Sophie Imbeault; p. 93 Sophie Imbeault; p. 96 LAC, C-104985; Archives de la Ville de Québec, N012732; p. 97 Morrin Centre; p. 104 Morrin College ca. 1890, Morrin Centre and Sophie Imbeault; p. 106 William Smith, ca. 1865, BAnQ-Q, P560,S2,D1,P87293; p. 108 Morrin College Seal in the 1860s, Morrin Centre; p. 109 Henry Daniel Thielke, *Doctor Joseph Morrin*, oil on canvas, 1854, collection of the Monastère des Augustines de l'Hôtel-Dieu de Québec and Théophile Hamel, *Joseph Morrin*, Morrin Centre; p. 110 Initial Collection, Beauport-Avenue Royale-Manoir Robert Giffard-Domaine Darnoc-Résidence, L. P. Vallée, *Portrait and Landscape Photographer*, ca. 1870, BAnQ-Q, P600,S6,D2,P52; p. 113 John Cook, Morrin Centre and Sophie Imbeault; p. 114 (c) 2016, Gilles Chiniara; p. 115 (c) 2016, Gilles Chiniara; p. 116 Dr John William Dawson, Principal of McGill College, Montreal, 1862, McCord Museum, I-4407; p. 118 Université Laval, Convocation Hall, LAC, PA-023511, Mikan 3382594 and Morrin College ca. 1890, Morrin Centre; p. 119 Sophie Imbeault; p. 120 BAnQ-Q, Fonds Fred C. Würtele, Quartier Vieux-Québec, avenue Saint-Denis, Quebec High School, Fred C. Würtele, ca. 1910, P546,D3,P62; p. 121 BAnQ-Q, P541,D183,P6, Staveley Family Collection, Morrin College – proposed building in "court," Harry Staveley, 21 June 1886; p. 124 Course Calendar for Morrin College, 1862-1863; p. 125 George Irvine, Dean of Morrin College's Faculty of Law, 1868, LAC, e010934026, Mikan 3469708; p. 128 Sophie Imbeault, *Quebec Daily Mercury*, 27 December 1873 and Henry Hopper Miles, 1867, BAnQ-Q, E6,S7,SS1,P30477, Fonds ministère de la Culture, des Communications et de la Condition féminine, Office du film du Québec, Neuville Bazin, 1946; p. 131 Sketch of John Theodore Ross by A.G. Racey, *Canadian Men of Affairs in Cartoon* (Montreal: Southam Press, 1922); p. 135 Memorials of Edwin Hatch, D.D. (London: Hodder and Stoughton, 1890) from University of Toronto, Robarts Library; p. 137 George Mercer Dawson, LAC, PA-026689; p. 141 Dr Salem Bland, 1925, Lawren S. Harris, oil on canvas, 103,5 x 91,4 cm. Art Gallery of Ontario, gift of the *Toronto Daily Star*, 1929, 1320-A; p. 142 Edith Sloane's diploma, 1889, collection Mary-Anne Bethune; p. 145 Euphemia MacLeod, 1919, LAC, FA-116, 3259831; p. 146 Margaret Ethel Fraser, 1918, Drexel University; p. 149 Morrin College, 1892, Morrin Centre; p. 150 Donald Macrae, 1891, William Cochrane et al., *The Canadian Album: Men of Canada* (Brantford, Ontario: Bradley, Garretson, 1891), vol. 3, 221 and Sophie Imbeault; p. 154 Sketch for a New Morrin College Building, 1902, *Quebec: Its Natural Advantages for Industries* (Quebec: Joint Industrial Committee of the City of Quebec, 1908); p. 156 Sophie Imbeault; p. 157 Annual Meeting of the Protestant Teachers Association, 1879, *Canadian Illustrated News*, 1 November 1879; p. 158-159 Morrin Centre; p. 160 IODE Room in College Hall, Morrin Centre; p. 162 Hubert Bauch, 2007, Patrick Donovan; p. 164 Morrin College, Morrin Centre; Architectural Drawing of Library in the Prison Cells, 1982, BAnQ-Q, Fonds P948; p. 170 Fire of 28 June 1845, Lithography by G.T. Stanford, based on a sketch by J. Murray, 1845, Archives de la Ville de Québec; Sophie Imbeault; p. 172 Quebec from the Twenty-One Gun Battery, Fanny Amelia Bayfield, LAC, C-002672K; p. 173 Sir George R. Dalhousie, Jarvis Frary Hankes, 1828, LAC, e008316040; p. 176 Jonathan Sewell, artist unknown, Morrin Centre; p. 178 LHSQ Coat of Arms and Seal, Morrin Centre; p. 179 Morrin Centre; p. 180 John Griffin, *A Practical Treatise on the Use of the Blowpipe*, Glasgow: R. Griffin, 1827; p. 183 A specimen from the Canadian Wood Collection at the LHSQ, Morrin Centre; p. 184 Samuel Sturton, "The Wild Flowers of Quebec," *Transactions*, vol. IV, App., 1861; Sophie Imbeault; p. 185 E.D. Ashe, "Water Power of Quebec," *Transactions*, vol. IV, part III; p. 187 *Carex laxiflora*, Royal Botanic Gardens, Kew, ID 10874664; p. 188 Louisa Blair; p. 190 Self portrait of Zacharie Vincent, Musée de la civilisation de Québec; p. 194 James MacPherson LeMoine, *Tableau synoptique de l'ornithologie du Canada*, 1864, Université Laval; Eider, Sophie Imbeault; p. 195 "Langton Forester Moth," archive.org; p. 198 Parliament Buildings, Quebec, Sarony and Major, ca. 1850, Archives de la Ville de Québec; Fire of 28 June 1845, G.T. Stanford, 1845, Archives de la Ville de Québec; p. 200 Sophie Imbeault; p. 202 Portrait of Philippe Baby Casgrain, by Charles Huot, Morrin Centre; p. 204 William Wood, ca. 1929, LHSQ collections; p. 205 Pileated woodpecker, illustration taken from *The Birds of America*, University of Pittsburgh; p. 206 Adèle Maud Stuart, ca. 1920, private collection, ministère de la Culture et des Communications, 88.039.20A; p. 208 Archives de la Ville de Québec, N032042; p. 211 Mrs. Taylor of Ongar (Ann Martin-Taylor), *Practical Hints to Young Females: On the duties of a wife, a mother, and a mistress of a family*, Boston, Wells and Lilly, 1820; p. 212 Pierre-Joseph-Olivier Chauveau, *Charles Guérin*, Montreal, John Lovell, 1852; p. 215 The Presentation of a Newly-Elected Chief of the Huron Tribe, LAC, e011160125-v8; p. 218 *The Constant Nymph*, www.royalbooks.com; p. 220 Georges-Barthélemi Faribault, Septentrion, 2007-11-071; p. 222 Playing card money, LAC, C-017059; p. 223 Silver Commemorative tray, 1997, LHSQ collection, Morrin Centre Collection LHSQ, Morrin Centre; p. 225 Royal Arms of France, Noël Levasseur, 1727, Canadian War Museum, 19940024-001; p. 226 Model of the Royal William, ca. 1930, LHSQ collections; p. 229 Wolfe Monument, BAnQ, P450_2009-03-006/118, Literary and Historical Society of Quebec collection, Post Card, author unknown, ca. 1908; p. 230 Horatio Walker, private collection; p. 231 Dufferin Terrace from Post Office, Quebec City, ca. 1885, McCord Museum, VIEW-1281; p. 232 Women in the Quebec tercentenary pageant, 1908, BAnQ-Q, P450; p. 234 Dufferin Terrace, n.d., collection L. Blair; p. 235 Mary Hilda Freeland Stephens, BAnQ-Q, P450; p. 236 Graham Fraser, BAnQ-Q, P450; p. 237 Rosemary Power-Cannon, Cameron MacMillan, Ross Cowan and John McGreevy c 1980, LHSQ Collection, Morrin Centre; p. 240 Map of the Province of Quebec, Ameri[c]an Atlas, William Faden, ca 1777, Lehigh University Digital Library; p. 241 Frozen pigs, St. Anne's Market, Montreal, ca. 1870, Alexander Henderson, McCord Museum, MP-0000.1828.2.82; p. 243 Literary and Historical Society library in 1999, Photographer Kedl, 2005, Morrin Centre; p. 247 Fourteen voyageurs and four gentlemen in Dalhousie's Vice Regal canoe, John Elliott Woolford, 1821, National Gallery of Canada, No. 42324.49; p. 253 Sophie Imbeault; p. 254 Sophie Imbeault.

PRINTED IN JUNE 2016
BY MARQUIS